THE
BEVERLY
HILLS DIET
LIFETIME
PLAN

ALSO BY JUDY MAZEL

The Beverly Hills Diet

THE BEVERLY HILLS DIET LIFETIME PLAN

BY JUDY MAZEL

WITH SUSAN SHULTZ

MACMILLAN PUBLISHING CO., INC.
NEW YORK

MACMILLAN PUBLISHING CO., INC.
866 THIRD AVENUE, NEW YORK, N.Y. 10022
COLLIER MACMILLAN CANADA, INC.

Library of Congress Catalog No. 82-184

10   9   8   7   6   5   4   3   2   1

DESIGNED BY JACK MESEROLE

PRINTED IN THE UNITED STATES OF AMERICA

*Recipes created and adapted
by Nancy H. Marcantonio*

This book is not intended as a substitute for the medical advice of physicians. The reader should regularly consult a physician in matters relating to his or her health and particularly in respect to any symptoms that may require diagnosis.

As stated in *The Beverly Hills Diet*, any eating regimen, including this one, should be supervised by a doctor. This regimen should not be followed by anyone who has diabetes, colitis, hypoglycemia, a spastic colon, ulcers, ileitis, enteritis, diverticulosis, or by anyone who is pregnant or breast feeding. Of course, anyone with a chronic ailment should undertake this eating program only under the direct supervision of his own physician.

give me your hand you little skinny
and i will lead you out of the
valley of the shadow of fat
and together we will revel in the land of
eternal slimhood

JUDY MAZEL
december 20, 1981

This book is dedicated to

YOU

YOU BOUGHT IT
YOU BELIEVED IT
YOU TRIED IT
YOU MADE IT WORK FOR YOU

"And with the fuel of your lost pounds and
contagious energy, The Beverly Hills Diet
ignited and word rocketed around the world".

Thank you for making my dream come true.

JUDY MAZEL

Contents

PART THREE

RECIPES TO FOREVER—FROM OUR KITCHEN TO YOURS

INTRODUCTION BY NANCY H. MARCANTONIO

INTRODUCTION BY JUDY MAZEL

CONTENTS

PART FOUR

UNFINISHED BUSINESS

A Word from the Medical World

The Beverly Hills Diet and the Beverly Hills Diet Lifetime Plan provide innovative, effective, new dietary concepts. Food combining, the basis of Judy Mazel's program, has long been a neglected area of nutritional research for which there are centuries of empirical history and experience. Proper food combining, an exciting concept that here seems to provide for easy weight maintenance, has captured the interest of millions. Because the Beverly Hills Diet Lifetime Plan permits food indulgences without guilt or deviation from the program, it is effective in preventing the relapses that are so common to other maintenance programs. No further words are needed to introduce and recommend this book, and you may stop here and proceed directly to this life-altering text, unless you have a special interest in the how and why of the ongoing debate sparked by the publication of *The Beverly Hills Diet*.

But, first, before addressing some of the controversial comments about the diet, the distinction between the Beverly Hills Diet and the Beverly Hills Diet Lifetime Plan should be made. The diet is a six-week reducing plan that begins with ten days of fruit only, after which carbohydrates and fats are added, and on the nineteenth day, animal proteins are reintegrated. By the sixth week of the diet, all foods are included.

From the first week of the Beverly Hills Diet Lifetime Plan all foods are incorporated into Judy's twenty weekly Food Formulas: meat, fish, poultry, fat, vegetables, bread, dairy products, and fruit. The weekly Food Formulas provide nutritionally-balanced, high complex-carbohydrate, high-fiber, low-saturated fat meals three times daily for a week. The formulas offer unlimited flexibility in terms of scheduling meals according to social, business, and family needs, making weight maintenance relatively effortless and painless. There is no calorie counting or portion control; there is no food that is forbidden. The key to it all is Conscious Combining, the system of eating that Judy introduced in the Beverly Hills Diet. Here the concept is expanded and developed into a way of eating that ensures proper weight maintenance and good health without deprivation.

Common to both the diet and the plan is Judy's belief that a low-salt, high complex-carbohydrate, and high-fiber eating program will keep us thin and full of energy. She shuns additives, artificial sweeteners, food substitutes such as non-dairy creamer, diuretics for healthy people, and diet pills of all kinds, and suggests keeping sugar and alcohol intake low. This approach to diet should be commended as it is now in the forefront of modern health principles.

Now, for a word about fad diets. The word fad in connection with diets is generally used by health professionals to refer to nontraditional diets; traditional diets are those used by dieticians, nutritionists, and diet therapists and doctors. These traditional diets are slow to go out of vogue and are used over and over again despite their high failure rate among individual dieters. For people with a fat problem, which is to say, people for whom no diet traditional or otherwise, works, after a period of time, *all* diets are "fad" diets because they go from one to another, to another and yet another, and their fat problem is never solved. The Beverly Hills Diet, which some critics have labeled a fad diet, may, in fact, be the answer to many people's persistent fat problem, and signal for them the end of "fad" dieting once and for all. Further, the Beverly Hills Diet Lifetime Plan is designed precisely to eliminate the need for fad diets.

The Beverly Hills Diet Lifetime Plan is a unique maintenance program. It may not work for everyone, but even if it proves only 40 percent effective—and Judy's records indicate better than this—the program exceeds the effectiveness of anything else available. Some dietary principles in this book may be at odds with those of orthodox nutrition experts, but at the same time may break ground previously unexplored by conventional nutritional research. Food combining is one such area.

In preparing for this introduction, I contacted a Ph.D. researcher in gastro-intestinal physiology at UCLA Medical School's Department of Physiology (these are the scientists on whom M.D. gastroentologists depend for research information). I inquired about investigation in the area of basic food combining: the work done in the past and presently under way, and the references available, especially with regard to gastric emptying times of combination meals. My old medical physiology textbooks were inadequate in this area, and current editions totally omitted all previous information dealing with gastric emptying times. The Ph.D. researcher informed me that no recent work had been done, and that at present nothing significant existed in the current literature to which he could direct me. The current trend in research about food in the stomach focuses on (a) food's buffering ability, and (b) its acid stimulating properties with regard to peptic ulcer. Thus, medical researchers have no significant data or scientific information to properly evaluate these principles.

Most of the work in food combining was done by hygienists in the early 1920's. Herbert Shelton, now in his eighties, founder of the San Antonio Hygienic Institute, wrote the classic *Basic Food Combining Book*, which Judy Mazel cited in her first book, *The Beverly Hills Diet*, as the source of the information she needed to break her own life-long diet-fat-diet cycle. The San Antonio Hygienic Institute operated for several decades as both a school and a retreat for fasting and natural healing. Recently, Dr. Shelton was honored for fifty years of meritorious work in the health and nutrition field when an issue of the *Hygienic Review* was devoted to him. Certainly, then, these principles are not untried and untested, as claimed by critics. In fact, the first references to food combining were recorded in the oldest medical textbook in existence, *Classics of Internal Medicine of the Yellow Emperor* (2606–2598 B.C.). In traditional Chinese medicine, foods were classified according to Yin and Yang qualities and combined to balance one another. One ate from Yin to Yang, in that order. And in ancient Persia, foods were similarly classified as being heat- or cold-producing and were combined to balance these properties. At present, there are 500,000 practitioners of traditional Chinese medicine using these same Yin-to-Yang principles within the framework of mainland China's Public Health Administration, adding another 4,000 years to Judy's clinical experience.

Judy Mazel's scientific tool in her dietary studies is the one common to all modern medical research and that is *observation.* Too many of us are far too caught up in the busy and complicated lifestyle of today's demanding society to sort out our food combinations, to make reliable, basic observations of our own eating habits. In addition, there are emotional aspects to eating that involve us with it personally to the point where we cannot clinically observe and evaluate our own habits. How many of us, after an uncomfortable and restless night of feeling overstuffed, can recall the next day what we had for dinner—in what combinations and in what order—much less when we had a similar combination and how we felt then? Or what meal combination, even though huge and highly caloric, left us hungry, unfulfilled, and snacking for the rest of the evening? How many of us have accepted this as a matter of course instead of keeping a log of these observations for analysis? It is comforting to know that Judy has done some of the work for us and has stimulated interest for further research in this field. It is difficult to understand why she should be criticized so severely for this original work for which no refutable evidence is available.

Here, I believe that some shortsighted critics have focused on Judy's lack of traditional scientific background and her inability to translate her basic observations into appropriate medical terminology. She may explain her observations by saying that "only undigested food gets 'stuck' in your body . . . and accumulates and becomes fat," or that "potatoes get locked in your stomach and ferment to vodka"; or by referring to the "fat-burning properties of enzymes" which may be inappropriate or incorrect ways to describe what are in fact correctly observed results. Some of these code phrases, Judy admits, are only picturesque attention-getters for the dieter to stress important facets of her program. Judy's use of "Mazel talk" should not automatically stimulate an unscientific, emotional response.

Some critics have declared, for example, that you will invariably get weak on the Beverly Hills Diet because of protein deficiency. Untrue. My good friend Gypsy Boots, age seventy, well known on Los Angeles television and distributor of his specially selected fruits to health food stores, eats three or four dozen tangerines a day and can jog up a mountain like a high school student on the cross-country track team. Anne Marie Bennstrom runs the world's toughest conditioning health spa in this country, The Ashram, immediately next door to me. I visit frequently and see her guests on fruit diets hiking all day in the Malibu Mountains, without evidence of muscle weakness. Clinically, in conditions of muscle wasting, quadriceps (thigh-muscle) weakness, which results in difficulty climbing stairs, is one of the first symptoms noticed. How could these people accomplish such feats on a protein-deficient fruit diet? Anne Marie and I did a vigorous exercise routine while she was on a fruit and juice fast for over forty days. With regard to the nutritional value of fruit, obviously nutritional experts were overlooking something here. Perhaps their calculations of protein deficits on Judy's diet were incorrect.

In checking scientific tables, I found that fruit is not nearly as low in protein as is commonly believed, especially when considering the percentages of protein available *per calorie* of fruit consumed. To cite the percentages of protein in fruit by weight or traditional portions only, as is commonly done, gives a false, low impression. What is important to evaluate for a reducing or maintenance plan is the percentage of protein and nutrients *per calorie* consumed. In the practical sense, for dieters and maintainers, new charts should be available (something Judy is now working on) that would allow the individual to calculate grams of protein and/or other important nutrients per hundred-calorie portions of food consumed. Evaluating foods in this way is a real eye-opener when comparing the protein content in fruits to that present in other foods.

For example (admittedly an extreme one), did you know—or does your diet expert know—that a *lemon* has more protein per calorie than a hot dog, bacon, sausage, many cheeses, bologna, or most nuts? Did you know—or do your vegetarian friends know— that per calorie, a banana has more protein than an avocado? In comparing other nutrients, did you know that watermelon and cream cheese have about the same amount of protein per calorie, but that surprisingly watermelon has more calcium *per calorie* than cream cheese does? More dramatically, there is twice as much calcium per calorie in papayas as in cream cheese. And, yet, there have been complaints of calcium deficiencies in the Beverly Hills diet.

John McDougall, M.D., Assistant Clinical Professor of Medicine at the University of Hawaii, who has responded to complaints about possible protein and calcium deficiencies as a result of following the Beverly Hills Diet, states that much of the criticism was incorrect, inasmuch as it has concerned the protein and calcium content of an all-fruit diet.

"It is easy to create a diet only of fruit which meets the World Health Organization's (WHO) requirements for these nutrients.

	PROTEIN	CALCIUM
WHO Rec.*	37 grams	400 mg.
Pineapple**	22 grams	963 mg.
Mangoes**	33 grams	633 mg.
Bananas**	39 grams	289 mg.
Papaya**	45 grams	1,538 mg.
Strawberries**	55 grams	1,690 mg.
Watermelon**	57 grams	785 mg.
Oranges**	63 grams	2,519 mg.

*Based on the needs of an adult male consuming 3,000 calories per day.
**Based on an all-fruit diet in an adult male requiring 3,000 calories per day.
Reference: U.S. Dept. of Agriculture Handbook, No. 456.

The ubiquitous presence of protein and calcium in foods should be no surprise, since plants also have requirements for these important nutrients. Our requirements are small enough that all natural diets provide adequate amounts. Calcium deficiency of dietary origin is unknown in man. . . .

If you think about it, it seems only reasonable that nature would design our foods whole—complete with protein, fat, vitamins, calcium, and other minerals. Man, for millions of years, has survived by only satisfying his hunger, without the slightest thought of calcium, protein, or amino acids.

[The published] statements that an all-fruit diet can lead to gout, kidney stones, coronaries, and strokes are in direct conflict with current theories on the cause of these diseases. Gout and uric-acid kidney stones are more common on diets high in uric acid. Calcium kidney stones occur with diets high in calcium and protein. Coronaries and strokes are associated with large intakes of sodium (salt), cholesterol, and saturated fat.

Fruits contain no cholesterol and are very low in sodium, saturated fat, and uric acid. The protein and calcium content are not large enough to promote calcium kidney stones. Therefore, fruits would be ideal in the diet of someone who wished to avoid these diseases."

In *The Honolulu Advertiser* (9/3/81), Dr. McDougall responded to a nutritionist's criticism of the diet in the same paper:

"Unfortunately many lay people and professional nutritionists share critics' misunderstanding of the protein and calcium content of fruits (and often vegetables). Because of this an excessive amount of meat and dairy products are encouraged in our diet. This results for most Americans in a high-fat, high-sodium, high-cholesterol, low-fiber diet which contributes to the major cause of death and disability in our country — heart disease, high blood pressure, breast cancer, colon cancer, diabetes, and obesity to name a few problems. For this reason it is essential that the public receive correct information on the nutritional value of foods."

With regard to the public receiving correct information, something should be said here about the nutritional misinformation commonly presented on protein needs. Minimum daily requirements of proteins by the USDA and the National Academy of Science are calculated with an excessively high margin-for-safety factor, which many scientists believe leads to overconsumption of protein. Nothing unduly critical can happen to the healthy human body under normal living conditions due to short-term dietary protein deficiency. Until 1968 there was a margin-for-error of 50 percent on the excessive side. Many cases of diarrhea and death in infants have resulted from overfeeding of high-protein milk formulas, which may possibly have been related to this excessive amount recommended by the USDA. Recently, the margin for error in national recommended protein requirements has been cut from 50 percent to 30 percent. However, critics of Judy Mazel's diet conveniently ignore the existence of this margin-for-error factor when stating how much protein a dieter should consume. We should be aware of this. It is interesting to note here that the United Nations and the World Health Organization advise universally lower protein requirements than the United States Department of Agriculture does.

How does the Beverly Hills Diet measure up in terms of protein? An eighteen hundred calorie reducing diet of papaya affords thirty-five grams of protein per day which would not result in protein depletion during the recommended period.

The reason I chose eighteen hundred calories when Judy avoids specific calorie counting is to focus on another fallacy of traditional dietetic theories. It is dogma that you must sacrifice thirty-five hundred to four thousand calories in order to lose one pound of fat. This is wrong. Where did this "sacred" fact originate? Although it has been passed down over the years and currently appears in diet manuals handed out by physicians to their obese patients, the origins of this caloric theory appear not to have been closely questioned. The basic figure was arrived at by calculating the number of calories per gram of fat and then converting grams into pounds. It is felt that there are nine calories in one gram of pure fat. So if you give up nine calories, you can lose one gram of fat. Thus, when you calculate the number of grams in a pound and multiply by nine, you get the figure of approximately four thousand, which equals the number of calories per pound of fat.* This conclusion applies to pure fat itself, but it is incorrect to apply to people who are fat.

We don't carry our excess weight around in solid little packages of fat like those standard one-pound blocks of butter displayed in supermarket bins. We carry around excess *fatty tissue*, which contains millions of fat cells, cell membranes, several yards of extra blood vessels with millions of extra blood cells and extra supporting connective tissues with considerable extra intracellular and extra-cellular fluids. These extra solid components alone would be calculated at only four calories sacrificed per gram of tissue lost, close to the figure for protein. Also, the water in all these extra components of fatty tissue and excess intracellular and extracellular fluid would then be calculated at zero calories sacrificed per gram of tissue lost. So, that is why you can lose weight a lot faster on the

---

*Basic scientific tables show pure fat contains nine calories per gram, pure protein and pure carbohydrate each contain four calories per gram. Diet therapists are only accounting for pure fat loss on this caloric counting system.

Beverly Hills Diet than can be calculated using the traditional system counting four thousand calories sacrificed per pound lost. And this does not consider the significant associated loss of other tissue that supports all this extra fatty tissue. Have you ever noticed that grossly obese people often have very large and very muscular, but not fat, legs? Fat people also have a greater mass of supporting musculature than thinner people. When you lose fifty pounds of *fatty tissue*, your supporting muscle tissue also decreases. Supporting muscular structure decreases at a sacrificial cost of only four calories per gram lost for the solid portion of muscle tissue, but also remember muscle tissue is composed of 72 percent water which can be lost with a sacrifice of no additional calories. Interestingly, this may explain in part the long misunderstood enigma of dietary plateaus. Additional loss of hypertrophic (or over-developed) supporting tissues and their fluid components will not occur when these tissues have stabilized to accommodate a lower body weight. This stabilization in decrease of muscle size and associated cellular fluid occurs until a new lower weight requiring less muscle to carry about has been reached, resulting in a "sticking point." Even supporting bone weight decreases gradually and slowly after a patient has lost a large amount of weight over a long period. Because these compensatory changes in fatty tissue and supporting tissue have not been sufficiently accounted for, they should be examined in greater detail before dogmatic statements are made as to how many calories must be given up to lose a pound.

The decrease of supporting muscle tissue in an obese person also provides a naturally built-in and traditionally overlooked *"protein-sparing factor"* in reducing diets. You may have observed what has happened when an arm has been in a cast for a few weeks. The muscles shrink to a fraction of their size. This muscle protein obviously is assimilated and used by the body.

Misconceptions of body protein requirements have frequently resulted in dieters' overeating in their worry to meet these allegedly necessary requirements, and is another cause of dietary failures. Too many people, even though satisfied on a diet, feel uneasy that somehow they may be subclinically malnourished in terms of protein needs and, therefore, daily consume additional unnecessary protein foods. This preoccupation with meat and other high protein foods may in fact also be a hangup passed down from the Depression era when these could not be afforded. Then, a table without meat meant deprivation.

Critics of the Bevely Hills Diet have warned repeatedly that the body does not store protein. While it is true that there is no specific storage organ for protein, there is, in the large mass of skeletal muscle (twenty-one kilograms in a seventy-kilogram man), what may be considered a *"labile protein reserve."* It has been estimated that two kilograms (two thousand grams) of the eleven kilograms of pure protein in the average seventy-kilogram man can be lost without serious results.

Complaints of loss of hair and depletion of skin proteins because of low protein intake in early phases of this diet originally brought my attention to misstatements by nutritional experts; however, these hair and skin problems occur only when people with little or no reserves, under almost starvation conditions, go on an obviously protein-deficient diet. Further, trouble does not occur without a coexisting severe caloric-intake deficiency, which causes body proteins to be broken down and used for daily energy requirements. That, indeed, can be a dangerous situation. Obviously, anyone going on a reducing diet will have sufficient fat reserves to be broken down for their energy requirements so that protein tissue will not have to be used.

While a resident in dermatology at the University of Michigan Hospital, I monitored the department chairman's hospitalized obese patient closely who was on a zero calorie intake program for more than ninety days. There was *no* significant muscle wasting nor negative effects on skin, hair, or nails. Admittedly, this is an extreme example, and not recommended to readers, but it should make one wonder about the validity of complaints that such problems would occur on the Beverly Hills Diet.

What about ulcers on the diet? There have been misstatements by critics in this regard. In folk medicine among Cubans and natives of the Caribbean Islands, it is believed that papaya is the best food to eat if you *do* have ulcers. The traditional Sippy Diet, which is no longer prescribed—the bland "milk and cream" medical regimen for ulcer patients—has been incriminated as actually aggravating ulcers by continued stimulation of gastric-acid secretion long after the original buffering action of milk and cream has been exhausted. Even milk is regarded by some physicians today as dangerous to ulcer patients. Acidity in fruit cannot add significantly to the stomach's acidity to aggravate an ulcer. Its acid strength is minor in comparison to the strength of normal stomach acid. Of course, if you have an ulcer problem, you should check with your doctor before going on a diet or maintenance program, including this one.

What about diarrhea on the Beverly Hills Diet? On an all-fruit diet you must carefully select good-quality, well-ripened fruit, and you must follow the food-combining rules in *The Beverly Hills Diet* book to the letter. Medical literature reports the incidence of "osmotic diarrhea" from high fruit intake, occurring when partially broken-down fruit sugar is trapped in the large intestine too long, causing osmotic resorption of excess water into the intestine. But if the rules of the diet are followed exactly, severe diarrhea is extremely rare. The specific rule that governs this is that nothing else can be digesting in the intestine at the same time as fruit. If for some reason excessive diarrhea proved to be a problem for a dieter, it would not persist unless an extraordinary lack of common sense compelled the dieter to continue a regimen not working for him or her. Gassiness and bloating from fruits can occur when the fruit ferments in the intestine; many people have such problems already, because of miscombining. The incidence should be less on the Beverly Hills Diet and Lifetime Plan, which stresses correct combining.

An interesting anecodote, though undocumented in medical literature, is that when some South Sea islanders want to rid their bay of sharks, they feed them heated melon along with fish. This kills the sharks. A basic food combining rule from many sources is "eat melon alone."

What about the fact that some nutritionists, with their computerized bank of tables of recommended requirements, found that this diet was low in salt? Low in sodium? Should that be a complaint? By the computer, the diet was also low in calories and low in fat, which, using the same computer logic, could also be "complaints." Americans, in addition to consuming far too many calories and too much fat, consume many times the required amount of salt. In fact, many senior citizens go into heart failure from fluid retention caused by high-sodium diets of canned soups, TV dinners and other pre-prepared foods. In this country, with its high incidence of hypertension and cardiovascular disease, a low-salt diet should be welcomed instead of criticized. A low-salt diet should also be welcomed by women with tendencies toward fluid retention. Under tension and emotional stress, some women secrete excess amounts of a hormone called aldestrone, which acts as a specific antidiuretic agent causing salt and fluid retention. Such a patient can accumulate as much as fifteen pounds of excess water before that weight gain can be clinically discerned as a recognizable edema or "bloat." Many women do not have to be told that, during periods of premenstrual edema—the fluid in the fingers and around the ankles and the swollen abdomen—does not represent true weight gain. Why should they be given potent diuretics for this? Diuretics to combat sodium and fluid retention are certainly more harmful than any facet of the Beverly Hills Diet or Plan. Too many diet doctors today prescribe diuretics to aid patients on crash diets. This *is* dangerous. If you are carrying excess fluid and can lose it by eating large amounts of fruit, why complain? Losing excess fluid should be regarded as beneficial! Certainly, some of these fluid losses may be regained later, but if you are a "bloater" (Judy's term), suffering fluid retention, and you could stabilize to a normal level on this low-salt diet, what a blessing this "weight loss" would be especially since you never would have sacrificed any calories at all.

And that brings up the word, sacrifice. There is really no feeling of sacrifice, deprivation, or frustration on the diet or on the Beverly Hills Diet Lifetime Plan. That is what is unique and exciting about both, and perhaps one of the main reasons Judy Mazel's system works. All dieters and weight maintainers are painfully aware that no one thinks of food more, and more intensely, than someone struggling to lose weight or keep off those newly lost pounds. It can be a problem of every waking moment that feeds and grows on itself. Under such circumstances, resolution dissolves and the smallest self-denial is magnified until all sacrifices become sacrificed. Further, the guilt of eating compounds the problem. Increased guilt, because of inevitable failures, leads to increased eating, which leads to increased guilt, until the dieter or maintainer yields and gives up and now has to compensate even for the guilt of giving up. And thus the failed dieter or maintainer can be even worse off weight-wise than before attempting the program.

Judy has broken this cycle with an evolutionary, entertaining, and innovative philosophy, and with more than a smattering of clever behavioral-modification psychology. I cannot overstress the importance of this aspect of both her books. Indeed, defeating the guilt and will power problems may be one of the most important reasons for this program's success. Once again, food can be your friend. If you make the Beverly Hills Diet Lifetime Plan your own, you really *can* eat three chocolate mousses in one sitting without a pang of regret or guilt. The Plan takes into consideration every aspect of a full and active lifestyle: travel, holidays, banquets, parties, emotional upsets, etc. You make the choices and gain control without the effort and the intensive self-will so necessary, but also so ultimately self-defeating, in other diet and maintenance plans.

ALBERT R. MACKENZIE, M.D.

Sherman Oaks, California

ALBERT R. MACKENZIE, M.D., a specialist in dermatology and skin cancer, former associate clinical professor of medicine (dermatology) at UCLA, has contributed to medical literature in the form of textbooks, journals, and basic research.

Although Dr. MacKenzie's private practice is devoted exclusively to dermatology and skin cancer, he has always maintained a special interest in the field of health and nutrition. While a dermatologist at the U.S. Naval Academy, he conducted a study challenging the widely accepted belief that chocolate causes acne, at a time when dietary restrictions were printed on all over-the-counter acne medications. Several hundred weekly photographs of a controlled population of midshipmen on and off dietary chocolate showed no statistical difference in acne severity in either group, disproving longstanding, traditional beliefs.

Here again, he produces new information to test long-accepted nutritional theories.

Acknowledgments

Success doesn't happen by itself:

My world
My life
My success

has been a composite of hands to hold, laps to lay my head upon —
the support and encouragement, pride and love of friends who
let me be me
and made this magic
become a reality.

Thank God you were there — I couldn't have done it alone:

Joan Stewart, Norman Brokaw, Susan Shultz, Marion Wheeler,
Margie and Herman Platt, Donna and Jerry Roth, Barry Haldeman,
Jackie Applebaum, Phyllis Morris, Joan Perlette, Alex Silverman,
Cindy Griffith, Nancy Marcantonio, Charlie Hayward, John Callas,
Nancy Kerrinickx, Judy Sakawye, Jay Bernstein, Gary Belkin,
Armando Cossia, Lil Peloso, Nini Policapelli, Lorraine Rachich,
Michael Carlisle, Dominick Anfuso, Lindley Boegehold, Paul
Zegler, Mary Lou Dell, Mari Falt, Harry Langdon, Lori Marsh,
Donna and Victor Kovner, Shelly Nadell.

Home is where the heart is and whether it was The Beverly Hills Hotel, The Regency Hotel, or The Kahala Hilton—you kept the home fires burning. Ernest Brown, Jean Majors, Muriel Slatkin, Hollis Polodna, Norma Argenzio, Walter Markowski, Mr. Fernandez, Mr. Vecht, Mr. Jamier, Dragon, Charlie Goodness, Terry Dudak, Willie Kissner, Bobbi Krewson, the people at the "Special Services desks," Bob Davis, Red John Haddad who got me there—the whole cast and crew.

Thank you, Thank you, Thank you.

PART ONE
GETTING IT OFF

I

The Beverly Hills
Diet — Forever

The diet phenomenon of the '80s has become a reality — a fact, a way of life. The verbal and the visible, the socially elite of Beverly Hills began eating a new way, and the world followed. Across the country, throughout the world, hundreds of thousands braved the traditionalists and led the way, giving testimony and credence to the wonders of Conscious Combining. For no one could deny the simple truth: It worked. The world was getting skinny. THE BEVERLY HILLS DIET HAD COME OF AGE!

Welcome to the world of the little golden pineapple — to the land of eternal slimhood. Welcome to the land of dreams come true — to a diet that is a dream come true. Welcome to the Beverly Hills Diet Lifetime Plan — a diet in the classical sense of the word, a way of life.

And life is no longer about diets and dieting, giving up and going without. Can'ts and nevers — shoulds and shouldn'ts: a trade-off without a pay-off. Now is the time for living! Because eating and living is what life's all about, and that's what the Beverly Hills Diet Lifetime Plan is all about.

You're off the merry-go-round; you've got the brass ring. You're not fat anymore, and you'll never be fat again. You've reached that pot of gold at the end of the rainbow, and just as I promised, it isn't empty. I didn't promise you slimhood and then

3

take away everything you love; *au contraire*, that pot of gold holds it all: hamburgers and hipbones, cheesecake and cheekbones. Tomorrow is here, and unlike the tomorrow of yesterday, filled with unfulfilled good intentions—broken diet promises and regained weight, it is here for you to enjoy. Because at long last you can look in the mirror with pride. YOU DID IT! YOU'RE SKINNY! And now I'm going to make sure you stay that way. Forever.

Forever. Now the focus shifts to beyond. To giving up the fear of ever becoming that fat person again. Forever. To locking in that energy and that vitality. Forever.

Over and over I hear, "I'm scared, I'm afraid I'll blow it." "It will never last." "I've been there before." And it's true, we've all been there before. How many pounds do you think you've lost in your life? How many new wardrobes have you bought only to find yourself looking at them longingly six months later knowing you'll never squeeze back into them before they go out of style.

Well, now you can throw out those fat clothes because this is it. Once and for all and Forever! All those new clothes will still be caressing your thighs six months from now, they won't just be fondled by your fingertips. You're skinny now and you're going to stay that way Forever.

Dick Smothers is still flaunting his hipbones, Pat Harrington is still as slim as he was two years ago, and petite Mary Ann Mobley never gained back those ten pounds that used to bother her so. If they can do it, if they can stay thin, you can too.

And look at me. I still love to eat, and live to eat, and when food is in my mouth, my heart sings and my soul soars. If something is good, more is better, and too much is not enough. Four months of travel, a sumptuous restaurant every night and I still weigh 102. If I can do it, if I can stay thin, so can you. And you will, because I'm going to help you. We're going to do it together. I'm going to take that skinny little hand, and together we are going to discover the wonderful world of eternal slimhood. I showed you how eating could get you skinny: well, now I'm going to show you how eating will keep you skinny. We are going to experience and enjoy the goods of the good life, and that part of our life that is so crucial, so vital. Eating.

Food is no longer your enemy. How can anything so beautiful and wonderful that has given up its life to create our life, something that has the potential to bring us so much pleasure, continue to bring us pain? How can anything so essential be so destructive? Anything so nurturing be so ravaging? Well, it won't any longer because at long last we have regained our touch with the meaning of food and with our ability to experience it. Experience it not with fear and guilt but with permission and pleasure. Food is your best friend and it's your lover and you are going to embrace it, not fight it.

For the next six months I am going to hold your hand and show you how to make food, even the most heretofore considered fattening food, work for you and that new body, not against you. You are going to eat your way through every excuse you've ever had for not staying skinny. And with the Beverly Hills Diet Lifetime Plan there will be no place for fat. You will have no excuse whatsoever. Holidays, work, travel, parties, even emotions are all allowed for in your BHDLP. You are going to eat your heart out at the Taj Mahal, you'll learn how to say no without losing your lover, your son will get arrested, and your daughter will run away with a punk rocker. You'll go to a Sunday night wedding reception in the grand ballroom of the Plaza Hotel, and *you'll stay thin*. You are going to eat your way through the next six months without gaining a pound. The exceptions will become exceptional, and Conscious Combining, the technique of eating foods in specific combinations for maximum nutritional value, digestibility, and weight maintenance, will become as easy and natural as buttoning your shirt or driving your car.

And as you learn and experience that the yo-yo is over, vast freedom will be yours. Those lost pounds will be banished Forever.

That newfound energy will be yours always. Skinny is no longer a fleeting moment on the black road back to fat. Now you will stay as thin as you like for the rest of your life without deprivation or denial, heartache or hunger.

These next six months are the crucial months. This is the period when your little fat body still aches to burst forth, when the deception of Forever is piled on the tentativeness of that newly skinny body. It is during these first six months that your Debilitating Fat Consciousness, your (DFC), and the physical roller coaster of keeping off lost weight combine to exploit you. And just as you didn't get fat or thin overnight, so it is with maintaining. Understand that the yo-yo is not truly smashed until six months of consistent weight maintenance. Remember those fat cells are ever poised to plump up again, that your poor little doubting body, subjected to the indignities of convoluted eating for oh so many years, requires at least six months to stabilize, to internalize skinny.

The Advanced Nonphysical Exercises (Chapter VIII) are the tools that will fix the Beverly Hills Diet Lifetime Plan Forever in your soul, and by the time we are through, you will have banished your DFC Forever. Your little, skinny voice will ring triumphant, outshouting the screaming, strident voice of fat.

Your life will continue to be about eating, but you will no longer think about life as being on or off a diet. "Diet" will become a way of life, a way of eating that lets you luxuriate in food smugly secure — secure in the knowledge that you are now and will be Forever thin.

Your life will continue to revolve around eating: business and social lunches, family brunches, hot dogs at ball games, ice cream at the beach, popcorn at the movies, glamorous soirees with candlelight and champagne, banquets, buffets, cocktail parties, dinners out, and holiday feasts. You'll continue to eat your heart out, to swallow your feelings, to turn to food for solace and comfort, fun and frolic. Nothing can change that. The magic will be in your control, in knowing that you have the power to have your cake and eat it too. In knowing deep in your heart that despite it all, you can maintain your weight and maximize your health for the rest of your life.

Beloved foods are no longer banned from your life to be used only as a reward for your fat person; instead, they caress your skinny self. You'll get hugs from hamburgers and kisses from cookies. You will revel in your favorite foods, without fear, without guilt.

You will learn and internalize the Three Golden Rules (Chapter IV) that will keep you thin Forever, how to embrace the skinny person within you, how to synergize your mind and body to release your skinny soul and make it sing. And these three rules will ensure that you stay skinny, no matter how social you are, how sensitive you are, or how compulsive you are. You will experience food without fear because you will know just how far you can stretch the rules and just how much you can get away with. *Excuse* is a word of the past, a concept cut out of your world. Holidays or happiness, misery or migraines, there are no food exceptions, no suspensions, no on or off. No more spurts of dieting! The Beverly Hills Diet Lifetime Plan is a constant—a sure—a Forever.

Eternal slimhood, that place where you can be as thin as you like for the rest of your life, is yours. It is that place where pie in the sky is a reality. In this book you will find Food Formulas for maintaining the good life. Eating formulas that run the gamut from Thanksgiving and its leftovers to treating yourself after an afternoon at the laundromat.

You will learn how to tally your nutritional and skinny quotients, how to mix and match to stay healthy and thin. You will begin to think in terms of weekly food quotients to maintain the skinny you while fulfilling your every food fantasy and your nutritional needs as well. You will realize that Conscious Combiners do not live by fruit alone, that virtually every natural food has a purpose on this planet. Once you define it, you can digest it. And what you choose to eat determines what you have to eat. You are not ruled by nos and nevers, portion control and time limits, foods you can and cannot have. Instead, there are rules, rules that guide your life and dictate that for every food you eat, there are foods that best precede it and foods that best follow it. Each bite you take will be a commitment to the next. That's the key to the Beverly Hills Diet Lifetime Plan.

Using the Food Formulas, the guidelines, and your Workbook to Wonderland, you will develop your own eating plans. Some days you will even give yourself permission to gain, testing your outer limits, testing to see if that fat person within you *really* is gone forever. Some days you will gain without permission, we all do, you know. And it just might happen despite your best intentions, despite your not eating anything wrong, despite your not miscombining (see Glossary) or breaking any rules. No one can rigidly hold the same weight day in and day out. But you'll luxuriate in the assurance that for every pound you gain, there is a specific Corrective Counterpart, an after-the-fact. In Chapter VI you'll meet the maintenance recoups, the three-day fruit feasts that counteract every indiscretion, every body-gorge you can dream up. Although as a Conscious Combiner you'll tend to blow it less and less.

When you have gained control over your body, over your little fat soul, you will experience that innate satisfaction that can come only from being a genuine skinny. You will know that you never have to be fat again because the Beverly Hills Diet Lifetime Plan is an exercise in living, a plan for always.

And as you begin to embrace your thin self and unleash your skinny soul, you will control not only the way you look and feel, but the kind of life you'll lead as well. "You are what you eat" is simple fact. Your eating plan will orchestrate the quality and the quantity of your energy.

Beverly Hills Diet maintainers combine not just to look good (they already do); they combine to feel good. The stars who know that their looks are their livelihood, who zip to every fad, have clung to Conscious Combining when statistics would insist that it's time to move on. They know it really works. Have you ever wondered how Liza Minnelli's energy output per pound must exceed all records? Again and again, on my frenetic, record-breaking four-month tour crisscrossing this country, talk-show hosts who had seen it all continually expressed incredulity at my stamina and sparkle. Well, my energy isn't "just there"; that body and vitality doesn't just happen—it has to be fed a daily diet of BHD. And you bet I do!

You'll learn to cook it Beverly Hills Diet style, although there's no need for complicated processes or special cookbooks. I'm going to show you simple recipes that I use that will make every meal a song. Not just for you but for every member of your family, and your guests as well. Plus you'll see how simple it is to adapt your favorite recipes from any cookbook you name. I'll share special recipes from my favorite restaurants across the country, and tell you where I ferret out the best—from bagels to pasta, pizza to cheesecake. You will begin to choose what you cook based on how it makes you feel, not merely on how it tastes.

Beverly Hills Diet maintainers are not losers, and we maintainers have special secrets and special tools for those special challenges that threaten our hard-won slimhood. We live in a rarefied world where every day we celebrate the good life, where we eat well and feel great. Now you, too, can share in our secrets and experience the good life: the world of the Beverly Hills Diet Lifetime Plan, the world beyond the golden pineapple.

Whether you've lost weight on the Beverly Hills Diet or on another weight-loss program, if you want to maximize your success and internalize those hipbones, if you want to stay skinny Forever, the Beverly Hills Diet Lifetime Plan is for you. It offers a way of eating for everyone who cares about feeling good and staying slim Forever. Even if you are one of those lucky souls who has never had to battle your weight, one of those natural skinnies to whom food is not a glorious, notorious obsession—even if you just want to fine-tune your energy, then join the BHDLP revolution. Participate in this exciting new way of eating and learn how you can make food work for you.

Whoever you are, wherever you live, whatever you do, this is an eating plan designed just for you. There is a golden network out there to support you, and it is yours for the asking. So come on, eat to your heart's content, because you'll never again have to eat your heart out. You don't have to be fat anymore, and you'll never have to be fat again. You have confronted your fat, you acknowledged your fat, and you've let it go. Now you have nothing left to lose, except the fear that it won't last. And trust me, it will!

Welcome to the world of the golden pineapple. Welcome to the world of Conscious Combining and the Beverly Hills Diet Lifetime Plan.

II

Going Public —
The Beverly Hills Diet
Explosion

On April 19, 1981, I left Los Angeles to share my diet discovery with the world. A simple three-week author tour soon turned into four months of travel to thirty-eight cities. I had no idea that the wondrous effects of the Beverly Hills Diet had preceded me. The book had been filtering into any number of cities for several weeks, and from New York to Minneapolis, St. Louis to Kansas City, they awaited my arrival, they came to say hello, scores of new skinnies. They had made the golden pineapple their own. And their enthusiasm and their energy were boundless. You could tell who they were by looking at them. They weren't just thin. Their hair gleamed, their eyes sparkled, and their skin glowed. They were slim and they didn't look as if they had ever been on a diet. They didn't look as if they had ever been fat!

The enthusiasm for the diet was explosive, and as I crisscrossed the country again and again, the response became more deafening, more heartening. The Beverly Hills Diet phenomenon was literally being devoured by a ravenous world, and thousands of new skinnies were the proof that it worked.

And you came to my autograph sessions in droves, to brag, to ask questions, and simply to say thank you. And you were just as ecstatic about how you felt as how you looked. And you couldn't help but share it with anyone who would listen. You didn't have to

11

be fat anymore, and you never had to be fat again. And, like me, you wanted to show the world how they could do the same.

In the beginning you tried to be quiet about what you were doing, because you knew the Beverly Hills Diet was different. You knew you'd been scorned by friends who had watched you bob up and down on the diet yo-yo as you touted every new weight-loss scheme only to fail. Well, who wants to be a target again and again? But it's hard not to be noticed when you're eating only pineapples at lunch. It's hard to be unobtrusive when you're served watermelon balls at a black-tie affair, or platters of pasta or stacks of steak. And it's hard not to be the center of attention when you're getting thin and feeling great. So, with the fuel of your lost pounds and contagious energy, the Beverly Hills Diet ignited, and the word rocketed around the world.

There was a run on pineapples in Butte, Montana; papayas could not be found anywhere in San Francisco; New Jersey blueberries had never seen such a season. There were riots over ripe bananas in mid-Manhattan, and caches of watermelon were hidden in lower desk drawers on Capitol Hill. In Aspen, Colorado, celebrities tried ripening their mangoes in their ovens so that they could return to Beverly Hills with slim thighs. Produce people across the country were besieged by new Beverly Hills dieters demanding bushels of grapes, pounds of plums, and scores of strawberries. A newly knowledgeable constituency sniffed, squeezed, and fondled barrels of fruit as never before. Only the most golden pineapple, the most resilient watermelon, the juiciest grapes, and the most scarlet strawberries would satisfy. No one could have predicted the breadth and enthusiasm of the demand.

And it wasn't only the grocers who were overwhelmed by this revolution in eating. Beverly Hills Dietfare made its debut on restaurant menus, in delis, and even in fast-food houses. Overnight the language of Conscious Combining became the common tongue of the slim and slimming.

The Beverly Hills trend setters, whose menus had been reprinted to tout their Beverly Hills Diet specials, were in the mainstream. In Beverly Hills, it was Le Bistro, Le Bistro Garden, Jimmy's Le Dome, Kathy Gallagher's. Tony's in Houston, Delmondo's in Milwaukee, and Doro's in San Francisco were among the first to follow suit. You only had to mention the Beverly Hills Diet; not only did they accommodate you, often they joined you. Time and time again a waiter, a maître d', or a chef would confide that he, too, was a Conscious Combiner, that he, too, owed his newfound slimhood to the Beverly Hills Diet.

From little Rock to Modesto—from Toronto to Tallahassee, the pounds were dropping like ripe mangoes. And I just kept traveling. There were books to sign, skinnies to congratulate, fatties to slenderize, and cynical talk-show hosts to convert. Despite my frantic and frenetic schedule, my energy and my glow were living testimony to the benefits of the BHD. Whatever it was I was doing really worked, that was obvious. Whether it was a 6:00 A.M. television show or a midnight radio phone-in, the magic of the pineapple was indisputable. I was an energized Beverly Hills Dieter. I was thin and felt vibrant, I couldn't have had more energy. And that energy became a magnet that drew converts by the thousands to the BHD.

It seemed that almost everyone was embracing the Beverly Hills Diet. The room service clerk at the Omni International in Atlanta gushed his enthusiasm at 4:00 A.M. while I was prepping for an early talk show. Stewardesses stood next to my seat waiting for me to open my eyes to bombard me with questions. When I arrived at the Mayfair Regent in Chicago, the desk clerk flung open his jacket with pride to reveal his newly thin waist. What began as a way of eating for the jet-setters, the stars, the avant-garde, what started out as a fat cure for celebrities willing to be different and flout tradition, became the diet for America! Students, computer operators, taxi drivers, corporate executives, housewives, socializers, garbage collectors, legislators, lawyers, and retirees made the Beverly Hills Diet their own. One grande dame toted Tupperware color-coordinated to her costume; an insurance salesman gave a watermelon party; a gaggle of grandmothers gathered over pasta at a Cleveland eatery. And for the first time in their lives, people were sticking to a diet and losing weight. Their excuses were gone. They had new priorities in eating, and they were learning they had a choice. Feeling good was all that mattered, and they couldn't wait to talk about how good they felt. You talked, I talked, and the word spread.

Books were sold out again and again, straining the tolerance level of even the most patient convert waiting to shape up with his own copy. Havoc reigned on famed Rodeo Drive when store owners were actively bribed for copies of the book that were being used as window displays during a week-long promotion. Bookstores clocked record numbers of calls, copies were sold right out of packing cartons, and, when Crown Bookstore had a sign in their window that said "We've got it," everyone knew they meant *The Beverly Hills Diet.*

And as we scoffed at the traditional emaciated dieters who commanded, "Cut the fat off your steak," "Skin those chicken breasts," "Snub that cheesecake!" "You can't eat pasta and lose weight," the uninitiated would stare at us in shocked disbelief. "What do you mean you're on a diet?" they would demand, as piles of pasta disappeared from our plates. "Oh," they'd sneer, "you don't really have to diet." Because no matter how fat we once were, no matter how much weight we lost, no one could tell we'd ever been fat. Certainly not by what we ate and certainly not by how we looked either. We didn't have that gaunt and haggard look that comes from diets that deplete our systems rather than nourish them. We looked like those lucky natural skinnies who never had to diet.

Reuben sandwiches were replaced by triple orders of strawberries. Papayas and pineapples crowded out bacon, eggs, and toast in the traditional breakfast eateries. Steak supplanted stew. Suddenly, there were new priorities in eating. People were learning they had a choice, and they were making it. Feeling good was all that mattered, and they were feeling it. They were experiencing food from a whole new vantage point. It wasn't important to have it all right now because they knew that sooner or later they were going to get it all. And along with the pounds went the excuses. They knew nothing was leaving the planet. It wasn't now or never anymore, instead it became now or later.

And the Beverly Hills Diet wasn't just for women. Men showed up and they spoke up. They, too, began taking pride in their new slimhood and began showing off their midriffs sans the bulge. Men like Pat Harrington and Dick Smothers publicly admitted to having hipbones.

More celebrities became devotées. Article after article appeared featuring yet another personality glowingly praising the Beverly Hills diet. Jaye P. Morgan said, "It's the greatest." The chanteuse set was singing its glories. No matter where I went, good reports abounded.

Bill Palmer, the owner of the beauty salon at the Beverly Hills Hotel, reported working on a project with Christina Ferrare as she touted the wonders of the Beverly Hills Diet. At my book gala at Le Bistro in Beverly Hills, I spied my girlhood idol, Robert Mitchum, looking spectacular, though thinner than I remembered. I was thrilled, THE Robert Mitchum at my party! Later that evening his wife, Dorothy, told me that they were celebrating their fourth week on my diet. The word kept coming in: the business heavies were lightening up, pound-wise, that is. Cubby Broccoli, Sam Spiegel. Arthur Kelly, former chairman of Western Airlines, spoke his success in a speech at a convention in Hawaii. Everyone was embracing and celebrating the Beverly Hills Diet. Hawaii Senators Matsunaga and Inouye hosted a party for me on Capitol Hill, my chance to give a copy of the book to Senator John Warner for his wife, Elizabeth Taylor. There were other parties in Washington, Detroit, and New York. In San Franciso society doyenne Dottie Cartwright gave a party for me complete with a twelve-tiered cake decorated with all my sayings and topped with a pineapple decoration. A big Welcome Judy sign spanned the entire front of the house. She had discovered the marvels of the Beverly Hills Diet and she wanted to share them with 250 friends and honor me as well.

It was after one of these gala affairs that I finally learned when enough is enough. It's interesting, no matter how thin we get or how involved we get in the process, there is still some semblance of that little fat soul lurking within. Stella Adler, grande dame of the theater, gave an enchanting party. Though I had planned on eating, the thrill and excitement of it all: the party, the success of the book, the rave reviews, the illustrious in the flesh, I just couldn't eat. I wasn't hungry. Or shall I say, it was one of those times when eating wasn't a priority. I began with a vodka, but never made it to the lush expanse of food. I socialized instead. We were driving to Philadelphia later that night for an early TV show, so I left the party with a bundle of goodies to eat on the way. It was 3 A.M. before we finally got going, and by that time I was ravenous. Ignoring all my rules, I began eating with both hands. Oh boy, did I get sick! Unhappily the gorged pasta, the vegetable tempura, and the chocolate cake were a little too much for my body to consciously combine, and did I suffer! I didn't gain weight, but I sure didn't feel great either.

It's interesting how "the moment" shoves aside "the always," how "right now" shoves aside "later," how instant gratification blots out feeling good and looking good. Our old DFC remains ever poised to snuff out our new skinny soul. I wasn't thinking about tomorrow or how I would feel as I ate my way into oblivion. I was thinking about the talk-show host I had to confront the following morning, who, six months earlier, had made fun of the Beverly Hills Diet and had ridiculed it in no uncertain terms. I only knew that at that moment I needed to eat. Pure and simple.

Well, thank God for the wonders of the BHD and the magic

of the mango. I ate it to start the day and it turned me on and kept me going. Undaunted by a mere two hours sleep and a stomach at war, I steeled myself to meet my critic. The host opened the show with an apology for past criticism, announcing that he had devoured my book and believed it to be the best of all diets. After a sigh of relief, I took advantage of the situation to revel in his praise and concentrate on the positive. So often we Eaters (see Glossary) swallow even our good feelings and fall prey to our DFC, precisely my behavior of the night before, after the party and the excitement were all over. Well, you don't think that I consumed that inordinate amount of food just because I was hungry, do you? I had been so looking forward to the party, there had been an intense buildup of excitement, and then suddenly it was over. I was experiencing the letdown, the emptiness that's left after something is finished. You know, that feeling of "please don't let this magic end," but it has, and there you are left clinging to the memory. So you swallow your feelings and you eat. Lucky for me I have my technique of Conscious Combining. I know that I'll never have to be fat again or give up my feelings either. And neither will you.

Thousands of letters have poured in from every corner of the country, and one by one we have answered them all. People seem to understand that I am one of them, that I, too, have fought fat. They know that I have won the fight, and if I can do it, so can they. I am not a pontificator from on high, a judgmental guru handing down diet edicts from a sterile environment. I don't live in a vacuum. I enjoy everything this good life has to offer, and among its best offerings are food and the pleasure of eating. I said it before and I'll say it again, I love to eat and I live to eat. Believe me, eating is as important to me as it is to you. I'm no different from you in that respect. Except that I've found *my* cure for fat. I studied, experimented, and synthesized the best food and nutrition theories to create a way of eating to keep myself thin, satisfied, and healthy. A way to eat to my heart's content without ever eating my heart out. A way to be thin without giving up my favorite foods, feelings, or changing my lifestyle. And now, so have you.

You have written to me as you would your best friend, from your heart, sharing your experiences, your hopes, and your joy in your new skinny souls. I rejoice in the pleasure I have helped you create for yourself. You have exulted, cheered, and celebrated. It was YOU that have made the golden pineapple the success that it is. That's right, it was YOU who did it by your slimhood. You deserve every iota of praise and happiness. You've made me very proud and very happy. I congratulate you. And I thank you. You've made my dream come true.

Roger Briggs, flight attendant, mid 30's, Beverly Hills: "By the time I was 15 years old I had a flabby 42-inch chest, enough to warrant a bra. . . . I hated myself . . . until the Beverly Hills Diet. . . . I lost 13 pounds in 10 days. Lost my stomach once and for all. . . ."

Doris De Quinze, "the Pineapple Kid," Largo, Florida, 53: "I've been on diets since I was 13. . . . This morning, my friend the scale read 135, my long-sought-after goal. I really can't believe it. I get in front of that mirror and just stare. . . . I have been so frustrated for so long, so fat . . . My husband very affectionately calls me 'Skinny.' . . . I will be a Conscious Combiner for life. . . ."

Katie Sill, Ellicott City, Maryland: "Each day I feel great because I know I'm not going to have to choose between being hungry and being thin. . . ."

Laurie Johnson, Augusta, Georgia: "I'm 54 years young. I've been married for 35 years and after this wonderful diet, my husband is chasing me around the house again! . . . I went from 142 to 129 and I felt terrific. . . ."

And as the Beverly Hills Diet became a family plan and you began to acknowledge each other's slimhood instead of ignoring and disavowing each other's fat:

Mr. and Mrs. John A. Coia, Laysville, Pennsylvania: "The Beverly Hills Diet plan is the greatest. My husband and I started the diet July 20, 1981, and we are still on it. This will be our way of eating for the rest of our lives. . . ."

As the book climbed to #1 on the Best Seller List, the critics called, "Fire!" But when the critics began shouting, it was you who shouted back for me; and when a detractor appeared in the crowds, it was you who hushed him up:

Jason Ross, Los Angeles, attorney: "Your book and your diet have turned my life around. I am sick of seeing critics attack you every day in the press for God knows what reason. . . . I tried cutting down on portions, calories, eating more protein, less carbohydrates, etc. Nothing worked . . . I have now lost 23 pounds in less than six weeks (including a ten-day Hawaiian 'misadventure into foods'). . . . I have never felt better! I am sleeping one or two hours less per night, and, when I awake in the morning, I experience a feeling of strength and virility (as opposed to feeling groggy, loggy and soggy as was the case before I went on your diet). . . . People tell me how much younger and stronger I look and my tailor loves me because I have had to take my entire wardrobe in for substantial alterations. What more can I say?"

There were letters to the editor:

Tessa Jane Hancock, New York City, Mitchell/Giurgola Architects: ". . . I am entering the fourth week of Judy's plan and have never felt better nor looked healthier. I have never had diarrhea, my complexion has cleared up and my hair has a shine that I haven't seen in years. . . ."

George Schlatter, Los Angeles, television producer: ". . . Only recently, I read that amphetamines for weight control have finally been made illegal in New York because they are dangerous—yet many of the doctors who have for years prescribed this drug are now 'horrified' at Mazel's suggestion that we live off fruits, nuts, vegetables and meat. People have died from amphetamines, but there is no record of anyone OD-ing on pineapple. Then when the AMA announces it has no intention of divesting its huge holdings in the tobacco industry, it makes you wonder if some of these doctors are more interested in finding cures or customers. Even your own article says the diet does work. You owe your readers a follow-up piece based on people who have benefited from the diet (I lost 47 pounds over five months and have never felt better in my life)."

The endorsements and raves have been stunning. Because, we former fatties know, Conscious Combining works. And the word is out. "No-sacrifice slimhood on Beverly Hills Diet" headlines the *Seattle Post Intelligencer*. "Dieters are going bananas" trumpets the *Detroit News*, relating the story of a doctor who shed 20 pounds in 22 days, and of two produce vendors who declared: "All we're hearing about is the Beverly Hills Diet. . . . We can't keep pineapples, mangoes and papayas stocked. . . . Our fruit sales have tripled." The *Oakland Press* quotes one Beverly Hills Dieter as saying, "I have so much energy. I'm off thyroid pills and other medication, and I never felt better."

The *Houston Post* reports, "It is in Beverly Hills where Judy Mazel found success and happiness with a diet that emphasizes the power of pineapple and wonder of papaya," and *Bazaar* declares, "It has been called the diet phenomenon of the 1980s—and it's no exaggeration. A unique, boldly original new food program, now sweeping across the U.S. has already been tried and tested in Beverly Hills among the movie stars, the trendsetters and the ultra-body conscious. It is, literally, an adventure into the world of food." And, from the *New York Post*, "Unbelievable as it may sound, Beverly Hills Dieters can eat lots of pasta, pizza, cake, whatever they desire and still lose weight. . . ."

The accolades piled up in literally hundreds of publications. *Newsweek* and *US* devoted multi-page spreads to the BHD phenomenon. Staffers from myriad local papers, tabloids, and magazines showcased hundreds of new Conscious Combiners exulting in skinny. No wonder one million of you have bought *The Beverly Hills Diet*! And hundreds of thousands more have shared its secrets with friends and relatives. Your voices have joined to propel the word to every inch of the country, to firmly fix *The Beverly Hills Diet* as the diet revolution of the 1980s and Conscious Combining as the way of eating for the '80s. An accepted way of life Forever.

III

How We Got There — The Proof Is in the Skinnies

At long last you now go to sleep feeling good about yourself, no more last-minute recriminations over the diet you didn't stick to. You can walk through any room with your head held high, your shoulders flung back, and be inspected by any skinny eye without flinching because you're perfect. And as you fling your head back and demand, "Do you think it's easy being gorgeous?" you know that you are. And when you get on the scale, it simply confirms it. Not only do you not have to lose one more pound, if you did, you would be too thin! Whether you had five pounds to lose or fifty pounds to lose, you did it, you lost it all. And now you're there — in the land of the little golden pineapple, the land of eternal slimhood.

Now you know what it means to feel good about yourself. And when people tell you that you're too thin, you simply smile and say, "Thank you." You hold the cure for fat. You're free; a giant weight has been lifted from your shoulders. You are rid of that obsession of "If I could just lose five more pounds, then I'll be perfect." And no one, no one can topple you from your pedestal of perfection. No one can ever push you off that cushion of control. You've replaced "now or never" with "now or later," and you know that nothing is leaving the planet.

You don't worry about what you're going to wear anymore because not only does everything in your closet fit, everything you put on looks great. You can turn to any snippy salesperson, wrap that little tiny hand around that little tiny hipbone, and with the utmost of panache say, "When you're as thin as I am, everything looks terrific." You can blow-dry your hair with the lights on, you can take a shower with your eyes open, and you no longer have to make love in the dark.

You don't have to dress in the closet or worry about what diet you will or will not go on today because you are on a diet, a diet that means Forever, a diet that means a way of life, and it's your way of life. You are secure in the knowledge that you'll never be fat again.

What you choose to eat now determines what you have to eat. *You* make the choices. *You* are in control. You're getting exactly what you've always wanted; the foods you love and a body you can be proud of. Hamburgers and hipbones, cheesecake and cheekbones, you've got it all. A little bit of a trade-off, but a great big payoff.

Why does the Beverly Hills Diet work? As Michigan librarian and a writer pointed out, "The Beverly Hills Diet was six years in the making. Ms. Mazel may be a layperson, but she has done her nutritional homework, consulting extensively with medical doctors and nutritional experts, reading and experimenting." And according to a report in the *New York Post*, "No wonder [the BHD] is . . . popular. There are no 'nevers.' Eat whatever you love best but combine it intelligently with other foods to lose or keep down weight."

But regardless of the whys, one thing is obvious: You didn't shed pounds because of calories. If you ate the amounts you should have during the six weeks, if you ate enough, then you averaged 1,200 to 1,500 calories a day. Not exactly low-calorie! And you didn't lose weight because of portion control, since there was none.

It wasn't the pills, the additives, or the artificial supplements, because they were shunned like the plague. The Beverly Hills Diet is special, not only because you learned a new way of eating that works, but also because you assimilated a whole new way of thinking that works, a way of unleashing your skinny soul. You learned to assume and accept responsibility for your body and to get in touch with it.

Because the Beverly Hills Diet is for the emotional you as well as the physical you, because it feeds your heart as well as your body, because the DFC pervades us all, fat or skinny, it is important that you new Beverly Hills Dieters grasp the essence of the Beverly Hills Diet. Remember, the Beverly Hills Diet is not just a cure for fat, it is also a way to maximize your energy and feel great, a philosophy as well as a methodology, it is a way of thinking interlocked with an eating program, each indelibly dependent on the other. It is a way of eating and thinking to make you feel good inside and out, regardless of whether you were fat or not.

So, if you haven't already done so, I strongly urge you to read this book's predecessor, *The Beverly Hills Diet*. We BHD skinnies are devout in our worship of the enzymes. We know that they represent our salvation, and that once we understand how they work, we can work with them and be thin Forever. The Beverly Hills Diet Lifetime Plan, like the Beverly Hills Diet, doesn't take our hearts out of our stomach, it just puts our heads in. We think about food as little family units and how they go together best. We understand how food becomes us. We've learned to experience food in its most fundamental form: we experience it as our energy and as our strength. We experience our body as a synergy of its parts, each dependent for its very existence on the food, on the fuel we give it. We'll always love to eat and live to eat, but now we are also eating to live. We have learned to make food, all food, work for us, even while indulging in our most glorious food fantasies. For those of you who followed the six-week program outlined in the original Beverly Hills Diet, the BHD entered your consciousness and altered it immeasurably and Forever.

For those of you who lost weight through another program, and for all you natural skinnies who want to become Conscious Combiners like Mary Ann Mobley because it will just plain make you feel good, I offer a recap of the Beverly Hills Diet.

THE BEVERLY HILLS DIET REVISITED

Simply, the Beverly Hills diet is a six-week program devoted to weight loss by feeding your body rather than starving it. The program is divided into three distinct phases, each of which serves a very specific physical and psychological purpose.

Phase I is the cleansing or detoxifying. For nine days, unlimited quantities of highly nutritious enzymatic fruits are eaten in ordered combinations designed to burn up fat, soften surplus flesh, and then wash out the residue.

Phase II begins on the tenth day with the reintroduction of the other carbohydrates and fats, such as breads, potatoes, salads, vegetables, butter, and oil. On the nineteenth day, the animal proteins appear. The continued emphasis is high carbohydrate, although at least 25 percent of the diet consists of protein from traditionally classified protein sources.

This brief but effective period further cleanses your body by allowing it to use its stored reserves. It also develops your sensitivity and awareness to foods. By isolating and then reintroducing individual foods, the effect of each food is amplified, making eating choices occurs naturally.

Phase III is devoted to maintenance. How to blow it without blowing it.

Essentially, Conscious Combining, the technique of the Beverly Hills Diet, means consciously eating foods together that digest together best. Foods that do not digest together, foods that cannot be processed by the body simultaneously, are termed miscombinations. In BHD lingo, it is the miscombinations that are the cause of our excess pounds, they are the main reason we are fat. It is not what we eat or how much we eat, but what we eat together that counts. Nothing and everything is or can be fattening.

CONSCIOUS COMBINING
REVIEWED

Conscious Combining is most concerned with digestion, the breakdown of food into nutrients, or how a hamburger with everything on it becomes vitamins, minerals, amino acids, glucose, lipids, and water. How human food becomes body food. As I understand the process, digestion of food is achieved through the work of enzymes, little chemical reactors that appear in the food we eat or are promoted in our bodies by the food we eat. Each food group (see pages 79-87) has its own set of enzymes and each is fired up to digest its own food group. Typically, a protein enzyme can only work on a protein, a carbohydrate enzyme can only work on a carbohydrate, and a fat enzyme can only work on fats. Often the presence of one enzyme will offset or thwart the presence of another.

The speed and complexity of digestion is an important cog in the Conscious Combining equation, too. As I see it, fruit digests the most easily and the most rapidly, literally slipping right through your body. Before you can even finish eating a whole pineapple, your body will most probably not only have digested what you've eaten, but absorbed it and metabolized it as well. Fats, which we usually don't eat by themselves (unless of course you have a fondness for eating butter or oil), slow down the digestion time of whatever they are eaten with by as much as several hours. Unlike protein enzymes, whose presence zap the work of the carbohydrate enzymes, the fat enzymes don't attack or neutralize other enzymes, so they can be eaten with carbs or proteins without serious consequences. Thus:

- Fruit goes alone, not to be combined with anything else, and not to be eaten after anything else.
- Fats go with other proteins or carbohydrates.
- Carbohydrates go with other carbohydrates and fats.
- Proteins go with other proteins and fats.
- Proteins and carbohydrates fight one another, digestively speaking.

The more complex the carbohydrate (I subgroup carbs into mini, midi, and maxi—see Chapter V), the longer it takes to digest. Now, just because something takes longer to digest that does not mean it is fattening or forbidden. However, they do require a little extra attention and you will simply learn how to combine them effectively.

Protein foods are the hardest to digest. And the slowest. Most notorious and ornery of all are the dairy products. Once again, you don't have to avoid them; *au contraire*, you'll just eat them at the right time. If, for instance, you love a glass of hot milk and cinnamon before you go to sleep, there is a way for you to enjoy it; there is a time and a place in your diet for everything. Surely, the Cheese Stands Alone (see page 107) is the perfect appeasement, or should I say *pièce de résistance*, for any cheese lover.

In simple terms, a slower-digesting food in one food group will block the digestion of a faster-digesting food in another food group if the two are eaten together. Now, to truly maximize efficiency (and weight loss) according to my theory, each different food type needs to digest independently; that means on its own, uncluttered by competing food groups. For example, the spaghetti in spaghetti and meatballs clumps up in your stomach while it waits for the meatballs to digest. The spaghetti in Spaghetti alla Olio however, cheerfully zips right through your stomach unfettered by the cumbersome protein. Now what this means in dollars and cents (sense, too!), or shall I say in pounds gained and lost, is that you will be able to eat a lot more Spaghetti alla Olio than spaghetti and meatballs and eat it much more frequently without having to worry about gaining weight.

Now remember, according to my theory of Conscious Combining, foods from antagonistic food groups that do not digest happily together are "miscombinations," and it is basically the miscombined foods that pile on those extra pounds. Not only does miscombining make us fat, it also saps the nutritional value of those foods because they aren't being broken down into nutrients as they should be.

Now, how could I ever boast that I've created a diet that is an Eater's dream come true if I insisted that foods never be "miscombined"? After all, man does not live by potato alone, or pasta alone, or steak alone, or even ice cream alone. Obviously, many miscombinations are far too splendid for us to continually and/or Forever pass them by. I, for one, am not willing to give up pizza, or my sandwiches, or my soufflés. Are you? Come on, let's get serious about this. Now you'd better believe that when I'm in Chicago, I'm going to go to Due's for pizza just as often as I can. A trip to Houston is not complete without a chocolate soufflé from Tony's and The Mile High Ice Cream Pie in the Caribbean Room at the Ponchartrain Hotel in New Orleans catapults me into hot-fudge heaven. The key is in making each and every miscombination count. The magic is in knowing how to use the enzymatic power of specific fruits to counteract the effects of a particular miscombined overdose. How to effectively and efficiently use the precidotes and the antidotes (see Chapter VI). The truth of the matter is, if you want to stay thin, you can only get away with just so many miscombinations. You have to know how to make food work for us, how to enjoy it as often as possible, and how *not* to get fat. Or, how to eat enchiladas tonight and pineapple tomorrow and be as thin as you'd like for the rest of your life.

Getting thin and staying thin is a product not of what you eat or how much you eat. Rather, it is a function of what foods you eat together and when you eat them. And what you eat before and after them. This is the essence of Conscious Combining, the heart of the pineapple.

THE FOLLIES OF THE FORMER FATTY

Again and again, that old Debilitating Fat Consciousness intruded into the minds of Beverly Hills Dieters and like an assailant in the dark, giving us a quick, rabbit punch in the neck, threatened to smash the best of intentions. Unpredictable and unfair, the DFC appears where and when it is least expected, in a sneaky variety of disguises ever armed to smother our newfound skinny souls. The screaming, strident voice of fat booms. No one is immune.

As you lost weight BHD style, you mended your mind/body split, and with each pound you lost, that healing continued, pound by pound. You became a thin person by becoming a thin person; by confronting, acknowledging, and letting go of the fat person; by feeling and confronting all those emotions that made you a fat person in the first place. None of us did it without a few jolts along the way. After all, you didn't get fat simply because you ate too much; you had to feel all those feelings you once swallowed in order to let go of them. None of us became skinny without a skirmish. How do you ever develop a skinny voice until you use it!

While many of the games you played were as unique as you are, there were certain similarities shared by BHDers in every nook and cranny of the country. For one reason or another many of you thought you knew how to do this better than I did, you thought that you could improvise on the diet "just a little." What you discovered in the process was that you were sacrificing your ultimate success. Oftentimes I would find myself having to remind people about *who* wrote the book. Or, as I said to a heckler at a Cleveland autograph session when all other efforts to silence her failed, "Excuse me, please, but who is the thin one and who is the fat one?"

The Six-Week Waffle

Many of you were so terrified of not losing fast enough or of gaining or of giving yourself over totally to Conscious Combining, of really becoming hooked, that you feverishly paused at the end of Week Five just when many of your favorite foods get reintegrated into your diet, just when you began to assume some responsibility for your own diet, you became convinced that there was no way you could eat pizza and live to tell the story; or, shall I say, face the scale. So you stopped after Week Four because you were afraid of Week Five, or, if you completed Week Five, you were afraid of doing Week Six.

Even if you have attained your goal weight within the first four weeks, all Beverly Hills Dieters should complete Weeks Five and Six. These weeks are not just about losing weight: they are also about balancing your brain, synergizing your head and your heart—your mouth and your stomach. Believe me! It really takes six weeks of a controlled program to break those old habits, to pry loose your DFC and replace it with that singing skinny soul. When I first began working with people in my Beverly Hills office, it was on a week-to-week basis. It evolved into a month-to-month program, and ultimately the Beverly Hills Diet became a six-week regimen. I discovered that the success and effectiveness of a permanent integration of the tenets of Conscious Combining were only truly accomplished over a six-week period. It took six weeks of experiencing this alternative approach to eating to change a person's food and diet consciousness. Now, I'm not saying that this change is 100 percent, but the difference is so dramatic that one's life is markedly affected, and it is an effect that lasts Forever!

Let's face it, if your way of life includes hamburgers, pizza, and ice cream, then you'd better learn to make those foods work for you. And by making them work, I mean not only counteracting their negative side effects, their fattening potential, I mean eating them without feeling guilty and without being afraid. You must prove to your skinny soul that those foods are a part of your life and will remain one. That you can indeed eat them with pride and pleasure, without guilt or fear, *with* permission, and *even out in public!* Only when you experience that you can really eat anything on this planet without losing control, and without getting fat, only when you internalize that experience, then and only then will your skinny soul really truly be free.

Well, it's Weeks Five and Six that help internalize your skinny soul, that make the difference in Forever. If you don't complete them, you never convince your skinny person that you are creating a new way of life, a way of eating that is Forever. If you didn't eat your favorite foods, then diet wouldn't mean a way of life. And just like every other diet that has failed you it would always mean a suspension of time and reality. Nancy Keenan, a Detroit lady, was stuck on a three-week-long plateau. She broke it with a three-pound weight loss after her pizza night. It's easy to say, "I can have all the pizza I want anytime I want it" and never do it and never prove it. . . .

Under the influence of the DFC, every day must be a weight-loss day, or panic consumes you. But what human body doesn't fluctuate—down and up? It's that old unrealistic expectation syndrome, the setting-yourself-up-to-fail debacle. Big deal if you gain a pound! So what? That's the beauty of the Beverly Hills Diet. The magic of Conscious Combining. Unless you experiment, unless you experience, how are you ever going to see just how much you can get away with?

I can't wave a magic wand and wipe out the extra pounds gained from pizza. That's not where the miracle lives. The miracle exists in those magic little enzymes. It's the enzymes in the potent fruits eaten in the right combinations that make this diet different.

The miracle exists in the precidotes and in the antidotes. The truth is that you will always gain weight if you eat certain things, nothing can change that. But if you eat the proper things before them and after them, you'll lose the weight just as easily as you gained it.

When Conscious Combiners worried that they would lose too much (joy of joys!), I advised them to take real advantage of their Open Meals. The worst that can happen is that you'll have a lot of fun gaining back some weight.

The Week-One Cling

Many of you were so anxious to perpetuate your dramatic weight loss of Week One that out of fear you kept repeating it. You thought it was the only way you would be able to continue losing weight. Despite my telling you not to repeat that first week, well, some of you thought you knew better, and you went ahead and did it anyway.

After you have done the nine days of fruit, you have completed your fruit cleansing, the burning, feeding, and washing. Not only do you not need to do it again, your body will not repeatedly respond in a positive way to that much fruit. The magic of Week One cannot be duplicated or re-created.

Once you have become a Conscious Combiner, once you have completed your six weeks' "training," you should not eat fruit exclusively for more than three or four consecutive days. Remember, man does not live by kiwi alone, any more than he lives by meatloaf alone. It is the proper balance of all foods that is going to keep you slim and healthy.

You can only go back to the first week of the Beverly Hills Diet if, heaven forbid, you've totally slashed fruit from your repertoire of foods. I mean, *only* if you have gone completely crazy, miscombined like mad, and unequivocally ignored the Golden Rules and Ten Commandments of the Beverly Hills Diet for at least three months. Highly improbable, but not impossible!

The Case of the Missing
Nonphysical Exercises

Just as I suspected, most people think they were too sophisticated for the Nonphysical Exercises. They were too embarrassed or they thought they were silly or, that they were just not necessary. Yet true to form, the elite got a real kick out of doing them. The stars and the jet-setters were far from ashamed. They did them at the slightest provocation.

The Nonphysical Exercises make you aware of all the things that made you a fat person to begin with; all those pounds and perversities you had to confront, acknowledge, and let go of. Getting thin is more than just losing weight. Being thin is a state of being; it is a way of thinking, an attitude. The Beverly Hills Diet is a way of relating to food and to yourself that ensures eternal slimhood. You develop a skinny voice by using it, you develop a skinny dialogue by developing it. You become a thin person by confronting, acknowledging, and letting go of the fat person. You have to see what you are to choose what you *don't* want to be, and you have to see what you want to be to become it. A bridge isn't built before it's someone's idea. You won't have a beautiful body until you can see it.

If you can't be proud of yourself (The Proud Sheet),* if you can't accept positive reinforcement (The Three Questions),* if you can't see yourself in perspective as an entity (Seeing Yourself as Others See You),* if you can't acknowledge your fat and how you hate it (The Sharon Assignment),* and if you can't Talk Back* to your detractors and believe every word you say, the answer is obvious: You'll never achieve eternal slimhood and you'll never luxuriate in the land of the little golden pineapple.

Oh, you might get thin. You might even lose all the weight you set out to lose. You might even get thinner than you've ever been before. But you'll never stay there, it will never last; you'll

*See Glossary.

just repeat the same old habits, make the same mistakes. You'll just stay hung up on that same gain-loss teeter-totter. Listen, I don't have to tell you about it, you've been there, you know what it's like.

Well, what's the point of getting thin if you can't stay there? What's the point of getting thin if you have to experience the pain of getting fat all over again? And again, and again? In my little outstretched palm I am offering you the secrets of eternal slim-hood. I've experimented, I've tested, I've tried and I've tribulated. I've attempted to get away with everything I could. Believe me, I've hacked all the nonessentials from the BHD. Do you really think I'd clutter up your life with trivia and busywork if it wasn't essential to becoming skinny? I know what it takes because I've been there. I have done it. And I've succeeded! To be skinny Forever you must do everything I've outlined in this book, and I do mean *everything*. All I want to do is put a smile on your face and unleash your hipbones and cheekbones so that you can be as skinny as you'd like for the rest of your life. No matter that you're skinny without the Nonphysical Exercises. Trust me, it won't last if you don't do them. The Beverly Hills Diet, after all, was con-ceived to free you to live a full life, unconsumed and unriddled by fat hang-ups.

Soooo . . . if you haven't already done the BHD Nonphysical Exercises, I urge you to do them, to confront that little fat person who is rebelling, that little fat person who doesn't want to confront that part of himself that the exercises might unfold. Is the heartache and misery that go hand and hand with Fat worth the alternative? Because there are more coming up, because the new Nonphysical Exercises are just as critical to maintaining your weight as the original ones are to weight loss itself, the BHD Nonphysical Exercises will set the stage and get you ready for Forever.

P. S., I still do them. Whenever I'm insecure I'll ask the Three Questions (see Glossary). I still keep my Proud Sheet going, I create situations to apply The Sharon Assignment. And every wall in my bathroom is mirrored. You know people are constantly saying, "Oh, come on, you can cheat just this time," or "You can have just one little bitty bite, it won't hurt you." And I am forever reminding them that it isn't easy being gorgeous!

So don't be afraid of them because I'm here, and so is your little skinny soul. And best of all, now you've got your hipbones to hold on to.

Plateau Panic

"Help! I'm at a plateau, what do I do?" The question, like weight, always comes up. Well, I warned you. Plateaus are not only inevitable, they are deviously unpredictable. They are the ultimate test of your skinny voice. Your DFC is poised, ready to pounce on plateaus. Oh, you can use them as an excuse to blow it. You can do what you did in the past, when day after day you would get on the scale and have it not move. You *could* say, "Oh, the hell with it!" kick the scale, and go eat just like you used to. Then you're sure to accomplish one thing. You'll get that scale to move all right, but it will go UP instead of DOWN. And if you think you're angry and frustrated when it's just standing still, imagine, or, better yet, remember how lousy if felt when it started going back up.

When you hit a plateau, your old fat self said, "What's the point of getting thin? I'll just get fat again when I start eating what I want." And all you can see is this dreary, endless trade-off without a payoff. No more pounds lost and no food you love; not now, not ever! But *never* doesn't exist for you anymore, now that you have become a Conscious Combiner. *Never* doesn't exist in your skinny vocabulary; it has been replaced by *later*. If you can't have it now, big deal, you can have it later, and if you don't have it later, then maybe tomorrow, *nothing is leaving the planet*. It will all be there, in abundance, waiting for you.

Plateaus allow you to internalize, integrate, and welcome that new skinny person into your life. To experience, embrace, and most of all accept it. They allow you to experience yourself as you are, at that very moment, to mend the mind/body split that so pervades the weight-loss process.

The sublime security of knowing you can outlast a plateau is one of the great thrills of life. When you smash a plateau, when you get on that scale and it says, "Yes, you really are thinner. You've Won!" Then oh, boy! Your heart will sing and your soul will soar. The joy of slimhood, the joy of success will outweigh any happiness you've ever known.

The Measure of Thin

People are always asking me, "Am I thin enough?" I, with my skinny bias, often say no. I really believe you can't be too thin or too rich . . . well, maybe there are some exceptions to the thin part. While developing this book on the beach at the Kahala Hilton in Hawaii we saw some skinnies who really were too thin. Their arms and legs were like sticks, and I had to admit that they were rather unattractive.

How do you judge for yourself? Which is, after all, the only way to judge. Forget all those charts. Don't bother asking everyone else's opinion; remember, your fat friends are intimidated by your new slimhood and your slim friends certainly don't need you for added competition. Forget about your mirror, because all you'll see is what you want to see, not necessarily what really exists. When I feel low and I look in the mirror, that old fat, unhappy person will fleetingly reappear. You'll see, that fat image doesn't go away just because you've lost weight.

I'll never forget my first shopping trip after I had become thin. When I gleefully discovered that the ladies' size 4s were too big, I went to the children's department. I tried on an adorable (though somewhat youthful for my thirty years) dress with a pink ruffled top and dirndl skirt. The kind that aren't even in the frame of reference of a fat person. My first reaction when I looked in the mirror was that it made me look fat; ruffles and a dirndl, PUHLEEZE! Now, let's get serious. I had begun wearing dark chemises when I was thirteen. You know, I might laugh at it now, but at the time I actually had to remind myself that a person can't look fat when she is wearing a little girl's size 10 and weighs ninety-seven pounds. But since you can only be so chic when you have to shop in the children's department, even if it is Saks Fifth Avenue, I thought it a good excuse to gain back a few pounds. And what fun that was!

So how *do* you know when you are thin enough? The one impartial observer in your life, the one thing you can always count on to tell you the truth is your scale. It's when you can get on that scale and say, "I don't have to lose one more pound!" and really, really mean it, then and only then are you perfect. If you still have even one pound to lose, your world is colored, you're chained to a diet. But when you get on that scale and you experience the high of knowing you can have anything in the world you want because you have nothing to lose . . . well, at that glorious point, nothing is fattening and the world takes on a new aura. You are no longer separated from your goal. And when your goal is realized, you break free into the world of rewards. And then you've got it all. Everything you've ever really wanted, your dream has come true.

Just to be sure your weight is perfect, you may have to go a little below your goal first. Remember, I had to get to 97 pounds before I could happily stabilize at 102.

Not long ago I was at a celebrity cook-off at Le Dome Restaurant in Beverly Hills. The tables were piled high with very tempting, devastatingly fattening hearty fare. I had a special sense of security. I had the luxury of being two pounds under my ideal. I could have anything I wanted, anything at all, because it really didn't matter if I gained weight. The irony? Nothing on the table appealed to me more than my sense of security. Once I could have anything in the world (and, believe me, it looked like it was all on the table), I wanted to eat, I didn't even want it; all I wanted was to stay perfect.

By the way, I've been skinny now for seven years, and despite many emotionally charged periods and four months of perpetual travel, my weight hasn't fluctuated by any more than three pounds. And still, my scale goes with me wherever I go. We still carry on our fervid love affair, my truth teller and me. It's the first thing I unpack, and it's the last thing that goes into my bag when I check out. It's my ultimate security. Make your scale your best friend and your lover, allow it to become your ultimate security, and it will be.

So, if I may suggest one more time, you little skinny you, before you embark on Forever, before you read another word in the Beverly Hills Diet Lifetime Plan: If you haven't already done so, read *The Beverly Hills Diet*. You will be grounded in the fundamentals of Conscious Combining, and you will be mentally prepared for our world of eternal slimhood!

PART TWO
KEEPING IT OFF

IV

The Rules and Tools—
An Advanced Primer

You want to believe, but you're tentative. How many times have you heard the promise of Forever? You think it's too good to be true. You've heard so many vacant promises; you've believed, but again and again your belief was battered and denied. Well, I don't blame you for being a skeptic; the odds are 9–1 against you that you'll keep off those lost pounds. According to a *New York Times* article (June 30, 1981), obesity specialist Dr. Theodore von Itallie of New York's St. Luke's Medical Center claims that 90 percent of all dieters fail to stay thin.

After one month, according to doctors in the *Treatment and Management of Obesity*, most "losers" in their study groups have begun to gain back their weight. About a year and a half after the beginning of two types of diets and therapy, Dr. Per Bjorntorp reported in the *American Journal of Clinical Nutrition* in 1980, patients' weights were about the same as they were before they started the diet program. In other words, the odds of keeping your weight off pre-Beverly Hills Diet Lifetime Plan were practically *nil; zero*. Dr. Albert J. Stunkard, writing along wih Mavis McLaren-Hume, M.S. in the AMA Archives of Internal Medicine, told us what we already know: "Results of treatment for obesity are remarkably similar and remarkably poor. . . . It is a terribly difficult business, one in which our experts achieve only modest success and the rest of us even less." In a study Dr. Stunkard conducted with one hundred intensely supervised patients, only two were still clinging to a respectable weight loss after two years! You have every right to be terrified. The statistics are devastating!

But trust me, because no matter how many pounds you have gained and lost in your life, you can put your fears to rest. Every trick I use to stay thin will become yours. Every ploy I use to feel good will become yours. And as Conscious Combining becomes Unconscious Combining, the Beverly Hills Diet Lifetime Plan will become your Lifetime Plan.

I'm going to give you the rules and the tools that will guide your life, tools to use in every case, in every confrontation. Tools that will become a support system; your support system. A support system you can depend on because it exists within you. A support system so secure it will override any excuse you will ever have for ever getting fat again. And once the BHD Lifetime Plan becomes your own, it will be literally impossible to ever wreak havoc on your body again.

Maintenance doesn't mean losing weight; it means staying put. Maintenance means Forever. You were fat and now you're thin. The power of your knowledge, your newly acquired tools, your support system, your self-respect, and your pride are going to keep you there. Maintenance means being in control. It means making choices, taking chances, and being secure that they are okay—you accept responsibility. Maintenance means throwing away your food scale, your calorie charts, and your regimen of denial. Maintenance means internalizing where you are and eliminating your DFC once and for all and Forever. So perk up your pineapples and prepare for the rules and tools, plump up those papayas and get ready for the Food Formulas, the precidotes and the antidotes, and your Workbook to Wonderland, the critical cogs in your own food equation for eternal slimhood.

THREE GOLDEN RULES
TO FOREVER

These three little rules mean the difference between thin and fat, life and lifelessness, happiness and misery, temporary and forever; going to bed feeling good about yourself and going to bed feeling bad about yourself. Well, what's worse than being fat? All of our lives we've been absorbed by our bodies, with being thin; with how we look, how we feel, especially how we look. Somehow we've been victimized into believing that we have no responsibility, no choice.

We either have a slow metabolism or an underactive thyroid. It's genetic, our parents were fat. We're doomed to be fat because we love to eat. And eating, we've been taught, and being thin are mutually exclusive. Our kidneys don't work well, we bloat, we're prone to colds, whatever the excuse, we accept it. We give up—and we give in. We bemoan our fat and our fate, and as we pull that French doughnut out of the bag, that French doughnut we were dying to have, we apologize for it because we have no right to have it, let alone enjoy it, because we're fat and we're getting fatter, and it's fattening, and everyone is watching and wondering why we're not on a diet. While we never really admit it, we've given up. Well, what's the difference you say, sooner or later you'll eat everything you love, and sooner or later you'll just get fat again. So why not, might as well have it sooner rather than later. Why postpone the inevitable? The inevitable? Well, it's not what it used to be, not anymore.

We're so sophisticated about food. Its meaning has become so convoluted in our minds that we've mentally smothered its simple and original purpose. It creates flesh and blood and it is our energy. Food will always be an excuse for a social situation, an emotional stopgap, an expression of love, an instant and temporary cure for boredom. Eating will always be a time for families to get together to celebrate, to rejoice and unite. It's a time to do business, it's a reward and it's a punishment. All true, but above all, food is you. You are what you eat. Pure and simple, no more, no less.

Our lives, our food, our eating have been dictated by habit and tradition. Our hearts rather than our heads have ruled our eating. Now, you know me, I'm the last one to take your heart out of your stomach. I know how it feels. I have those moments, those moments of madness when my head says no and my heart says go, and most of the time, I listen to my heart. But that's okay, because my choice in those moments of madness is not to eat or not to eat, it's not to get fat or stay thin. My choice is what to eat to make it all work. What to eat to stay thin and feel good. I'm an Eater, and as we Eaters know, those "moments" happen quite frequently. What has saved me, what's kept me skinny, are three little rules; rules that are as important to me as the moral code that guides my life. And just as I wouldn't commit murder, well, I wouldn't break these rules either. The Three Golden Rules have the potential to ensure your eternal slimhood just as they do mine.

I know, you're wondering, "What about all those other rules and tools?" While they are all vitally important, any of them can be broken occasionally without fat taking over or your energy being instantly zapped. But, no matter how flagrantly I may abuse any of the other rules, never do I trifle with these three. The Three Golden are sacred, never to be abused.

Keep in mind that the rules and tools were first discovered when I was seeking my personal cure for fat, when I was struggling alone through that mire of misery. There were a few physical laws to guide me, but the methodology, the philosophy, the rules, and the tools all came first out of my own personal experience and experiments, and later those of my clients. People often ask me, "Didn't you break the rules when you first started, didn't you slip up once in a while?" I remind them that there were no "rules" when I started, the rules as we know them are simply a product of what worked and what didn't work. They only became etched in bronze as they were stretched to their limits, as I went along and experimented.

Since then, with the help of well over a thousand Beverly Hills Dieters whom I have personally supervised in my Beverly Hills clinic, I've experimented and refined, honed and hacked. Only then did I put the Three Golden down indelibly as guidelines for all of us. Believe me, my clients and I have tried stretching them to the limit. We know that the Three Goldens are inviolable.

I'm asking you to take these rules and put them on a pedestal, to internalize them so that they will always guide your eating. To make them as much a part of your life, as much a part of your moral code, as I have done. And just as you wouldn't commit armed robbery or lie in front of a moving car, establish these few simple parameters when it comes to eating. Make a commitment to me and to yourself. I'm not asking you to eliminate anything from your life, I'm asking you to *add* to it.

And together we can revel in the power of the hipbones and frolic in the land of Forever skinny.

Golden Rule One
The Waiting Time
When you switch foods, wait the appropriate time

- From one fruit to another, wait two hours.
- From fruit to anything else, from one food type to another, wait three hours.

These are minimum waiting times, the least time you can get away with without running the risk of FAT. Remember, according to my theory of Conscious Combining, you gain weight because food is not processed properly. In simplest terms, if food doesn't leave your stomach when it should, if it gets held up or trapped by other antagonistic foods, the nutrients it should generate will not be properly processed by your body, and you'll gain weight.

I know. You're hungry and you just can't wait. But be honest, you have only yourself to blame, you didn't eat enough! The trick, of course, is to not leave yourself those long gaps between eating so that you're starving when food finally does come your way. When you know that you are going to change foods, give yourself enough time to fill up first. Be sure you check your watch so that you wait the appropriate time. Don't let yourself be a victim. There is *no reason* to let yourself get hungry. Maintenance means eating until you're full. If I, the compulsive eater of all time, can wait, so can you.

Golden Rule Two
Fruit First

· Once you have gone off fruit in the course of the day, never go back to it.

I don't care if the last mango in paradise is at the peak of perfection on your kitchen counter and all you had was a one-inch square of day-old pot roast six hours earlier, or if it was only the mere crumb of a crust of bread when you cut your son's peanut butter sandwich. Once anything else has passed through those infamous portals, once absolutely anything other than fruit has gone into that mouth, that's it!

Once you have eaten something other than fruit in the course of the day, fruit no longer exists for you until tomorrow. Forget about it, wipe it from your consciousness. It's not leaving the planet; that pineapple will still be there tomorrow.

You Beverly Hills Dieters will remember when I first told you about fruit and its magic. Your reaction: "Fruit is fattening. You can't eat fruit and lose weight." "I always get bloated from fruit!" "It makes me gassy." "That's because," I responded, "of when you ate it. You probably didn't eat it on an empty stomach." Fruit is so supercharged it must work alone. It's been my experience that it simply cannot digest properly after anything else. If inhibited in its processing, if stymied by noncompatible foods, if eaten after anything else, its explosive enzyme action will be offset by bloating and gas. Your savior will be transformed into your tormentor.

I'll never forget a dinner party where a grape at the end of a meal literally spelled the near demise of one of the guests. The only non–Beverly Hills Dieter in the crowd, she ate everything and anything with wild abandon. Much to my disappointment she fared quite well, at least until she began nibbling on the grapes out of the centerpiece. They were the corker or, shall I say, the uncorker. It wasn't long after that first grape that she had to excuse herself and was shuttled off with an excruciating stomachache.

The only exception to the Fruit First rule is when you know in advance that you will be eating an Open Human (a meal including all food groups [OH]) or an Open Dessert (dessert in lieu of the meal [OD]). If you know in advance that you're going to an Open Meal that contains fruit you will be able to minimize the consequences by preceding that meal with the appropriate fruit precidote (see Glossary). Really though, only under the most exceptional and rare circumstances should you include fruit in an Open Meal because, believe me, it will be the most devastating part of that whole meal.

I plugged into the potency of fruit to make you thin, and I am doing the same to keep you there. That pineapple perched on the cover of this book is there for a reason!

Golden Rule Three
Once Protein, Always Protein

· Once you have eaten protein in the course of a day, stay with protein for the entire day.

While no rule is maintenance unto itself, this golden rule verges on it. If I had to choose only one rule to magically ensure slimhood and vivid energy, this would be it.

As I see it, enzymatically, there is no way your body can

properly digest carbohydrates once the full enzymatic response of your stomach has been activated by the presence of protein.

Let me explain the digestive process as I view it, based on the facts as I understand them. Bear in mind, this is my interpretation of how food becomes you. Understand that I've taken a very complicated process, digestion, and simplified and described it so that you and other BHDers can identify, visualize, and understand it. I believe the reason most of us are so far removed from ourselves and our bodies is because the subject matter, our bodies, has always been described in a manner that made it foreign to us, in textbook terms that only the chosen few in "the Golden Circle" could understand.

There are three steps to protein digestion as I perceive it. First, the hydrochloric acid shower shoots out of the walls of your stomach. When the hydrochloric acid shower stops, those tough little pepsin enzymes begin to bang away, breaking down the protein. The presence of the pepsin then reactivates the hydrochloric acid, and those two potent agents work together to finish off the job. Once pepsin and hydrochloric acid are holding hands, or rather, working together, they set up a chemical reaction that neutralizes or negates the carb-digesting enzyme, ptyalin. This means that any carb eaten after a protein cannot be digested properly. Also, recall that protein digests far more slowly than any other food type. Thus any carb that appears in your stomach with a protein will sit around waiting for the protein to be digested, before it can be properly digested. And it's a long wait! In an average, happy (meaning efficient) stomach, I have experienced that waiting time to be as long as:

3 hours for Nuts
5 hours for Fish
6 hours for Chicken
8 hours for Beef
12 hours for Dairy Products

Of course, the times aren't cast in stone. There are so many variables. It could depend on your own particular stomach, how you feel, what you ate earlier, or even the time of the day. As far as I'm concerned, the bottom line is that as long as there is a smidgen of protein left in your stomach, as long as pepsin and hydrochloric acid are working together, that carb is going to be fattening.

For you non-BHDers, this won't be a hard rule to follow, because you haven't become carb-conscious yet. You are probably used to a high-protein diet. For those of us who know better; for those of us who have experienced the joy of a carb day, for those who have become addicted to bagels and pasta without guilt and fear, well, waiting until tomorrow will be tougher.

But remember, everything will still be there tomorrow; that sourdough bread that you're looking at so longingly as you gnaw on that steakbone can be yours in the morning if you stick to your protein tonight.

And what you are really doing if you don't follow the Golden Rules is depriving yourself. When you break them, guilt will monopolize you. And how can you possibly enjoy anything you eat when you know you shouldn't be eating it? You know you're doing something you shouldn't and you'll have to pay the price. Not only are you depriving yourself of the pleasure of now, you're also depriving yourself of the pleasure of later; the joy of tomorrow. You won't be able to have what you want tomorrow. You won't be able to have what you want tomorrow because of what your scale will tell you and because of the way you'll feel. Instead of hamburgers and hipbones, you'll be dooming yourself to heartache and hunger.

And you'll be setting yourself up for future problems. Once you blow your discipline, you'll do it again and again. Not so long ago I broke the Once Protein, Always Protein rule. Yes, even me! I ate bagels *after* steak. Of course I got away with it, I didn't gain any weight. The reality is you aren't going to gain every time you blow it. But suddenly I found myself breaking that rule again and again; it kept getting easier and less important somehow. Until I yanked myself back to reality. Until I admitted that even *my* DFC was ever lurking and had almost knocked me off my pineapple. If the Beverly Hills Diet and the Beverly Hills Diet Lifetime Plan weren't my life and my mission it would have been easy for me to ignore that rule once I had broken it. So beware, if I could do it, so can you.

The Three Golden Rules are the cornerstone of your maintenance plan. They are your foundation, the rules you will live by. They will allow you to conquer fat forever, to feel spectacular and finally to be free.

However, as we all know, nothing worth having happens as easily as one, two, three. Did your terrific marriage just happen or have you worked at it? Were you born into that great job or did you have to work for it? A beautiful body? Well, having and maintaining it is no different. Remember, it's not easy being gorgeous!

So, Now for the Tools— Your Support System

When you were losing weight, the rules were rigid, unrelenting, uncompromising. Part of doing it was doing it all the way, no ifs, ands, or buts about it. In the process of following those rules they have become a part of you, easily and naturally; many of them you don't even have to think about anymore. They have become your tools, the foundation of your support system, the tricks you rely on to keep you thin, to keep you on the straight and narrow.

Now that you've lost it, now that you're thin, well—now the fun really begins. Sure, your life will still be guided by a series of rules, but now they become *your* rules, *your* tools; *your* very own *individual* support system. Your foundation for eternal slimhood.

Some will be the same as those you followed during weight loss. Some are modified. Some are new. All are flexible. How much you can adapt them and get away with is up to you.

MENTAL RULES— MIND OVER MATTER

The Beverly Hills Diet Lifetime Plan is for the total you. Like the diet, the lifetime plan is a philosophy, a way of thinking, as well as a methodology, a way of doing. It is a completely new way of relating to food and to yourself that guarantees you eternal slimhood. It is a revolutionary new way of thinking. It's thinking right as well as eating right.

Mental Rule One
Think about Food

If you think about food when it doesn't count, you won't have to think about it when it does. When eating is not going to be an orgasmic experience, when it really doesn't matter what you eat, when it's a choice between an ordinary dinner salad and blueberries, hard-boiled eggs or papaya, when you aren't going to remember it ten minutes after you've eaten it, then you should think with your head and not with your heart. You should choose to feed your body. Because if you feed your body when you can, you can feed your heart and soul when you want to.

Revel in your love affair with food. Make every bite count. Obviously you can't eat everything you want every time you want it. You will have to make some choices. The reality, for every bite that goes in your mouth, something else can't. How many bland tuna salad sandwiches and slices of processed cheese have you crammed in without tasting them, without feeling them? How many times have you grabbed something, anything, just because it was the most convenient thing around? Remember, if you plan for

it, nothing, not even that chocolate soufflé, will be fattening.
When you make every bite count, when you feed your body the
food that is ultimately going to make that nine-course Chinese
meal work, when you allow what you choose to eat to determine
what you have to eat and do it graciously without a struggle, when
you can honestly say, "I surrender, I give up, I'll give in to thin,"
then your heart will sing and your soul will soar, and eternal
slimhood will be yours evermore!

Mental Rule Two
You Are What You Eat

Food is energy, your energy. You are a product of what you
eat, pure and simple. Think not only about how you react sensu-
ally to food but about how you react physically as well. Think of
food in terms of later and how it will make you feel later, not just
in terms of the transitory now. How you feel, how you look, how
people relate to you, how your life works for you, all depend on
your energy. Your energy is a magnet, its strength and power
determine what will be drawn to you. And your energy comes from
one source, the food you eat. Food is your life, and your life
depends on it.

When I choose not to have cheesecake, believe me it's not
because it doesn't taste good, it's because it doesn't feel good. One
of the benefits of the Beverly Hills Diet, of those first six weeks, is
that the cleansing, the elimination, the gradual reintegration, and
the isolation of foods develops a heightened sensitivity and awareness so that you can feel the precise effect that different foods have
on your state of being, the real role food plays in your life. You
experience that bagels make you feel different than hot dogs, that
a pineapple gives you energy and a potato calms you down. I'll
never forget a client who has spent years alternating between
uppers and downers. She described the effect of a baked potato as
better than that of a tranquilizer.

When you choose not to "miscombine" (see Glossary), it

won't be because you can't, it will be because you don't want to, because it doesn't feel as good.

Mental Rule Three
Nothing Is Leaving the Planet

If you don't have it now, you can have it later; if not later, then tomorrow. Nothing is leaving the planet. Because at long last tomorrow is here, and it is here for you to enjoy. It is not the tomorrow of yesterday, filled with unfulfilled good intentions; it's filled with hope and promise, hamburgers and hipbones. It includes the foods you love and the body you've always wanted; cheesecake and cheekbones.

No longer will you look at a plate of french fries and inhale them at first sight just because they're there. It's not now or never anymore; you have permission to have french fries anytime you want them. You'll be able to sit in front of your favorite pizza and eat grapes, without flinching. You will be in total control. Pizza will be there tomorrow. You don't have to stop at McDonald's and eat a Big Mac just because you happen to be driving by; you'll pass another one later. You don't have to have the Veal Pepper and Fuselli every time you're at Adriano's; they aren't closing, you'll be there again and again. If you don't have Gia's quesadilla every time you lunch at the Bistro Garden, it isn't the end of the world; the quesadilla is on the menu every day. So what if tonight you can't have the Mozzarella Marinara you love so much at Matteo's; you'll be there again next Sunday night.

Your favorite restaurant, your favorite foods, your favorite chef, they'll all still be there tomorrow. And if they aren't, if that chef quits, he'll go to work someplace else; if the restaurant burns down, another will take its place. Always remember, this beautiful, wonderful life we lead is like a cruise: There's plenty of time, plenty of food, and plenty of opportunities to enjoy it. And if we don't have it now, we can have it later, and if we don't have it later, then maybe tomorrow. *Nothing is leaving the planet!*

Mental Rule Four
Stand Up and Be Counted

I am an Eater (see Glossary), and I am proud to admit it. I have accepted it, I have acknowledged it, and I have embraced it. I've surrendered, I've given up, I've given in to thin. I've let food and eating become a positive thing; I've learned how to make them work for me. And so can you.

The Beverly Hills Diet Lifetime Plan is the salvation for people who love to eat and who live to eat. For those of us to whom food is important, it is *really* important. Our energy and the way we use it, our power and the way we direct it, are all contingent on how we feed ourselves. The sooner you are willing to accept the role that food plays in your life, the sooner you are willing to stop fighting reality, the sooner maintenance will work for you.

Stand up and proclaim yourself an Eater. It's okay. You're thin now, no one will point a finger at you. You have nothing to be ashamed of. You must acknowledge that fat person, to let go of him or her once and for all and Forever. You confronted your fat person and in doing so got thin; now acknowledge that person and stay thin.

When you were fat, you couldn't deny you were an Eater because everyone could see it. But now you're thin, and that's a trap all its own. Suddenly you try to lead a double life, you become furtive about food. It becomes important to the "newly thin" person to hide the fact that he was fat. God forbid anyone should know. It becomes important to play the game of "I can eat whatever I want, I'm thin now, I don't have to give food or eating a second thought." The problem is you do give it a second thought, and a third; and that's what sets you apart from the natural skinnies. You think about food, a lot! But this time you think you'll get away with it, this time it's different. Well, you can't, and you won't, so forget about it. Surrender, give up and give in to thin. Always remember that you are a fat person, a fat person in a thin body. What once was can always be again. Those fat cells won't ever go away; they just hang out, waiting to plump up again at the slightest provocation. Accept who you are and embrace it. It's okay, you're skinny now and you have the tools that will let you stay that way always. Tools that will let you lead a normal life devoid of the Forever of "dieting."

You are an Eater now and Forever, so don't try to deny it. Acknowledge it and let it be a positive thing. I'm asking you to take your negative energy, your DFC, and turn it into a positive. It will make the difference between now and Forever.

The sooner you stop being jealous of those natural skinnies who eat everything, the sooner maintenance will become Forever. Give up the dream once and for all and Forever that you can be one of "them," a naturally skinny "outsider" just because you have *become* a skinny. Give up the idea that you can eat whatever you want, whenever you want, and however you want without thinking about it as they do, *because you can't.* "They" don't think about food the way you do; "they" don't care about food the way you do. Food isn't important to them the way it is to you. You are not one of "them" and never will be. So give it up. Give up *that* dream, once and for all and Forever.

But, by all means, don't give up your pride. And don't give up your joy in eating. The love of eating is as basic to mankind as any sensual pleasure. A lady next to me at lunch the other day at Jimmy's was obviously relishing her Duck with Strawberry Sauce. Her lunch partner leaned across the table and sneered, "Boy, you really like to eat, don't you!" As if she were indulging in child beating. Don't be ashamed. Eaters are real special people. Enjoying eating means enjoying life. You don't feel guilty when you are entranced by a magnificent concert. You aren't scorned because you adore the smell of roses. You aren't ridiculed because a morning mist makes you gasp with the beauty of it. You aren't mocked because you enjoy making love. Far from it! So why should you deny your feelings for food?

When you truly feel good about who you are and what you are, then philosophically you can never be the same, be buffeted by food whimsies, smothered by diet "advice," cuffed by your DFC. You can't deny your little fat soul—you can't deny from whence you came. So stand up and be counted.

THE TOOLS

The skeleton of your eating program will be the Beverly Hills Diet Lifetime Plan. I will provide you with the backbone, and you will furnish the meat. The flesh will be your own. I will give you the guidelines, you will adapt them. I will provide the Food Formulas, you will make your own food choices. Remember, this is your diet, your way of life, based on the food you want to eat and the food you like to eat. There is no going off the Beverly Hills Diet Lifetime Plan. There is no cheating. Cheating is a word that doesn't even exist for us. There is nothing you can't have, so you won't have to cheat to have it. This isn't a plan that you "sort of" do. It is a commitment to Forever, a commitment to slimhood and health.

I am offering you the guidelines to the world beyond the golden pineapple; the rules and the tools; the keys to eternal slimhood. If you want to win, you'll have to play by those rules, just as you do in the rest of your life. In every area in which we succeed, we are bound by rules. Most social rules, for example, have become so automatic that we follow them unconsciously. If you want to be socially acceptable, you don't eat with your hands in public, you don't wear a bathing suit to a dinner party, and you don't tell your host what an ugly sport jacket he's wearing. If you want to stay skinny and energetic, you'd better play it by the rules, too. Remember, it's rules, not nos and nevers, that will make the difference in Forever.

I'm not a fool. I don't expect perfection and conformity. I'm going to show you how to experiment with the rules by stretching them—so that you can get away with murder and not serve a life sentence. I'm going to show you how to stretch the rules and not add insult to injury, how to accommodate your diet to your life rather than accommodating your life to your diet. The thing that will make it work for you is following the rules and using the tools.

I've divided the tools into General (those that apply to all situations), Home (those to use at home), and Social (you know what that means). Use them, stretch them, don't abuse them. They are your salvation!

General Tools

1. *Experience and enjoy*. It's not how much you can get in in how short a time, it's how long you can make the pleasure last. You have permission to experience and enjoy it, so eat slowly. Taste it, luxuriate in it, and understand how it makes you feel.

2. *Ease into maintenance*. When you begin maintenance and resume "regular eating," do it gently. Ease into it. Start miscombining with trepidation, always being prepared for the worst. Keep in mind that it takes a full six months of maintaining before your body is truly in balance at your new weight, before your heart is in harmony with your new world of eating.

3. *Isolate your eating experiences so that you can isolate their effects*. Know your enemy so that you will know how to defend yourself. This is a very important tool. It is the keystone to learning to stretch the rules. If you find that you gain weight from a particular eating experience, it's not the end of the world, that's how you'll learn to correct it. Repeat your experiments; often those most devastating in the early stages of maintenance (particularly salt) will be quite

successful after your body has had more time to stabilize, after the first six months.

4. *Experiment —stretch every rule to its limit*. Don't be afraid. Only in this way can you identify the parameters of your skinny kingdom. If you don't know for sure just how far you can go, you'll never be able to stay where you're at. Find out what works for you and what doesn't. After all, we're talking about Forever. Try café au lait at the end of a protein day. See how many Open Humans you can manage in a week. Find out what happens if you eat as much as you want of your favorite pizza, how it feels to be buried under mounds of mozzarella. Eat pancakes until you turn into the Pillsbury Doughboy.

Juggle your combos of precidotes and antidotes (see Chapter VI) and learn what works best for you and when. Relish your control. Play with those enzymes until you know every nuance, every possibility. Take control once and for all. Don't cower in the safety zone. You have nothing to be afraid of. There is no damage you can't correct, no pounds gained that you can't lose. You're on the Beverly Hills Lifetime Plan and that's Forever. You're skinny now and will be Forever.

5. *Don't deprive yourself*. Schedule in your favorite foods and eat them with wild abandon. They are the exceptions, so make them exceptional. Consume them, or they will consume you. If you don't schedule them in, you are setting yourself up for failure. If you turned to ice cream when your mother yelled at you, if you buried yourself in barbecued spareribs when a romance soured, if you're used to turning to chocolate to blot out a bad day, be alert! If you're not careful these foods will continue to be your refuge. You'll continue to indulge yourself in them in emotional moments.

But if you schedule them in, in the clear light of day, unshadowed by feeling and with permission; if you allow yourself to experience them unemotionally and happily, without guilt, you'll win the battle of the binge. You'll not only diffuse the emotion of food, you might even find out, that unmasked by emotion, many of the foods you thought were so terrific really aren't. Somehow they lose their flavor when they aren't covered with salty tears.

If you can't eat your favorite foods now that you're perfect, when can you, and then, what's the point? In your devious little mind, you'll still be on a diet that means deprivation, a diet that you have to "cheat on." You will have opened the door to your DFC to move in and crowd out your skinny soul. If you don't schedule in your favorite foods, you're denying the heart of the BHD Lifetime Plan. And you're not making it yours. Remember, this eating plan focuses on what *you want* to eat, and that and only that determines what you have to eat. So stop denying yourself. You deserve to have what you really want. You've earned it!

6. *Weigh yourself every day*. For the first six months, write down your weight in the chart provided in your Workbook to Wonderland in Chapter VIII. When you travel, take your scale with you. Perpetuate that love affair; your scale is the only important observer of your perfection.

7. *Midnight does not a new day make*. A day ends when you go to sleep, and the new one begins when you wake up, not when the clock strikes twelve. If you awaken hungry in the middle of the night, continue eating the last thing you ate before you went to sleep.

Fats Do Not Equal Fattening

OIL   Use oil at will to round out your fat quotient. To be readily digestible, it must be expellor, or cold-pressed. Heat destroys the oil's digestibility by destroying the lecithin, the ingredient that is naturally present in all oil and that functions as its digestive agent. For this reason, oil used in cooking does not count toward your nutritional fat quotient.

Use oil in pasta (add after cooking), to marinate vegetables, and in salads. When you use it in cooking, use as little as possible. You can add more later for flavoring. Try seasoning your oil with fresh garlic cloves, tarragon, basil, thyme, and/or other fresh herbs.

As long as it is cold-pressed, you may cheerfully use all kinds. Sesame oil is the most nutritious; but now, as a maintainer, you can and should take advantage of the more exotic oils. Engineer some taste-test treats and have fun. Different oils, different tastes.

Don't be shy about premixing your salad dressing and taking little bottles of it with you to restaurants. It certainly didn't bother Margie Platt in her chic, sleek, black dress when we dined together at the elegant Ma Maison. She whipped out her little bottle of dressing without flinching. At this point why eat sugar (hidden in almost every restaurant salad dressing) when it doesn't count? Really, if you are going to have sugar, wouldn't you rather have the chocolate mousse for dessert instead? You do have another choice in restaurants: You could ask for plain oil and vinegar and make your own. But please, why subject yourself to those two awful little bottles that you have to mix on the spot and never get it quite right?

Match your oils whenever you can and everything will digest so much more happily. If, for example, you're having something with corn, use corn oil. For deep frying or tempura-ing you'll want to use the lightest oil of them all, safflower oil. The only oil that you shouldn't use is soy oil; anything made from soybeans is a legume, that betwixt category of foods that refuse to digest well.

One further reminder: Once it has been opened, keep your oil refrigerated lest it get rancid.

BUTTER   Use unsalted butter whenever possible. You'll find that most restaurants do have it; they use it for cooking. Raw butter (the cream hasn't been pasteurized or homogenized) is preferable. Unfortunately, the process of pasteurizing and homogenizing dairy products requires high heat. Recall that heat destroys lecithin, and, along with the lecithin goes a good part of the digestibility.

There is no limit to the amount of butter you can have, but be reasonable. Foods like potatoes and bagels will gladly soak up as much butter as you'll give them so, don't go crazy.

Now, there is butter, and there are vehicles for butter. Let's be realistic. You can't have unlimited vehicles and unlimited butter and not gain weight. Be aware of what it is you really want; is it the vehicle or the butter? If it's the vehicle, then use discretion in the amount of butter you use so that you'll be able to eat more of what it's going on. While driving from New York to Baltimore on my tour I munched eight, yes, eight, big beautiful New York bagels. If I had loaded each of them with butter, I would have been very nauseous and would have bulged unbearably. But it was the bagels I lusted for, not the butter, so I didn't go crazy with it. In fact, most I ate absolutely plain (they were sooo good), and I was fine the next day. In fact, I was fine that night, I ate my pasta with pleasure.

Now that you're on maintenance, try testing garlic and herb butters. You can use them on bread, fish, chicken, and vegetables; I'm sure you can find a host of things to do with them.

Why is butter so acceptable when other dairy products are not? Because most dairy products qualify as proteins and all that digestively implies. Butter, on the other hand, is a fat, made from the thickest cream, the fat portion of the milk. Thus butter doesn't activate the protein-digesting enzymes and, along with the other fats, heavy cream, and sour cream, it will cheerfully digest with both carbs and proteins.

HEAVY CREAM AND SOUR CREAM   Don't be afraid to use these fats either. Although, do use some discretion. Creams are marvelous taste treats; try them on pasta, in salad dressings, in or on potatoes, in curries, for dips. You've got the idea. If you use cream with moderation, it won't turn on you. Now when I say heavy cream, I mean *real* heavy cream, the kind you can whip, not half-and-half. Again raw is best because of the lecithin, but you already know that by now.

Please don't renew that old habit of adding cream to your coffee; you've become used to drinking it black, so keep it that way. Cream is fat, and as you know, fats will slow down but won't prohibit the digestion of anything else. Anything else, that is, except fruit. Remember, FRUIT DOES NOT DIGEST WITH ANYTHING, not even a fat. So if you eat fruit while drinking coffee with cream, the cream in your coffee will really play havoc with skinny. For this same reason, don't add cream to fruit.

MAYONNAISE   You can use my egg-yolk version liberally. This also counts as a fat. Make exotic yet simple herb mayos (see pages 219–20 and use them to adorn your fish, chicken, salads, or whatever else fits your fancy.

While we're on the subject of herbs, let me recommend them to you. Now that you're not masking your food or your tastebuds with salt and chemicals, these fabulous seasonings take on a whole new dimension. Experience them, grow them, and you'll find that they will become a precious adjunct to your foods.

The Hardly Evers*

In the Beverly Hills Diet Lifetime Plan, just as in the Beverly Hills Diet, there continues to be a clump of Hardly Evers that should be fervently avoided. I didn't say eliminated, I just said avoided. Certainly, you should never go out looking for them. But if they should happen to sneak into your mouth now and again, well, that's something else. While it won't be the end of the world, always remember that they are the harbingers of fat. They can nix your energy and your weight, and should only happen by conscious choice.

*See *The Beverly Hills Diet* for the full exposé.

1. *Salt —The Sneaky Subterfuge*. In all cases, pass the salt. Leave it out. Don't add so much as a grain voluntarily to anything. Order your food salt-free in restaurants. Be adamant, you can get your waiter to understand. I was only salted (see Glossary) twice during my four months of travel, and I ate out every night.

I am not so worried about the occasional assault. It is the constant invasion of salt that is going to affect you. It is when the Hardly Evers are omnipresent in your diet, and your body, that the damage is perpetrated.

The fluids in your body are so distorted by the buildup of salt that you are likely to bloat miserably. In all probability, pre–Beverly Hills Diet and the Beverly Hills Diet Lifetime Plan, you wouldn't have consciously felt the difference. But now that you're in tune with your body, bloating and excess salt have become intolerable. If salt makes you feel so bad, imagine what the medical implications must be!

Now, obviously bagels and cheesecake are not exactly salt-free. Less obviously, neither are catsup, bread, cereal, diet drinks, most carbonated beverages, salad dressings, and precooked chicken. Pick and choose the times you opt to be salted. Be aware of how it makes you feel. Measure those times accordingly and *make them count!* P.S.: Medical problems notwithstanding, unless you live in a cave, subsisting on leaves, your salt needs will be amply fulfilled by the natural sodium present in food.

2. *Sugar —The Insidious Energy Convolutor*. Sugar triggers an instant high, then a dreary low. The same is true of white flour and other highly refined carbohydrates. You can get hooked on sugar, just as on a drug, and the effects are much the same: zapped energy and frenetic activity; nutrient drain, pits, pocks, and mucus in your intestinal wall; cravings and constipation. Not a good trade-off. Not now that you care as much about how food makes you feel as how it makes you look. Experiment, experience, be aware, and beware.

3. *Dairy — Do's and Don'ts.* Dairy, as you have experienced by now, is devastating to digest. Your poor body is tested to its max in the effort. Dairy products have a tendency to be mucus-forming and clogging. It's been my experience that people on a diet high in dairy products are often the same ones who are plagued by heavy amounts of cellulite. I call it the Dairy Derrière.

Believe me, I love cheese just as much as you do; ice cream, well, what can I say? Treat dairy products with respect and when you do have them try to have them on their own. Save your café au lait, the cream in your coffee, or that glass of milk for an Open Protein meal. (See pages 101–7 on Open Protein options.) You will enjoy them without them enjoining you.

4. *Chemical Additives and Other Foreign Substances — The Nemesis of the New Age.* Shun these aliens. Your body is no more capable of dealing with them than it is with rocks. They immediately ignite a "no compute" alarm in our digestive systems. Our bodies first have to figure out what to do with them and then they store what they can't properly process. Those that do get processed sap and destroy precious nutrients along the way.

Food Tools

Always remember, you lost weight on the Beverly Hills Diet by feeding your body, not by starving it. In the Beverly Hills Diet Lifetime Plan it is eating that will *keep* you thin. Eating the proper foods *before* and *after* those miscombinations and Open Humans is going to make them work, keep them from being fattening.

1. *When in doubt, it's pineapple.* Pineapple is still the closest thing to a miracle food that I have found. If you're in doubt and don't know what Corrective Counterpart to use (see page 114), you can't ever go wrong with pineapple. Don't overdo it, though. If you use it too much, it will diminish in its effectiveness.

2. *Neutral fruits can be eaten anytime you don't need a Corrective Coun-*

terpart. They can also be used as a precidote to an Open Meal (see pages 100–7). Enjoy them and take advantage of them. They make a welcome change from our trusty pineapple.

3. *Eat fruit roughly 90 percent of your mornings*. It will not only make you feel great, it's also a lovely, clean way to start your day. Fruit clears you out from the day before, and sets you up for whatever you will eat later. Unless you need a specific precidote, virtually any fruit qualifies; that includes the neutrals, such as peaches, pears, nectarines, and apricots. Of course, watermelon and grapes are the exception.

4. *Watermelon and grapes are all-day fruits only*. Once you begin eating them, because of their very special effects, you must continue with them (and only them) for the entire day. If you "blow" a grape or watermelon day, their special wash and feed effects will have been interfered with, and the odds are you will gain weight. If, however, despite all my warnings, you have to have something else or you'll go "mad," there are some *fairly* safe alternatives. Raisins (they are dried grapes, you know), bananas, another fruit, or even a plain baked potato will probably not be the end of the world. That "special" day will not be as effective as it would have been, but at least it won't be destructive.

5. *Dried fruits should be unsulfured*. Do not eat dried fruits that have been treated with sulfur dioxide or preservatives or that are honey-dipped. Soak all dried fruits for one hour in water (except raisins and dates), and drain the fruits before you eat them. That is exactly one hour, no more—no less. You want to deconcentrate and rehydrate the dried fruits, but not so much as to destroy their high concentration of vitamins and minerals. Dried fruits are a vital complement to our eating plan, so let's not dilute their potential.

6. *As a general practice, dried fruit should not be eaten the meal before, or for breakfast the morning following an animal protein*. It tends to cause gas.

7. *Don't begin the day with raisins or dates.* They are too concentrated, too intense.

8. *Nuts and seeds should always be raw and unsalted.* Unsalted for obvious reasons, raw for the lecithin.

9. *Nut proteins, including avocado, are best eaten at the end of a fruit day.* They do not combine well with other proteins, or even with each other.

10. *Whenever possible, use rice or malt vinegar (a carb) instead of wine vinegar (a fruit).* Salad dressings can be oil- or sour-cream based. (See recipes in Chapter XI and in *The Beverly Hills Diet.*)

11. *Learn to love your coffee or tea black.* A drop of milk in your morning coffee or your afternoon tea can be far more devastating than a pound of chocolates. Try adding cinnamon to the grounds before you brew your coffee; it's a great replacement for the sweetener you are no longer using.

12. *Plan your menus a week at a time.* Schedule in your emotional as well as your social and business needs. Be generous and imaginative! What you choose to eat determines what you have to eat. It's your life, it's your diet, and it's your agenda. (See Chapter VII on Food Formulas and Chapter XI for recipes.) Remember, you aren't on a "diet" anymore. You aren't trying to lose weight any more. Deprivation only breeds overindulgence. Enjoy food, enjoy eating, enjoy cooking, and enjoy entertaining. Enjoy and start living!

13. *Preparing for an Open Human, keep yourself "enzymatically open."* When you know that later that day you will be eating foods that do not combine an Open Human or an Open Miscom, a fruit precidote is ideal. *Don't not eat.* "Starving yourself" is just a perpetuation of your DFC. Not only will you be ravenous when the time comes to eat, your body, suddenly inundated by a barrage of food, will simply not be able to function efficiently. Consider how

long it takes a garbage disposal to start working when you first turn it on.

14. *As a general practice, maxi carbs (see food-type listings in Chapter V) should not be eaten the meal before or the meal after protein.* Don't, for example, have bagels for breakfast and chicken and ribs for lunch, lamb for dinner and pancakes for breakfast. You will be able to get away with it occasionally, but not as a daily practice.

15. *Ideally, a protein day should be divided into only two eating experiences.* If three, they should be separated by at least six hours.

16. *If you are on protein, you can selectively eat only the protein from a dish that mixes protein and carbohydrates, but you cannot do the opposite.* That is, you cannot eat the carb and leave the protein without making the carb indigestible. Take a chicken and rice casserole, for example. If you're on protein, you can safely pick out and eat the chicken, but if you're on carbs and think you can get away with eating the rice alone, you'll be in trouble. Protein from the chicken would have seeped into every little kernel, into the very soul of that rice, and will have rendered it a miscombination.

17. *To ensure the highest quality of energy when eating Open Meals, stay in the same family of foods.* Fish with seafood, eggs with chicken, two kinds of pasta. Different kinds of food generate different kinds of energy. But please don't take my word for it; experience it for yourself.

18. *Avoid soft drinks, diet or otherwise.* They are piled high with chemicals or sugar and/or sodium. Carefully check labels on club soda for sodium content. If you're going to bloat, I would hope it would be from something more interesting than a beverage.

19. *Lemons and limes —last but not least.* Do not add lemon or lime to your papaya or other fruits because they negate the very enzymes they are activating.

Home Tools

Your home should be a Conscious Combiner's haven, the epitome of the Beverly Hills Diet Lifetime Plan. Promise yourself that your home will be a sanctuary for feeling good and staying skinny. It's easy. Stock your shelves, your fridge, and your freezer. Rid your cupboards of packaged goods which are loaded with preservatives and chemicals; give them away, or better yet, throw them out. Learn to adapt your favorite recipes and learn some wonderful new ones (see Chapter XI). Remember, make every bite count. Why would you even have commercially processed oil in your house once you've started using cold-pressed, or mayonnaise made with sugar, or TV dinners, or crackers with lard and sodium propionate, or peanut butter with salt and hydrogenated oil, or salty potato chips, or sugary breakfast cereals?

Remember, there is a healthy equivalent for even the unhealthiest food. Your home should house only the best, and the rules and the tools should be the gospel. It's your choice, your territory, and your chance to really think about food when it doesn't count so that you don't have to think about it when it does. The more good you do when you can, the more bad you can do when you want to, or you have to.

The first giant step I took toward slimhood and health was eliminating foods with preservatives and chemicals from my "at-home repertoire." I prided myself on having what I called an "organic" home. Now, you can laugh and pooh-pooh me and say, "Organic shmorganic, that's a lot of poppycock," but I cannot stress strongly enough how important I think it is. As I explained earlier, the human body was not created to process all those artificial ingredients, and it has to figure out what, if anything, it can do with them. Many of them don't get processed at all and just get stored in the body. Others, during processing, cause damage to our bodies' vitamin and mineral supplies. Save the junk for the outside, where you don't have any quality control. You'll be able to feed your heart and soul when you want to if you feed your body when you can.

1. *Surely you have already tossed out your salt shaker, haven't you?* If not, do so. Well, its contents at least. There really is *no excuse for eating salt at home.* Remember, whether you are a bloater or not, your body can only handle so much salt without retaliating. Save salt for the outside, for when you have no choice, or for those foods that don't exist without it.

2. *Use unsalted butter. Raw if possible.* In fact, at home all the dairy products you use should be raw.

3. *Always have enough BHD Lifetime Plan foods in reserve* so that you will always be able to eat to your heart's content. Don't set yourself up for failure by running out of core foods. Toni Lopopolo found an easy way to avoid this potential problem. She moved next door to a twenty-four-hour greengrocer.

4. *Keep a hefty supply of pineapple and papaya* ripening on your windowsill and lying in wait in your refrigerator.

5. *Keep lots of dried fruits, such as prunes, raisins, and apricots, plus a supply of raw nuts and seeds safely stowed away.*

6. *Harbor a trove of low-salt, nonsweetened breads in your freezer.*

7. *Ban canned vegetables from your life.* Most contain salt and chemicals. Once you become a fresh-veggie convert, this will be a snap. Regardless of the season, there is always an abundance of interesting fresh veggies. Frozen vegetables are handy to have around and will do in a pinch.

8. *Eliminate powdered spices and herbs laden with chemicals and salt.* Again, discover the fresh ones. You'll love them. Remember, the fewer chemicals your body has to deal with, the cheerier it will be.

9. *BHDLP your family.* Cook Conscious Combining meals for your

family and they will not only love them, they will feel fabulous and will probably be more fun to live with.

10. *Save your Open Miscombinations and your Open Humans for when you go out.* At home, play it "straight" (see Glossary). Why stretch it when you don't have to, when it probably won't be for anything too terrific anyhow? For what? A few vegetables with your meat-loaf, a salad with your steak? When you realize the "straight" (see Glossary) splendors you can create in your own kitchen (see Chapter XI), your chubby little soul will be in perpetual ecstasy. Besides, at home you can make and have as much of anything as you want.

11. *Throw out your fat clothes. Clean out those closets. Go shopping. Get a new hairdresser or barber and get a new haircut.*

12. *Fill your house with mirrors.* Reinforce your emotional high by looking at your body and rejoicing in its perfection.

Social Tools

1. *Be selective.* Don't let others make your food choices for you. If you don't get what you want, you'll just be disappointed and unsatisfied. Since you know you can't have everything, stay skinny and feel good, save yourself for what you like best. Even if you've planned on an Open Human or an Open Miscombination, you don't have to go through with it, you don't have to finish it all. Make sure it's worth it, because remember you can only get away with just so many.

Don't be indiscriminate about the rule "to feed your body." Don't blow your special food experiences on those destined to be inferior. How long will you remember that greasy potato chip, that packaged coleslaw or that dry white birthday cake? Is that banquet for five-hundred really your choice for an Open Human? Do you really want to have your Open Miscombination at a restaurant you don't even like? Is that processed chicken breast covered with gravy and those overcooked string beans bathed in butter at that hotel luncheon really your first choice? Now, I'm not telling you not to eat those things, only that you make sure they're really worth it to you. If it's terrific coleslaw, then that's one thing; if it's not, then why bother? Why waste a miscombination that you may have to pay for? You'll only be disappointed and mad at yourself. You'll only be filled with the recriminations of the why-did-I-eat-that syndrome.

You wouldn't catch me eating just any pizza or any pancakes or any chocolate. If it's not Due's pizza in Chicago, if it's not Dupars' pancakes only at Laurel Canyon and Ventura Boulevard, if that chocolate isn't from Teuscher's, then why bother? The substitutes won't ever be as good, I'll compare them to the "real thing," I'll be disappointed and mad at myself for having them, and I'll wind up wanting and having to have the "real" thing anyhow. Unfortunately, knowing me, I'll remain fixated on having to have it until I do. Now aren't there better things to think about?

2. *Don't eat it just because it's there*. You don't need that excuse anymore, you know it will always be there. Remember, for every bite that goes into your mouth, something else can't. Cocktail parties and buffets are always the toughest. Get into the social aspect of the affair. Notice everyone trying to talk with their mouth full or choking down food to participate in the conversation. As you participate in the conversation with a mouth full only of words, think about where you'll stop on your way home to get what you really want. Consider cocktail parties and buffets a BHDLP challenge and each victory will make the next easier until these too become Unconscious Combining experiences.

3. *Advance it*. Before you decide what you are going to eat, inspect the buffet, study the dessert cart, memorize (well, not really) the menu. Think about later, then decide. As we Eaters know, the anticipation is as marvelous as the eating; often, it's actually better.

4. *Stick to your choice*. Once committed, don't change your mind. If your fork wanders to someone else's plate, make sure it stays in the same category that it started out in. One bite of that Veal Par-

migiana will blow all that Pasta alla Olio you're eating. If you've made a mistake, if you've ordered and started the wrong thing, something you've decided you don't want after all—too bad. You're stuck with it. Big deal, it's only one meal; you can have what you really want later, or tomorrow, or whenever. You can't, nor do you have to, now. Besides, it's not leaving the planet. It will *all* still be there for you to enjoy. You're making sure of that!

5. *Don't assume anything*. Steaks, chops, and chicken are often automatically seasoned with salt, MSG, and a variety of other things in restaurants. Premixed salad dressings harbor sugar. Garlic bread may well be made with chemical-laden garlic powder or garlic salt. Steamed vegetables are probably bathed in salt, as are potatoes and pasta. Know what you're eating. Make your decisions based on that knowledge. If you should gain, don't automatically blame the core food; think of how it was prepared. You will probably find that it was not what you ate or how much you ate but rather what was done to it to make it taste better. But you will learn by experience, and you will begin making choices based on that knowledge.

6. *Ask and ye shall receive*. If you want your food cooked without salt, ask, or rather insist upon it. Restaurants are there to serve you. You're paying for it. God gave you a mouth for more than just eating. If something isn't exactly as you would like it, send it back. If you want pasta without cheese, ask. If you want the avocados left out of your salad, ask. Don't allow yourself to be a victim.

7. *Don't isolate social and business eating*. Don't use them as an excuse. Don't worry that you'll make people uncomfortable because you're doing "your own thing." Believe me, no one else really cares what you're eating as long as you're eating. Remember, this will not be the only time you'll find yourself at a restaurant or at a party. If you always let these situations undermine your skinny, the BHD Lifetime Plan and skinny will never become your way of life.

8. *Entertain Beverly Hills Diet Lifetime Plan style*. You will not be depriving your guests. Far from it. Consider the menu socialite Margy Trevor created in her Phoenix home: stuffed mushrooms, borscht with sour cream, fresh French bread, unsalted butter, stuffed tomatoes, Linguine alla Olio and fresh vegetables, fettuccine with cream and butter—all presented resplendently amid shining crystal and smug Conscious Combiners, who were near speechless with the joy of it all.

Remember, the tools are just that, aids to help your little skinny voice shout, the helping hands to skinny. Thousands of compatriate Conscious Combiners and I can testify to their value. The Three Golden Rules are for Forever, never to be transgressed, never to be played with. The tools, on the other hand, are to be stretched, tried and tested. Experiment. See just how much you can get away with. Remember, the beauty of the Beverly Hills Diet Lifetime Plan is that it is yours, adopted by you and adapted to your way of life. It is a foundation on which you should grow, or should I say, shrink. In the first six months of maintenance, go easy. Your body is still settling into its final state of perfection. I've refined the tools, building on my own experience and that of my clients. I've honed them, chopped them, pushed them, and prodded them. The tools as here inscribed represent my ultimate secrets to maintaining my splendid hipbones and my 102-pound ideal. These tools are it for me; I can cut no more chunks out of them. But maybe you can; don't be afraid to try. The success of the BHD Lifetime Plan depends on your making it your own. Just remember that glorious pineapple spells your salvation.

Physical Exercise

During weight loss we deemphasized physical exercise, except that involving hand-to-mouth movements. Most people with weight to lose are riddled with so much guilt that piling on the extra burden of having to exercise when their minds should be on losing weight is self-defeating. Any change in eating, even to Conscious Combining, requires discipline. Physical exercise also requires discipline. Enough is enough, one thing at a time.

Now that you've lost your weight, now that your goal is maintaining and feeling good, diet no longer means discipline, it means way of life. You are no longer worrying about firming up a bunch of old fat and inhibiting the weight-loss process; all the fat is gone. Now you have to firm up some of those muscles you've softened. Now is the time to tighten up that flesh, to perfect that body for Forever.

Now it's time to integrate a new discipline into your life. Eaters thrive on discipline, if it makes sense. Rather than something you *have* to do, exercise becomes something you want to do. Now that you have a body you're proud of, you want to use it, to show it off. And exercise will help you do just that.

What type of exercise is best for you? Only you can be the judge. There is a plethora of organized, disorganized, and unorganized physical activities that range from a solitary walk to aerobics in a class of a hundred. Make a list of all the physical exercises that tickle your taste and try each of them. Decide which ones you like best. Do one or several until they no longer feel good. Then try something else.

If you get bored, if you begin to dread your chosen activity, don't push yourself and make yourself crazy, move on to something else on your list. Nowhere is it written that you must do one exercise forever. Ease into it and make it easy. Make it and keep it fun. Enjoy and delight in your new proud body.

I didn't begin exercising regularly until my weight was almost perfect, and now it's become a regular part of my life. I'm hooked. I can't make it through the day without some form of physical exercise. Not if I want to feel good. Experimenting with many different kinds of exercise has given me a wealth of choices, depending on my mood and how my body feels. It's a time I cherish, a time to reconnect with my body.

Supplements

The following supplements are an absolute must in your daily diet.

BRAN *First thing in the morning*, eat two tablespoons of unprocessed bran flakes, and then drink a hot beverage. Wait forty-five minutes before eating anything else.

As you weight-loss Beverly Hills Dieters know, bran is the ultimate nutritional broom. Bran only sweeps on an empty stomach. If it gets clogged up behind other foods, you will likely bloat.

NUTRITIONAL YEAST *At 4:00 P.M.*, eat one to two heaping tablespoons of nutritional yeast flakes in a small amount of water. I make mine the consistency of peanut butter. Do not eat for forty-five minutes before or after taking the yeast. The yeast will help keep your body's B vitamins in balance. Even if you are getting all the vitamins you need, your vitamin store can be depleted in sneaky ways. For example, certain foods deplete the B-complex vitamins. Tension and stress will sap your supply of these vital nutrients as well. If, like me, you get hooked on the way yeast makes you feel, have it twice a day. Or, if you're in an especially stressful period, have it three times a day.

SESAME SEEDS *At bedtime*, eat two heaping tablespoons of unhulled, raw sesame seeds. Sesame seeds are one of the richest sources of calcium imaginable. And all that concentrated calcium helps you sleep by relaxing your nervous system. They provide you with the three essential fatty acids you can acquire only from food and they feed you extra fiber.

Now that you're a maintainer, I recommend that you take a high-grade, one-a-day multiple vitamin with minerals, if you feel you need it as well as additional vitamin C. Also, I have no objections to a multimineral supplement. Recent studies have shown that since women do not absorb calcium as well as men, it is wise for women to take a calcium supplement. Your doctor can recommend one.

Under no circumstances should you take additional vitamin A. You're getting plenty in the food you're eating. For additional supplements, ask your doctor.

V

Your Nutritional Quotient — The Food Equation

How can you speak a new language if you don't understand the vocabulary? *Proteins, carbohydrates, fats* —words we've heard and used, and yet to many they are as foreign as Serbo-Croatian. And now for some new ones: *Open Miscombination, Open Protein, Mono Carb*. How can you apply them to your life, integrate them into your conversation, when you don't even know what they mean; when you've probably never even heard them before?

Obviously, you've got to be able to know what I'm talking about to be able to hear me. You've got to understand my terminology before you can adopt my technique, adapt to my way of thinking. You are going to have to be prepared to learn a few new things. While I'll never take your heart out of your stomach, I am going to put your head in it. I'm going to make you think a little bit. The Beverly Hills Diet Lifetime Plan means thinking about food. But unlike your food thoughts of the past, instead of the shoulds and shouldn'ts; the can'ts and the nevers. Instead of your food consciousness being ruled by ignorance, apathy, myths, and your DFC, it is going to be propelled by knowledge, understanding, positive food thoughts, and choices.

You have a choice now, a choice that is no longer to eat or not to eat but what to eat and when to eat it to make it work best.

I'm no longer going to be responsible for telling you what to eat. I am relinquishing that decision to you. Oh, I'll offer some suggestions, I'll give you a few hints; but from now on, *you* will make *your own* decisions. Decisions that will be ruled by your head as well as your heart, your body as well as your soul. Decisions that will be dictated by later and tomorrow, instead of right now, instead of just today. This is *your* diet now. This is *your* eating plan. To work it must be based on *your* food and *your* choices.

I know, I know, you're anxious to get on with it; bring on the food, you say, tell me what I can eat. Well, just hold on. Remember, we're building a support system, a support system that will never topple. A support system you can depend on, one that is going to ensure that you will be as thin as you like for the rest of your life. And just as carefully as we laid each brick in the foundation, just as carefully as I laid out the rules and tools for you to internalize and synergize, we are just as carefully, one by one, going to hammer in each nail to complete the structure. I just want to make very sure you don't hit your thumb in the process. You've got to crawl before you walk and you've got to chew before you swallow. Well, you've got to understand how this works before you can make it work for you—before you can do it.

First, I'm going to tally up the food groups so that you'll know which is which and what is what. Where a noodle and a lima bean fit into the scheme of things.

Then I'll define your nutritional equation. And just so you understand how expansive your choices can be, I'll grace you with a long list of sample meals.

Next you'll meet the Food Formulas, those magic eating combos that spell skinny. They'll be yours to mix and match, pick and choose, and you'll learn how to plug these Food Formulas into your own six-month chart for maintenance (Chapter VIII). Included in your Workbook to Wonderland is the month-by-month countdown, the new and even more enlightening Nonphysical Exercises, and the guide to do-it-yourself formulas that will move you from now to Forever.

Also, you'll learn the precidotes and the antidotes to fat. What to eat before and after anything and everything. They are the key to making your eating plan work, the critical cogs to being in control, Forever. You'll meet the three-day Fruit Flings, plus learn how to deal with all those lurking pitfalls once and for all. Step by step I'll lead you out of the Valley of the Shadow of Fat.

So sit back, relax, go grab a "nosh," something to eat, the best is yet to come. Freedom is just around the corner, just a few pages away.

THE FOOD GROUPS

There are three and a half food groups (these are not to be confused with the U.S. Department of Agriculture food groups): the proteins, the fats, the carbohydrates, and the "one half"—now remember, this is my interpretation of the facts—is the legumes. Each food group has a very specific purpose, and no one of them can fill all your nutritional needs. It is the proper balance of all three during a week that will keep you thin and healthy. A balanced diet, yes; a balanced meal, well . . .

We seem to be obsessed with the idea of the balanced meal. In actuality, the balanced meal is a contrivance of modern civilization, a product of our social evolution. Watch children eat. Instinctively they eat one thing at a time and will often get hysterical if the foods run together on their plates. Tell me, do you think early man ate a balanced meal? He'd eat some berries, maybe later some nuts, he'd pick up a rock and find some slugs or he'd kill a deer. Sometime during our social evolution it became convenient to eat breakfast, convenient to eat lunch, and convenient to eat dinner. Convenient to get all our nutrients in one, or rather three fell swoops. Convenient, yes; healthy—well, that's questionable. Heart disease, cancer, arteriosclerosis, high blood pressure, diabetes,; all are on the rise. Most often they are not congenital; rather they are a product of our lives, a result of our nutrition. To my way of thinking, glutting your body three times a day with a mishmash of foods does not necessarily add up to healthy. Just as you can't sing, dance, carry on a conversation, and play the violin at the same time, my experience has taught me that you can't gulp protein, carbs, and fats and expect to appreciate the full nutritional benefits of each or not gain weight.

But, before we can balance them, we've got to know them, who they are and what they do. Foods are classified according to their nutritional components, and by determining the major component in each. All foods contain some of everything, some protein, some carbohydrate, some fat. Proteins, by the way, are far more prevalent in other food groups than you might suspect. They don't only come on four legs, you know. If a food contains at least 51 percent amino acids, it is classified as a protein. If it contains at least 51 percent glucose, the nutrient derived from carbs, it is classified as a carb. And, if it contains at least 51 percent lipids, it qualifies as a fat.

Preceding each of the food group breakdowns is a brief description of what each food group does for us, the role it plays in our health equation.

Proteins

Next to water, proteins are the most plentiful substance in our bodies. Protein is the major source of building material for muscles, blood, skin, hair, nails, and internal organs. During digestion, the large molecules of proteins are broken up into simpler units called amino acids. The proteins are as follows:*

ANIMAL PROTEINS

Beef	Eggs
Fish	Lamb
Fowl	Pork

*Source: *Nutrition Almanac*, Nutrition Search. Minneapolis, MN, 1973

DAIRY PROTEINS

Milk	Buttermilk
Cheese	Kefir
Yogurt	Ice Cream
	Cheesecake

NUT PROTEINS

Nuts	Avocado
Seeds	

VEGETABLE PROTEINS

Sprouts

Fats

Fats are the most concentrated source of energy in the diet. In addition to providing energy, fats act as carriers for the fat-soluble vitamins: A, D, E, and K.

Butter	Cream (sour and heavy)
Oil	Lard

Carbohydrates

The chief functions of carbohydrates are to provide energy for body functions and muscle exertion and to assist in the digestion and assimilation of other foods. Carbohydrates provide us with immediate calories for energy so that our bodies can save protein for the building and repairing of body tissues. Carbohydrates also help regulate protein and fat metabolism; fats require carbohydrates for their breakdown within the liver.*

All fruits	Brandy
All liqueurs made	Champagne
from fruits	Cognac
	Wine

*Source: *Nutrition Almanac*, Nutrition Search. Minneapolis, MN, 1973

MINI CARBS

Arugula
Asparagus
Bran
Celery
Kale
Lettuce
Mushrooms
Mustard greens

Parsley
Spinach
Summer squash
Swiss chard
Watercress
Wheat germ
Zucchini

MIDI CARBS

Beets
Broccoli
Brussels sprouts
Cabbage
Carrots
Cauliflower
Cucumbers
Eggplant
Jerusalem artichokes
Jicama
Leeks
Okra

Onions
Parsnips
Peas
Peppers (green, red,
   and chili)
Radishes
Rutabagas
Seaweed
Shallots
String beans
Tomatoes
Turnips

MAXI CARBS

Artichokes
Breads
Buckwheat
Bulgur
Cake
Candy
Chewing gum
Chocolate
Cookies
Corn

Grains, all
Jello
Liquors, all distilled
   (see Glossary)
Millet
Oats
Pasta
Popcorn
Potatoes
Pumpkin

MAXI CARBS (*Cont.*)

Crackers	Rice
Desserts, except those	Rye
made with cheese	Winter squash

Legumes

Because of their high-protein and high-carbohydrate content they are not the most desirable of the Beverly Hills Diet Lifetime Plan foods. Their natural structure makes them an inherent miscombination.

Garbanzo beans	Peanuts
Kidney beans	Pinto beans
Lentils	Soybeans
Lima beans	Split peas

The ordering of carbs is based on the complexity of their molecular structure, the maxi carbs being the most complex and requiring the longest time to digest. But don't let that daunt you, don't be afraid of them. Maxi doesn't mean more fattening. What it means is maximum energy—long-acting, sustained energy. Remember, carbohydrates are our prime source of energy, the fuel on which we run.

Now, there are some foods that fall into several food groups. Cheesecake and ice cream, for instance, are high in carbohydrates, and one might logically expect them to be classified as such. But they contain so much dairy, a protein, that they require the protein enzymes to digest. So, for our purposes, or shall I say for Conscious Combining purposes, they are classified as a protein.

Obviously these proteins aren't exactly the life-building proteins. They will not provide your body with the powerful building blocks that a steak, a cashew, or a lobster will. They should not be scheduled in as one of your proteins in your food equation, as they don't quench your body's nutritional protein needs. You'll understand what I mean as we go along.

You will find some other exceptions to the orthodox food classifications. They too are slotted according to what I believe is their specific digestibility. Digestion is of course the key to Conscious Combining and skinny Forever. Again, trust me: Food classifications are not the result of an arbitrary whim. I have classified food only after long and extensive experimentation.

FRUITS—A SPECIAL CASE

Fruits are divided into two categories: enzymatic and neutral. Enzymatic fruits, our precidotes and antidotes, are those potent packages of fat-cutting enzymes and concentrated nutrients that spell skinny to us Conscious Combiners. I have no objections to the neutral fruits; in fact, quite the contrary. Remember, they don't have the special fat-fighting powers of their enzymatic brethren. Not only are the neutral fruits perfectly acceptable for maintenance, not only are they a welcome change from that papaya we've known and grown to love, but I highly *recommend* eating them when a precidote or antidote isn't necessary.

Eating a neutral fruit when you don't need an enzymatic will only enhance the effectiveness of the enzymatic fruit when you do need it.

You know you can overdo a good thing, even pineapple, and if you eat it every day your new healthy body won't stay that way.

Enzymatic Fruits

BURN

Pineapple   Strawberries

BURN/DIGEST

Papaya   Kiwi
Mango   Persimmon

FEED

Bananas   Prunes
Dried Apricots   Raisins
Figs

WASH

Watermelon

FEED/WASH

Grapes   Blueberries

FEED/BURN

Apples   Boysenberries
Blackberries

Neutral Fruits

Cherimoya   Passion Fruit
Fresh apricots   Peaches
Grapefruits   Pears
Guava   Plums
Nectarines   Tangerines
Oranges

Forbidden Fruits

Sorry, melons, other than our beloved watermelon, will bloat you.

CONDIMENTS, ET AL.

For some reason, we think of condiments as entities unto themselves, above and beyond the ingredients from which they come. When deciding what to do about condiments, take responsibility. Be logical. Type them according to their origin. Remember, maintenance means thinking for yourself. So if you think of something that is not included in the following list, for skinny sake, think about it.

Catsup is made from tomatoes, so it's a carb. If added to protein, it becomes a miscombination. But for that hamburger with everything on it, it just might be worth it. Make Beverly Hills Diet Catsup (see page 222) or buy it sugar-free. Of course, you've figured out that barbecue sauce, marinara sauce, and other tomato-based sauces are offshoots of the same breed.

Horseradish, freshly grated, goes with anything. If you buy bottled horseradish, inspect the label and decide for yourself.

Liquor in cooking (sorry!) should be treated as a miscombination. If you must use it, cross your fingers and hope for the best.

Mustard can be used on anything but fruit. Look for salt-free mustards and be wary of the "gourmet" mustards that translate into miscoms.

Free condiments that can be used at will with anything include cinnamon, parsley, garlic, and pepper (red, white, and black). All herbs that are fresh, bottled, unpickled, and unsalted can be indulged in with total abandon. Fruit excluded.

Pickled foods, such as sauerkraut and kimchee, are salty, salty, salty! Keep in mind that the process of pickling dictates salt and often sugar, the devastating duo. If you are a pickled food freak, check at your health food store; often they have some that are prepared without sugar and with much less salt, a slight nutritional upgrade. Remember, every little bit helps! The more good you do when you can, the more bad you can get away with when you want to.

Olives and pickles can be combined with other carbs. But I repeat, beware of the pickling—salty, salty, salty.

Canned sardines and sockeye salmon with soft bones are, for want of another place, included here. These are two canned foods I highly recommend; the low-sodium variety of course! They are oozing with potassium, calcium, and phosphorus and are just splendid for you.

Imitation bacon and its compatriots tend to be loaded with artificial chemicals. Watch it.

Soy sauce and tamari, a soy sauce derivative, both are wildly salty. Tamari is slightly less salty, hence, the preferable of the two.

Tartar sauce is a miscom of the first order.

Vinegar has different bases: *wine vinegar* is a fruit. *Rice and malt vinegars* are carbs.

THE FOOD CATEGORIES
CATEGORIZED

So that you newcomers understand our language and to re-charge the memories of all my BHDers, here are the food categories defined plus three shiny-new categories for the BHD Lifetime Plan. Maintenance is defined in these terms, so, until you know the difference between OC, MP, and OR, do not proceed any further. Each term refers to *individual meals* or eating experi-ences, not to entire days.

Mono Meal (MM)

A meal that is a single food, either one fruit (F), one carb (Mono Carb [MC]), or one protein (Mono Protein [MP]).

Open Fruit (OF)

Fruit combined with a fruit liquor—wine, champagne, brandy, or cognac.

Open Carb (OC)

A meal that combines three carbs, with no more than two being maxi carbs. Don't forget, fats go with anything. Examples:

Asparagus
Garlic bread and butter
Pasta alla Olio
Vodka

Baked potatoes with
    sour cream and chives
Spinach salad

Wide Open Carb (WOC)

A combination of as many carbs as you want with no limitations on even the number of maxi carbs included.

Open Protein (OP)

A meal that combines any three proteins, excluding nuts and seeds and sprouts. Nuts combine only with nuts. Seeds with seeds. Sprouts with sprouts. Examples:

Mixed Grill

Steak
Shrimp Scampi
Cheesecake

Caviar
Sour cream omelet
Canadian bacon

Wide Open Protein (WOP)

Eating as many proteins as you want at one sitting.

Open Miscombination (OM)

There are two types:

Miscom #1. A meal that combines one carb and one protein. You eat the carb first, then eat the protein. Don't go back to the carb after you have had your first taste of protein. Examples:

Salad
Barbecued chicken

French fries
Steak

Miscom #2. The entity unto itself. Those foods that wouldn't exist if they weren't miscombinations. When I contemplate the ecstasies that preside over my most-favorite food list, when I wallow in the sheer pleasure of these foods, I bless my pineapples and their magical enzymes a hundred times over. These to me are when a miscom is worth it. Miscom #2s are the foods that tempted us and taunted us in the old days. They were always the nevers. Examples:

Eggs Benedict	Stroganoff
Hamburger with	Corned beef on rye
everything on it	Beef Wellington
Pizza	

Open Dessert (OD)

Desserts instead of a "normal" meal. There are no restrictions on the kinds of desserts you may feast upon. Examples:

Frozen Snickers bar	Soufflé with fresh cream
Banana fudge cake	Fresh blueberry tart
Two chocolate brownies	Napoleon
Carrot cake	

Resnick Open (RO)

Some of us can't eat and drink at the same time without gaining weight. If you are one of those, then you will have to choose between liquor and food. If you choose to drink alcohol, then it's a Resnick Open, a particular meal or "eating experience." A Resnick Open must be treated like any other meal and separated from other foods by the required two- or three-hour periods between eating experiences.

Caution: Wine is a fruit and can only follow fruit. If you choose a grain alcohol, then don't go back to fruit; go on to other carbs or proteins. If you have had protein in the course of the day then you can't do a Resnick Open. As a maintainer, you may need to resort to ROs only on occasion or only in the first months of maintenance. Experiment and find out what works best for you.

Open Human (OH)

This is the true test of the maintainer, the challenge of thin. Open Humans give you the opportunity to prove once and for all that your skinny voice is in charge, that you are in control. Open Human means eating anything and everything you wish in any order you like. In the beginning, follow the lead of a natural skinny. Don't gobble up every morsel on your plate. Don't fill up on hors d'oeuvres or glut yourself with the first course. Stop eating when you are satisfied, before you're stuffed. When doing an Open Human you eat like a "mensch," with one hand, one bite at a time, slowly, tasting and luxuriating in the experience of every bite.

You will chart your success by the number of Open Humans you're able to experience and get away with in a week. If you can eat them without gaining weight you are moving into the land of Forever. You are becoming an Unconscious Combiner and you will finally banish that fear of never being able to eat like a real human being. Guilt will become a misery of the past. Never forget, it's not how much you can eat in how short a time, it's how long you can make the pleasure last.

Wide Open (WO)

Also referred to as Open Chozzer or a Pig-Out. This is a special maintenance category that goes along with the territory. Unlike an Open Human, where you eat with dignity and decorum, with one hand, one bite at a time, on a Wide Open you can eat everything and anything with wild abandon; with both hands and your hair flying, until you are so stuffed you can barely move away from the table. It's eating just like you used to eat. Only now it's different. For one thing, it won't taste as good because it lacks the bitter aftertaste of regret and recrimination.

A Wide Open is splurging with permission, without guilt or fear, and with confidence. The confidence that comes from knowing that this is an exception and it's okay because you are in control. The confidence that comes from knowing that any added pounds do not a fatty make because your little golden pineapple is perfectly ripe and on your windowsill waiting for you.

Now I'm not encouraging you to do a Wide Open, nor am I condoning it. I am only accepting the reality and trying to make it a positive one. And the reality is that we all "go crazy now and then."

I can't imagine that now that you're feeling so good you'll want to do Wide Opens very often. I mean, why would you ever want to feel bad? Who wants to feel like a bloated, beached whale when you're used to feeling like a glorious, graceful gazelle? Always, always keep in mind that eating and feeling good are what living is all about and that, you little skinny, is what the BHD Lifetime Plan is all about.

THE NUTRITION EQUATION

At this stage of the game, the number of fruit meals you are eating should be substantially fewer than those you ate during weight loss. Those cataclysmic enzymes are still the backbone of your thin body, but for maintenance you don't require the high concentration that you needed to skinnify yourself. I rarely resort to an all-fruit day.

Remember, it is the balance of all foods, all nutrients, carbs, proteins, and fats, that is going to keep you slim and healthy. As a Conscious Combiner, your ideas of a balanced diet will be dramatically changed; no longer will you think of a "balanced meal" but rather a "balanced day" or, more likely, a "balanced week."

The U.S. Senate Committee on Nutrition and Human Needs recommends, in their "Dietary Goals for the United States," that carbohydrates account for 55–60 percent of our diet. Further, they recommend that our unsaturated fat intake be reduced to 20 percent (poly and mono saturated combined). This leaves a balance of

20–25 percent protein. The Committee recommends that ultimately we reduce our protein intake to 12 percent.

Your nutritional quotient breakdown:

Carbohydrates	60%
Protein	20–25%
Fat	15–20%

Your nutritional quotient in sum:

2 1 MEALS PER WEEK

13 Carb Meals

5 Fruit breakfasts
2 Fruit lunches
3 Carb meals that include
unsaturated fat, i.e.,
butter, oil, sour cream,
or heavy cream
3 Carb meals without fat
13

6 Protein Meals

2 Free Meals, including
Open Breakfast, Open
Human, Open
Miscombination, Wide
Open, (all three
categories), or Open
Desserts

TOTAL   21

Don't let this scare you. I'm going to explain it all. And it's easier than it looks.

THE ART OF FINE EATING—
SAMPLE COMBINING

Although we are becoming untraditional and thinking in terms of eating experiences rather than three meals a day, we still have the three-meal-a-day point of reference to the rest of the world. Therefore, for simplicity's sake, we will talk in terms of breakfast, lunch, and dinner. But, as you know, I am referring to eating experiences, divided by pauses of two or three hours. Certainly there will be days or parts of days when you will eat meals in conventional timing. But there will also be many days without identifiable "mealtimes."

As a Conscious Combiner, think and tally by the week. Your nutritional quotient doesn't fix on individual meals, it hinges on your weekly intake. According to most standards, including those propounded in *Normal and Therapeutic Nutrition*, your nutritional needs are met if your average intake over a five- to eight-day period meets the required allowances, even if on a given day or days particular nutrients are in short supply. So, for nutrition's sake, think weekly!

Based on our three-meal-a-day point of reference, a week should be broken up into twenty-one meals or eating experiences. If 60 percent of our meals are carb meals and 20 percent are protein, then in a week we should have eaten a minimum of thirteen carb meals and five to six protein meals.

Because we don't eat fat by itself, we should make sure that about three carb meals a week include a significant amount of it. Actually, 15–20 percent of your calories (sorry to bring up that dirty word, but we need some common unit of measure) should come from unsaturated fats—oil, butter, sour cream, and heavy cream all qualify. The best, most nutritional source of unsaturated fat is cold-pressed oil. Some good examples of carbs with fats added are salads with dressing, marinated vegetables, Pasta alla Olio, and baked potato with butter.

Remember, heat destroys lecithin, so foods cooked in oil, deep fried or otherwise, do not count toward your fat quotient. Keep in mind that you are getting part of your fat requirement from your daily supplement of sesame seeds. If you eat raw nuts and seeds to fill your protein needs (remember, protein doesn't only have to come from animals—cows don't eat other cows, and chickens don't eat chickens), they also provide your body with high-quality, easily digestible unsaturated fats.

How many days should begin with fruit? A minimum of five. So, there are five carb meals in your nutritional equation. Another day could begin with a mini, midi, or maxi carb. The seventh could be a protein.

As a maintainer, you should allow yourself one Open Breakfast a week. Go on, give yourself permission. That's what maintenance is all about.

On the day you begin with protein, if you follow the rules, which I know you will, you will continue with protein for the rest of the day. Regardless of how you eat your protein, that day will tally up as *three protein meals*.

One day you might have a protein lunch and a protein dinner. That's five. A third day you might choose another dinner of protein. That's six. Or you might choose to have three protein dinners, or two all-protein days, or six protein dinners. Any combination will do so long as your total for the week is six.

Of course, carbs and proteins do not have to be isolated to meet your nutritional requirements. They may be mixed into Open Miscombinations and Open Humans.

In the first six months of maintenance, it's a good idea to go on a fruit day about once a week, regardless of what your scale says. This will continue the cleansing and detoxifying, firmly establish your discipline, and always ensure that you'll be safe rather than sorry. It doesn't have to be a mono-fruit day. As you'll see, it doesn't have to be only watermelon or only grapes or just pineapple or just papaya. Unless of course you've gained weight, and are applying the appropriate Corrective Counterpart. Your fruit day can consist of as many different fruits as you can get in as long as you wait the required two hours.

For good maintenance, at least two lunches a week should be fruit during the first six months. The more fruit you feed your body when you can, the more other things you can feed your heart and soul when you want to. It's those high-powered enzymes in fruit that clean you out from the day before and get you ready for the day that's coming. It is fruit, and fruit alone, that allows you to eat your heart out. Those enzymes and nutrients are the magic of the BHD Lifetime Plan. They are your hook to skinny.

As a Conscious Combiner, you will probably begin to choose to have fruit instead of other foods simply because you like it. And because you like the way it makes you feel.

I'll never forget my first trip to New York, long before my first book was published. A friend took me to lunch and at my request we went to a very chic Upper East Side French restaurant. I had chosen this particular place not because of the food, but for the ambience and the clientele.

I was going to a big dinner party that night and would be in a situation in which I would have no control over the meal. My choice of a triple order of blueberries was predicated on that and the fact that New Jersey blueberries were at the peak of their perfection. My luncheon companion thought I was very weird to order blueberries at a restaurant renowned for its gourmet fare. Her selection, a spinach and mushroom salad! Tradition, we are sooo bound by tradition.

And there may even come a day when, like Marlena Brauer, you take your raisins to Dan Tanas. Not because you have to, not because you are scheduled for them, but because that's all you really want to eat. The fact that she found herself at one of her favorite restaurants didn't deter her; she just ate what she wanted the most. Now that you have a choice, now that you don't have to eat anything because it's there or because you're there, isn't it about time you started eating what *you* want the most?

Now, on with the instructions! If you are on a day with two carb meals, it's a good idea to make only one an Open Carb. It cuts down on the temptation to overeat.

Remember, don't be afraid of the maxi carbs. I repeat, they are not maxi because they are the most fattening.

Several of your carb meals should be in the vegetable family. I also recommend one or two salads a week; those leafy greens help absorb fat.

But please, don't get carried away with the salads! Don't get caught up in the "I have to have a salad for lunch" syndrome. Salads are so bulky, and one has to eat so much of them to get full that they really require a great deal of digestive effort. In many cases, far more than they're worth. As a Conscious Combiner you're getting masses of fiber, so you don't need salads for that. And since salads are mini-carb combos, they don't pack as much supercharged energy as some of the other carbs.

I know, you want to eat them because they're low-cal. Well, you know how I feel about calories. Calories are energy, pure and simple. If you don't put it in (energy, that is), you won't have any to put out. Low calorie, low energy. There are lots of choices that are much more fun, will provide you with lots more energy, and are as, if not more nutritious than salads.

Try pasta, couscous, fried rice, a steamed-vegetable plate or a baked potato, some bread and butter or, just for fun (obviously not for nutrition) some white chocolate brownies. Don't stay locked into tradition. Conscious Combiners are creative thinkers. That's why food is so important to us. There's a world out there beyond the chef's salad and the tuna on whole wheat, a universe of food vastly more interesting than cottage cheese and canned peach halves. Stop longing for it, and live it. Use your imagination. Be creative. Now that you are leading the good life, take advantage of it.

Remove the diet plate from your consciousness. Welcome the good life, the life beyond the golden pineapple.

MEALS IN YOUR LIFE—
SUGGESTIONS FOR THE GOOD LIFE

As I've toured the country, a lot of you have asked me for meal suggestions. "Help," you cried, "give me some ideas." What else *is* there for lunch besides sandwiches? If I don't eat fruit, what can I have for breakfast? What should I cook at home for my family? How can I entertain as a Conscious Combiner?

So I'm going to prod your imagination. I'm going to give you some ideas of the kinds of eating experiences I and my clients delight in. Once titillated, you'll be able to come up with many of your own. I sure hope so; otherwise it will be my diet, and not yours.

Next, I'll introduce you to the three day fruit flings, and then we'll go on to the Corrective Counterparts or how to take the FAT out of FATtening, and then the magic Food Formulas for your first six months of maintenance. And of course I'll give you guidelines for putting together all kinds of terrific meals, and show you how to use your Workbook to Wonderland. In the recipe chapters, I'll share a glory of super-splendid Conscious Combining recipes with you. Gourmet delights that will be savored by your family and your friends as well as yourself.

Now, just to jostle your mind a little, to further prove our unconventionality, I've mixed the traditional and the untraditional in the following listings. Dinner can be lunch. Eggs can be dinner. Hors d'oeuvres can be breakfast. A meal can be just beginnings or middles or ends. Just because you're eating out, it doesn't mean you have to have an entree. How many times have you ordered a veal chop when all you wanted was the dessert? How many times have you eaten the whole meal when you would have been satisfied with just the homemade bread?

Remember, you are not confined to breakfast, lunch, and dinner. Think not in terms of meals but in terms of eating experiences separated by two- and three-hour increments. Start thinking in terms of longer eating experiences than the traditional half hour or hour. What's your rush, anyhow? I thought you enjoyed eating. Remember, it's not how much you eat in how short a time, it's how long you can make the pleasure last.

How many times have you eaten lunch knowing full well that you'll snack again in the afternoon? How often have you had dinner knowing you'll plop down in front of the TV and want to munch on something? How frequently have you eaten a meal "just to go along," well aware that you won't be satisfied and will eat again later? Well, you might just want to forget that meal in favor of the nosh or snack.

Change your time-frame mentality. Eat what you want, when you want it. You can have bacon and eggs anytime. Dessert anytime. Pasta anytime, even for breakfast.

If you were fat, believe me, it was conventional eating that did it to you in the first place. It was all those things you ate that you thought you had to eat and then what you really wanted to eat on top of them. No matter what, in the end we always find a way to eat our favorite foods, and along with them comes the guilt and the pounds. And the frenzy of guilt catapults us into a binge, and the cycle of FAT spirals.

But you're no longer a victim. You don't just take whatever comes and pile your own choices on top of it. Now you are consciously scheduling in only the foods you love. From now on you are going to eat just and only what you really want to eat to keep you feeling good and looking good, to keep you thin and healthy. You've taken responsibility, you're in control, and you'll never be fat again

Breakfast Bounties

FRUIT

- Do not eat grapes or watermelon unless, of course, you intend to eat them all day and night, because, as you know, they are all-day fruits only.
- There is no limit to the quantity of fruit you can have for breakfast, or at any "meal" for that matter.
- Because of their very special individual action, don't combine different fruits at the same time. You will find that combining fruits will make you gaseous and bloated.

You will note that there is no portion control indicated in the following listings. That's because none is intended. You are taking responsibility. You are making the decisions that affect your body. You're on maintenance now. Who knows better than you when you've had enough! Also, remember there are no time limits on your eating experiences. You can stretch them out as long as you'd like.

MONO CARB BREAKFASTS

Bagels

Bread, pumpernickel

Bread, sourdough

Brioches

Cereal, dry, to snack on

Cereal, hot, with butter

Croissants

Danish, fruitless and cheeseless

French toast, made with cinnamon and egg yolk

Onions, sautéed

Potatoes, any style (baked, cottage fried, french fried, hash browned, mashed)

Rice with herb butter

Tomatoes, baked

Yams, baked, with butter

Zucchini, steamed or pancakes (see page 260)

Remember, the fats—butter, oil, heavy and sour cream: They go with everything!

OPEN CARB BREAKFASTS

Asparagus, tomato, and zucchini, stir fried

Bagels with butter or sour cream, tomatoes, and onions

Borscht, hot or cold (see page 231)

Brioche with sautéed onions and mushrooms

Cornmeal pancakes with butter or sour cream (see page 269)

English muffin with butter and sliced tomatoes

Gnocchi with Sage Butter (see page 249)

Grits and biscuits (watch the salt)

Hash browns with onions and croissants with butter

Mushrooms and onions, sautéed, and baked with sour cream over English muffins

Potatoes with green peppers and onions

Toast with cinnamon and noodles with heavy cream or butter and cinnamon

Tomatoes, sliced; zucchini, steamed; and green peppers, sautéed

Remember, heavy cream is not something to take lightly! Although it is a fat, it's not as easily digested as butter, and it will slow down your digestion. Use it with discretion, and don't use it in your coffee.

MONO PROTEIN BREAKFASTS

Bacon

Cheese or cottage
cheese (If you're
smart, you'll heed
my warning and
make cheese the
last food you eat
in a day, because
nothing will
digest very well
after it. But if you
must, you must!)

Chicken livers

Chops (lamb, pork,
veal)

Eggs

Grilled halibut with
Herb Butter (see
page 223)

Ham

Hamburger

Milk, regular or
buttermilk

Sausage

Steak

Yogurt

OPEN PROTEIN BREAKFASTS

All deli fish are fine.
They can even be
smoked, but keep
in mind how salty
they are.

Bacon and eggs

Bacon, sausage, and
ham

Canadian bacon and
café au lait

Caviar with sour
cream in deviled
eggs

Chopped liver and
hard-boiled eggs

Eggs and tuna, or
salmon patties

Eggs, scrambled, with
cream and bacon

Fresh trout stuffed
with crab

Ham and eggs

Hamburger and eggs

Kippers and eggs

Kippers, herring, and
sardines

Lox and eggs and
smoked cod

Mahi Mahi and eggs

Omelet (chicken
liver, hamburger,
ham, bacon,
crabmeat, lobster,
caviar, lox), with

Bacon or   Sausage and eggs
    ham or a
    combination of
    any two
    ingredients

Carb Lunches

Anything you would have had for breakfast, please feel free to apply to lunch. Following are some more excitements to whet your appetite.

MONO CARB LUNCHES

This category includes some multi-entities (*). However, their ingredients are so similar in makeup that they can be considered as little family units and thus qualify as Monos.

Artichokes with butter or
    Mazel Dressing (see page
    214).
Bulgur wheat
Corn on the cob
*Crudités with a dip of sour
    cream, Mazel Mayo, or
    Mazel Hollandaise (see
    page 219 and page 214)
Egg-yolk-only matzo balls
French fries
Fried tortilla chips
Marinated green beans, hot or
    cold
Pasta with simple sauces, oil,
    butter, or marinara, and no
    vegetables
Popcorn
Rice

*Salad: Mazel, L-T-O, or Sweet
    'n' Sour with Mazel
    Dressing, sour cream, or
    Mazel Mayo (see pages 225,
    214, and 219)
Saltless potato chips

Soups:
    Corn Chowder (see page 230)
    Creamed vegetable soups
    (remember the cream
    warning: asparagus, carrot,
    pea, vichyssoise,
    watercress—use your
    wildest imagination)
    Tomato Soup con Pesto
    Vegetable broth

Steamed cauliflower
Stir fried broccoli

OPEN CARB LUNCH

Remember, foods that go together are like family units. Conscious Combining is not only knowing what doesn't go together but also knowing what does go together.

What Is Lunch If Not a Sandwich,

So . . .

for the Sandwich Lover

The Mix and Match Carb Club

(PICK 1)

Bagel	Rye
Bialy	Sourdough bread
Brioche	Whole wheat bread
English muffin	ad infinitum
Pita bread	

FREE LIST (AS MUCH AS YOU WANT OF ANY AND ALL)

Butter	Horseradish Cream
Hollandaise (see page 214)	(see page 219)
Mayonnaise (see page 219)	Sour cream

You may use as many foods from within a single group as you wish, but don't mix the groups.

FAMILY 1

Celery	Parsley
Cucumber	Summer squash
Lettuce	Tomato
Mushrooms	Watercress
Onion	Zucchini

FAMILY 2

Broccoli   Cauliflower
Brussels sprouts   Mushrooms

FAMILY 3

Cabbage   Turnip
Radish (grated, raw)

FAMILY 4

Chili pepper   Onion—all varieties
Green pepper   Red pepper
Iceberg lettuce   Tomato

FAMILY 5

Asparagus   Mushrooms
Celery   Onion
Green beans

FAMILY 6

Beet   Endive
Carrot (raw)   Scallions or Leaks
Chard   Kale
Mustard greens

MORE OPEN CARB LUNCHES

Chips and dip
Chips and salsa
Endive
French-fried onion rings** and
    cottage-fried potatoes,
Sliced tomatoes and
    french-fried zucchini**

Stuffed mushrooms and broccoli
    or asparagus with
    garlic-herbed bread crumbs.
Grilled tomato and onion
    sandwich on your favorite
    bread

**The flour breading counts as a carb.

MORE OPEN CARB LUNCHES (*Cont.*)

Hamburger with Everything
Without (see page 270)

Gnocchi with Sage
Butter (see page 249),
and salad

Pasta, rice, or couscous (see
page 245) with
salad and bread and butter

Sloppy Sue (see page 270)

Spinach-Dill Tourte
(see page 254)

Vodka, tequila, Scotch, rye, or
bourbon, as an addition to
two other choices, so long
as only one of the other
choices is a maxi carb.
Remember, Open Carb
allows only two maxi carbs
in its trio.

MONO PROTEIN LUNCHES

Feel free to steal ideas from breakfast.

Beef Stroganoff without the
veggies

Broiled Chicken with Herbal
Mustard Coating (see
page 281)

Carne Asada

Carpaccio (see page 272)

Creamed chicken sans veggies

Ham hocks

Lobster with butter

Marinated Beef on a skewer

Prime rib

Ribs, beef or pork

Roast chicken

Sashimi

OPEN PROTEIN LUNCHES

If you'd like a more expansive list, see the breakfast and dinner
suggestions.

Fisherman's Platter

Liver and bacon

Rib and Wing (spareribs and
chicken)

Seafood Newburg sans veggies

Weiner schnitzel

Protein Picks (special
all-protein salads—use your
imagination and see the
special recipe section for
spices and dressings):
Chicken and egg salad

Chicken livers and egg salad

Duck salad

Lamb curry salad

Lobster, crab, or shrimp
  salad

Sardines and chopped eggs

Seafood Salad (see page 280)

Tuna and eggs

Dinners

MONO DINNERS

I've mentioned an array of Mono Meals for breakfast and lunch. Feel free to elaborate on the lists. I don't think you need any more suggestions to figure out what single foods you're in the mood for. It's the Open Meals that are likely to tax your imagination. But not for long. If I know you, you'll quickly get into the swing of things.

OPEN CARB DINNERS

Artichoke, baked potatoes, and
  salad

Asparagus Hollandaise, boiled
  new potatoes, and
  watercress salad

Onion Soup with bread and
  butter

Pasta (see pages 245–51), bread
  and butter, and salad

Potato salad, corn on the cob,
  and peas

Raw vegetables with sour cream
  dip and vodka

Rice pilaf, baked tomatoes, and
  sautéed onions

Risotto with mushrooms, and
  bread and butter

Salsa, tortillas, and beer

Soupe au Pistou (see page 232),
  watercress and tomato
  salad, and croissants

Vegetable rice soup, potato
  latkes, and sour cream

Vegetable tempura and rice

Vichyssoise, sourdough bread,
  and French-cut green beans

Don't forget that alcohol (but not wines, brandy, or fruit cordials or liqueurs) can be substituted at will for one of your three Open Carb choices.

OPEN PROTEIN DINNERS

Baa and Moo (lamb chops and steak)

Bouillabaisse (see page 240)

Moo-River (three steaks: filet, New York, and T-bone)

Mousseline de Poisson

Caviar
Cracked crab
Butterflied Leg of Lamb (see page 273)

Mussels à la Marinière (see page 278)
Oysters
Pheasant under Glass

Carpaccio (see page 272)
Veal with mustard (see page 275)
Cheesecake

Chops Ahoy:
  Lamb chop
  Veal chop
  Pork chop

Lox of Luck:
  Herring
  Lox
  Smoked cod

Sashimi

Surf and Turf

The Cheese Stands Alone:
  Your choice of any varieties of cheese

Deli-icious—(choice of three):
  Corned beef
  Kosher hot dog
  Pastrami
  Pepper beef
  Rare roast beef
  Salami

Hot-Sea-Tot-Sea:
  Seafood Salad (see page 280)
  Stuffed Mussels (see page 279)

Moon Liver:
  Chopped Chicken Liver—or Chicken Liver Paté
  Broiled Calves Liver and Bacon

Vealy Truly Yours:
  Veal Chop
  Veal Paillarde
  Veal Scallopini

Open Oink:
  Pork chop
  Spare ribs
  Baked ham

NUTS AND SEEDS

Nuts should be nibbled and only at night. Preferably at the end of an all-fruit day. You noticed I said nibbled. That is precisely how they should be eaten, very slowly. And chew, chew, chew. Nuts have a tendency to clog and unless they have become liquid in your mouth they will not digest properly. The beauty of nuts is that the more you chew them, the *better* they get. Obviously, they are not exactly the kind of thing you would sit down and expect to eat and finish at a "traditional meal" (see Glossary); rather they are an option you would select in lieu of a meal, for those "nosh" or snack occasions.

You should save eating nuts for the evening, because if you start them in the middle of the day, you'll get real bored with them by dinnertime, and then you'll be in trouble. You'll be hungry, and you will have ignited that hand-to-mouth action, and nothing other than nuts will really digest well.

As in everything else on maintenance, there is no portion control when it comes to nuts. Take it from a former cashew freak, you can't eat too many; your body simply won't allow it. If, however, you want a mixed bag (of nuts, that is), you would be wise to limit yourself to about eight ounces. Because of all the different tastes and textures you might have a problem knowing when enough is enough, and nuts seem to trigger all those old eating neuroses that are hidden deep inside and that threaten the demise of many a confirmed Conscious Combiner. It is for this reason that I don't recommend mixing nuts.

Seeds go with other seeds and nuts with other nuts, and never the twain shall meet. Everything I said about nuts applies to seeds as well.

DESSERTS, OPEN AND OTHERWISE

You can even have an Open Dessert instead of breakfast, although I caution you not to let that frivolity translate itself into a habit, not if you want to feel good.

Need I remind you, the beauty of maintenance is that you can literally eat anything you want to your heart's content. You don't even have to limit your Open Dessert portions anymore. Although, for myself, I try to stick to the guidelines I set up for *The Beverly Hills Diet*: one or two desserts for breakfast (I must confess though, I never do an Open Dessert breakfast, it would ruin my day), two for lunch, and three for dinner.

If you haven't gotten sick after four pieces of chocolate cake and you still want more, go ahead, but maybe you'd better tune in to your body. By this point you should know when enough is enough, or at least your body should, and you should be listening. But the problem with sweets is sometimes they just never stop tasting good, so you really do have to listen. Actually, I'm not that worried that you'll overeat. After all, who would gulp down ice cream when you have permission to let it linger? Why would you want to inhale chocolates when you can luxuriate in them?

Desserts such as puddings, cakes, and soufflés, while classified as carbs, are in actuality miscombinations because they all contain eggs. They will work in combination with an Open Carb meal despite their being a miscombination if you don't abuse the privilege, that is, if you don't do it too often. Because of their protein base, cheesecake and ice cream can be included in an Open Protein meal, but they do not combine with any other desserts, other than each other.

The best way to enjoy desserts, and enjoy means to eat them without guilt and fear, is as an Open Dessert. And quite frankly, the way they taste the best is on their own. This also gives you the opportunity to experience the full brunt of their—I hate to say it, but I will—malice. Be prepared to not like the way you feel afterward. I sure don't. In fact, I never do an Open Dessert if I have anything even remotely important to do within a twenty-four-hour period, that's how long the effects linger.

Readers of *The Beverly Hills Diet* were confused about the rule of never following a maxi carb with a protein, whereas an Open Dessert lunch requires that you follow it with protein. The reason for the Open Dessert exception is the effect that the protein has on sugar. If there is anything that will jar you loose from the sugar trip as you begin to crave more, more, more, it's protein. If sapped energy is a potential pitfall for you, I recommend that beef be your protein choice at dinner following an Open Dessert lunch.

If your Open Dessert comes at night, you'll have two choices the next day: Almost certainly you will need a Corrective Counterpart for one of two reasons. Either you will have gained weight or you'll be suffering with convoluted and sapped energy. If you've gained, refer to the Corrective Counterparts. If you haven't gained but are feeling the wallop of all that concentrated sugar, go on a protein day.

Remember, nuts are a protein, and not only will they make the dessert even more of a miscombination, they will also inhibit the digestion of the protein antidote you'll be eating later. Now, why add insult to injury? If I select a dessert that happens to have nuts in it, I just pick the nuts out. Not easy in a Bear Claw but at least it lessens the possibility of gaining. The desserts that nuts go best with are those that are typically protein-based, such as ice cream; then it isn't such a terrible clash of food types. Ask yourself if the nuts really add to that dessert you're about to eat. If the answer is yes—go for it and enjoy.

As you know, fruit does not really combine with anything else. So eating a fruit dessert is not really a great dessert choice. If you do eat a fruit combo dessert, such as a pie or a tart, do so only at the end of a fruit day. And don't you dare even consider having just fruit for dessert. If I ever catch you, we're through! Why destroy and convolute fruit's potency by cramming it in on top of a mishmash? With all the dessert choices, how could you even think of doing that, of breaking Golden Rule Two, when you can enjoy its purity and luxuriate in its benefits each and every morning?

And, speaking of fruit, when you schedule your eating, be sure to consider:

THE THREE-DAY FRUIT FLINGS

These Fruit Flings are feasts for your body and your soul. Hard to believe, but a lot of people make fruit a first choice not only because they love eating it, but also because they love the way it makes them feel, physically and emotionally.

Embrace a Fruit Fling whenever you feel like it. Do it for a three-day cleansing, to lose a few pounds, to gain energy, or just to take advantage of the fruits of the season. One of the main thrusts of their design is to take full advantage of seasonal fruits. Don't mistake a Fruit Fling for a Corrective Counterpart; their enzymatic values are substantially different.

- Do not do more than one Fruit Fling a month.
- If you choose to go on a Fruit Fling during your six-month maintenance program, simply stop wherever you'd like, preferably between weeks, have your fling, and pick up your Food Formula progression where you left off.
- When you embark on a Fruit Fling, eat one fruit at a time; eat as much as you'd like, for as long as you like, but allow two hours between the different fruits. Eat the fruits only in the order listed; that is, once you have stopped one and moved on to another, you cannot go back to the first.

Morning	*Midday*	*Evening*
	PRUNE PICK UP	
Prunes	Raspberries	Raisins
Watermelon	Watermelon	Watermelon
Bananas	Apricots (fresh or dried)	Blueberries
	BLUEBERRY BOUNCE	
Blueberries	Strawberries	Raisins
Cherries	Cherries	Cherries
Peaches	Nectarines	3 Bananas

Morning	*Midday*	*Evening*
	PEACHY KEEN	
Peaches	Nectarines	Apricots (fresh only)
Cherries	Cherries	Cherries
Prunes	Raisins	3 Bananas
	CHERRY TRA LA	
Cherries	Cherries	3 Bananas
Peaches	Peaches	Nectarines
Prunes	Plums	Apricots (fresh only)
	TOP BANANA	
Blueberries	Strawberries	2 Bananas
Watermelon	Watermelon	Watermelon
2 Bananas	Apricots (fresh)	Dried apricots
	BERRY TRULY YOURS	
Blackberries	Raspberries	2 Bananas
Apricots (fresh only)	Nectarines	Peaches
Plums	Prunes	Blueberries

P.M. SWING

The P.M. Swing is a special four-day Fruit Fling. And just like the person for whom it was designed, famed interior designer Phyllis Morris, it lives by rules all its own. This special plan was developed for Phyllis while she was wintering in Acapulco with Harold and Grace Robbins.

Choose between papayas, pineapples, mangoes, and bananas for three days. You *must* eat something every two hours. Eat one fruit at a time in any order you wish, eat as much or little as you'd like at each sitting. Do not exceed six bananas during the three-day period. Day Four, however, must be nothing but watermelon.

VI

Saving Graces—
Taking the FAT Out
of FATtening

CORRECTIVE COUNTERPARTS

Okay, so you blew it, big deal; don't panic! We all do, you know, even Liza and Mary Ann. Yes, even I blow it occasionally. The beauty, the magic, of the BHD Lifetime Plan is that you can do something about it after the damage has been done—an instant fix, after the fact. You weight-loss BHDers already know the wonders of the Corrective Counterparts, the magic of the potent fruit enzymes and their ability to erase fat by accelerating digestion.

Every day of your life, no matter what, turn to your daily pal, your scale. It will tell you whether or not you need a Corrective Counterpart by telling you in no uncertain terms what works and what doesn't work.

A weight gain could of course be a natural fluctuation, the result of causes beyond your mouth. After a few months of mainte-nance you should be able to discern pretty accurately whether the scale is up because of something you ate or if it's up for other reasons. If you have gained because of something you ate, or if you aren't sure and you want to play it safe, if you want to feel secure, then apply the appropriate Corrective Counterpart. Believe me, you'll only feel better for it. Besides, what's the worst that could happen: You'll drop below your ideal, revel in that special sense of security, and luxuriate in that place of too-skinny.

Apply the Corrective Counterpart following a weight gain as follows:

AFTER GREASY, CREAMY, OR CHEESY FOODS SUCH AS:

BURN WITH:

Avocado	Ice cream	Pineapple
Bacon	Lobster Newburg	Or Strawberries
Beef ribs	Mexican, Middle	
Cheesecake	Eastern or Italian	
Cold cuts	meals	
Creamed spinach	Nuts	
Dairy	Pork	
Duck	Quiche	
French fries	Rib eye steak	
French meal	Seeds	
Goose	Spareribs	
Hot dog	Wild Game	

AFTER PROTEIN SUCH AS:

DIGEST WITH:

Beef	Turkey	Papaya
Chicken	Veal	Mango
Fish		Kiwi

AFTER SWEETS SUCH AS:

FEED WITH:

Cake	Pie	Grapes
Candy	Soufflé	
Cookies	Sweet rolls	
Mousse		

AFTER SALTY FOODS SUCH AS:

WASH WITH:

Chinese food	Salty fish, caviar, lox,	Watermelon
Deli food	or herring	

AFTER OVERDOSING ON MAXI CARBS SUCH AS:

Bread   Pasta

Pancakes   Potatoes

UNPLUG WITH:

Prunes (8 oz.),
Strawberries,
Raisins (8 oz.).
Or Strawberries,
Prunes (12 oz.).
Be sure it is a carb overdose, not an overdose of what went with the carb (the butter or the cheese or the sugar).

Antidotes for Special Meals

These are special three-day antidotes that can be followed for one, two, or three days.

MISHIMISHIMA (see Glossary)   Can be used to correct an Open Mexican, Open Italian, pizza, Thanksgiving dinner, Christmas dinner, Open Human, or Wide Open:

DAY 1   Pineapple and Papaya
DAY 2   Papaya and Pineapple
DAY 3   Watermelon

EASTERN ESCAPE   To be used to counter the effects of an Open Oriental and the high-sodium content that affects us bloaters:

DAY 1   Watermelon (if your weight is still up, you must do the next two days)
DAY 2   Pineapple and three Bananas
DAY 3   Watermelon

When to Resort to the Corrective
Counterparts

Your scale will tell you whether you need to apply the Corrective Counterpart for the first one-third of the day, the first two-thirds of the day, or for the entire day. On the days that you need a Corrective Counterpart but it is only required for a portion of the day, keep your eating light for the balance of that day. Don't have Open Humans or Open Miscombinations; and by all means don't have a Wide Open. If you only need a Corrective Counterpart for one-third of the day, you can have anything else for the balance of the day, excluding the aforementioned categories. That includes Open Carb, Open Protein, Open Dessert, and of course any of the Mono Meals. You do *not* have to eat fruit all day. If your weight gain requires that you devote two-thirds of the day to a Corrective Counterpart, then the balance of the day should either be a Mono Protein or a Mono Carb; sorry, no Open Meals. Again, while you can always do another fruit, it isn't really necessary, and in some cases it might even do more harm than good. I don't ever want you to ever associate fruit with punishment.

If you have gained:

¼ to ¾ pound	Begin the day with the appropriate Corrective Counterpart.
¾ to 1¾ pounds	Eat the appropriate Corrective Counterpart for two-thirds of a day.
Over 1¾ pounds	Eat the Corrective Counterpart for the entire day.

Note: If the appropriate Corrective Counterpart happens to be watermelon or grapes and the scale does not dictate the necessity of a full day, the fruit itself does. I'm sure I don't have to remind you that watermelon and grapes are all-day-only fruits.

If your weight is still up despite the Corrective Counterpart, you have several options:

1. Continue with the appropriate Corrective Counterpart. There surely will have been some change in your weight, so you will of course change the Corrective Counterpart accordingly.

2. If your Corrective Counterpart was papaya the first day, use pineapple the second day. If it was pineapple the first day, do the reverse and use papaya the second.

3. If you need a second day after the "unplug," make it watermelon or grapes.

4. If there is any similarity at all between the "special meals" and what you ate, you could do an antidote for "special meals," following the instructions as outlined on page 115.

5. Select a three-day Fruit Fling (see page 111). This should only be done as a last resort, and only when you have gained three or more pounds and a one-day antidote barely budged them. As you know, the Fruit Flings are not really Corrective Counterparts and for the most part should not be treated as such. They will, however, put your body through a three-day cleansing, which should put you back on the track. Remember, once you have committed yourself to a Fruit Fling, you must follow it all the way through.

Every time you miscombine, every time you eat something off the wall, you will not a disaster make. Despite your expectations, you may just get away with murder and not gain an ounce. This happens to us skinnies, you know, especially as we move beyond the first few months of maintenance, as our bodies and our brains establish balance and harmony. You won't always have to resort to a Corrective Counterpart when you miscombine. There will be many times when you absolutely know you blew it, you've got your Corrective Counterpart waiting for you, but your scale informs you NOT NECESSARY. Celebrate and save those magic enzymes for another day. But always, always have that Corrective Counterpart scheduled, always prepared.

PRECIDOTES

These are the fruits you eat before something else, that is, before the fact. They are similar to the antidotes; the difference is in the timing. They won't always be necessary, and in fact should only be used when you know you are going to be eating to excess or when you are going to eat something that has a strong weight-gain potential. For instance, I would most probably use a precidote before an Open Mexican or an Open Italian to help diminish the effects of the grease and cheese. The precidote in this case would be strawberries. I'd save the pineapple for after the fact, the next morning.

Normally, if you just keep yourself "enzymatically open," you won't have to worry about what you eat before. If I was going to have a basic Open Human meal in a restaurant and my weight was fine, the only precaution I would take would be to follow Golden Rule Three, making sure I didn't have any protein earlier in the day.

In selecting the precidote, look to the list of Corrective Counterparts (pages 120–21) for guidelines to the appropriate fruit. Save the most potent (the first one listed) for the antidote for when you need it most—when it will be the most effective. A precidote, once again, refers to a food to be eaten before a possible indiscretion and should really only be used if you have serious intimations of trouble. Remember the fruit rule, and if you need a precidote, don't eat anything other than fruit before it.

SUBSTITUTES AND THEIR ILK

People keep insisting that there must be more substitutes than I list. I would love to be able to create some new foods with similar potencies, fruits that would have the same effect as our magic fruits of the Beverly Hills Diet, but sorry, it just isn't possible.

Unfortunately, the magic only exists in the small handful of fruits that are integral to the Beverly Hills Diet and the Beverly Hills Diet Lifetime Plan and it is the proper use of these fruits that is going to let you eat to your heart's content. I can't wave a magic wand and make food less fattening by miraculously making it more digestible, but the proper use of these fruits can. They are your life insurance, your ticket to Forever.

What do you do if you can't find the fruit you need to prepare yourself properly? What can you do to correct a huge Chinese meal if there is positively no watermelon on your immediate part of the planet? You can't, so you don't have the Chinese meal. If you know from past experience that you are going to gain from a certain eating experience, and the appropriate Corrective Counterpart is not available, that eating experience is not an option that is open to you. And why would you even want to have it under those circumstances? What fun would it be knowing the consequences; when you know you're going to gain and you can't correct it? Wait until you can. It will still be there tomorrow; it's not going anywhere; it's not leaving the planet! It will *all* be there waiting for you, along with your perfect body *and* your Corrective Counterpart.

If your weight is up after a miscombination and you do not have the appropriate food; if, despite your hacking your way through jungles and swamps, climbing mountains and riding rapids, you have been unable to obtain it, then and only then look for a reasonable facsimile. Try to stay in the same category. Study how fruits are combined in the Burn, Feed, and Wash listings on page 114, to give you an idea of what can replace what. Don't let the absence of pineapple be an excuse for blowing it; just because you can't find watermelon, that doesn't mean you should have Eggs Benedict. Use your good common sense. There's always a reasonable alternative, certainly something that is better than the worst. Your mind is now as committed to the BHD Lifetime Plan as your body. Use it!

If the appropriate fruit is not available, at least select another fruit as the most reasonable alternative. Almost any fruit would be better than nothing, or anything else for that matter. Even a grapefruit or an orange is far more desirable than a nonfruit choice. Tell me, where on this earth do you think you might be where you won't be able to find some kind of fruit, an apple or a pear? I cannot stress it strongly enough: *Always, always, always* eat fruit first.

There is one exception: the less fibrous melons which include: honeydew, cantaloupe, casaba, and company. All those melons that have a cluster of seeds in their centers should never be substituted for other fruit because, unhappily, they will do more harm than good: You will bloat. Melons are the only fruits that are worse than a nonfruit choice. Another convention breaker, but alas, my extensive experimentation with many a melon maven has proven its truth. Watermelon, of course, is a melon unto itself, an all-day fruit of special value.

Only resort to the substitute list if you absolutely must. Every fruit is unique in its digestive powers and no other can fully mimic its bounteous benefits.

Substitute Food List

Remember, if fresh is not available, you can happily substitute frozen.

Dried fruits can be substituted for fresh (pineapple and papaya excluded). But fresh fruits cannot be substituted for dried.

Bottled fruits with NOTHING added can be substituted for fresh fruits.

Under dire circumstances, *only, only, only* in an extreme emergency, can you use canned fruit, and then only in its natural syrup.

PROGRAMMED FRUITS:	SUBSTITUTE:
Strawberries	Pineapple, kiwi
Kiwi	Mango, papaya, persimmon, apple
Figs or dates	Prunes or raisins
Papaya	Mango, kiwi, persimmon
Pineapple	Strawberries
Prunes	Figs
Strawberries	Pineapple
Watermelon and grapes*	If you absolutely cannot unearth them, go on either pineapple for two-thirds of a day and two bananas in the evening or apples for the entire day.

*Reminder: If you find yourself on a watermelon or grape day and have actually begun eating the assignee, if there's been a plague, if one more bite will make you jump out the window, if a fire consumes your secret grape cache, there *is* an alternative to giving in to a hamburger with everything on it:

· raisins or bananas after grapes
· bananas after watermelon
· baked potato with *nothing* on it.

VII

Countdown to Forever — The Food Formulas

We all know these first six months of skinny are deadly. We've been there before. Your fat is on hold, ready to pounce back at the slightest sliver of opportunity. It doesn't need much provocation. It's in the beginning, when you are newly thin, that you are at your most vulnerable, physically and psychologically. Physically, although gorgeously and radiantly thin, your body is unstable and still dangerously prone to fat. Mentally, you are subject to alternating states of euphoria and complacency. Your Debilitating Fat Consciousness is primed for action and will take mental advantage in an instant. It has always made its comeback before, and it's lying in wait, coiled to strike.

These first six months are just as important to those of you who aren't newly skinny, to those of you who have never been fat, as they are to all my old friends from the Beverly Hills Diet and all other former fatties. It takes six months to acclimate your body and your brain to your new lifestyle, the Beverly Hills Diet Lifestyle (see Glossary), to make Conscious Combining unconscious. Remember, your goal is not to lose weight, your goal is not only to look terrific; more important, it is to feel terrific.

I am going to show you how. The Food Formulas will allow you to maximize the quality of your life by eating, enjoying, and embracing food and all it has to offer. Man doesn't live by pineapple alone any more than he lives by steak alone. And now I'm going to prove it to you.

I absolutely insist that all you "dieters" go off your rigid regimen of weight loss and move into the wonderful, wide-open world of maintenance! A world where you will soon see that you can be as thin as you'd like for the rest of your life while having your cake and eating it too. A world where you can participate and partake in all the things the good life has to offer, including whatever you want to eat and a body you can be proud of.

The Food Formulas will show you how much you can get away with, how far you can stretch the rules without stretching yourself. They mean doing your own thing, but with a crutch. They will dispel that nagging trepidation, that inevitable doubt harbored deep in your mind that is all "too good to be true." The Formulas will allow you to experiment with real living and eating with confidence. You will continue with the cleansing, both physically and emotionally, and you'll learn in the process. You will get a better sense of what follows what and why, firmly fix how this is done, see how really easy it is, and make Conscious Combining your own. You now have permission for everything!

The following Formulas are your ticket to Forever. There are twenty carefully blended, nutritionally valid Formulas to mix and match during your first six months of maintenance. No two are the same. Their nutritional and emotional quotients are perfect. They all contain 20 to 25 percent protein and a license to luxuriate in the fun of eating.

Just to make sure you understand exactly how to interpret them, I am giving you sample menus for each Food Formula. I remind you, these are samples, not prescriptions. If you love them, terrific, you're welcome to adopt them. But I'm not telling you what you should eat; that must be your decision, no one else's, not even mine. To make the Beverly Hills Diet Lifetime Plan a way of life Forever, you must include your favorite foods on a regular and consistent basis. Don't only use my examples. Replace them with some of your own selections. The six-month Food Formula program is your recipe for Forever; it is training for your consciousness. If you become too dependent on me, you will have trouble making it on your own when the time comes.

Each week is an entity unto itself, carefully designed to maintain the weight you began the week with. The weeks may be juggled and rearranged, but only as seven-day units. The foods within a single week are properly ordered, in terms of precidotes and antidotes. They are models of Conscious Combining. They will demonstrate what naturally follows what and show you how to slot in your favorite foods. They will demonstrate how to schedule in Open Carb and Open Protein meals, and how to follow and precede your Open Humans and Open Miscombinations to maintain your slimhood and vitality. The Formulas are designed to teach you how to skillfully create food formulas for your own weeks, weeks that you will weave into my Food Formulas each month.

I've come up with every miscombination and Open Human meal I could imagine and included every Open Carb and Open Protein combo conceivable to my food-loving brain. Don't let that stop you, I'm hoping you'll come up with lots I've forgotten about and many I haven't yet discovered.

Many of the Open Carb and Open Protein suggestions are examples of how foods can be combined as interconnecting family units. They are foods which I believe combine best together, both nutritionally and digestively.

Two perfect examples are the Mazel Salad (see page 225), a spinach-based salad with a variety of vegetables, and the L-T-O (see page 225). Those rich, dark green vegetables in the Mazel Salad, fill your body with chlorophyll, vitamin A, and vitamin C. The diuretic qualities of the L-T-O exist because of the combination of the iceberg lettuce (high in water content), the tomatoes, and the onions, which feed your body concentrated forms of sulfur, potassium, magnesium, and yes, even *natural* sodium.

Is One Week Better Than the Next?

Everyone is different, physically and emotionally. As we all know, a big part of the way we process our food depends on the state of our heart and how well we're feeding it. As far as our individual nutritional needs are concerned, they are very individualized; RDA's (Recommended Daily Allowances) have replaced MDR's (Minimum Daily Requirements) as a standard of measure because what might be minimum for you may be twice as much as is necessary for me.

Which week will be best for you? How can you best satisfy your needs? You will discover that for yourself as you begin filling them. You are creating your Forever diet, and in the process you will discover for yourself just what your needs really are, physically as well as emotionally.

You may find that you do better on a week that includes mostly protein dinners, a week that specializes in carbs. Hopefully you'll find happiness in a mixture of weekly Food Formulas. Variety is the spice of life.

If you are over the age of sixty, it is a good idea to concentrate on weeks that have more protein. In fact, I would suggest protein almost every day. If you don't have protein for a day or two, follow those days with a double or triple protein day. Protein is a body builder, and after the age of sixty your cells need that extra protein boost.

No Food Formula week is more "fattening" than another, so don't be afraid of the weeks with all the Open Humans; if you eat like a human being, you won't gain any weight. The reality, easier said than done! We've always had those real good intentions. Now, knowing you as I know myself, I considered the possibility that you might not eat like a human being, and that you will gain weight. So I've compensated for that inevitability, I've taken care of everything, and the weeks will take care of themselves. Trust me and trust the weekly Food Formulas. I promise I'll help keep you thin so please, don't try to prove me wrong; you'll only be hurting yourself.

There will be some Food Formulas that you will adore and others that will bore you. While you do not need to do all twenty of them, I want you to do as many as possible. Repeat the weeks you like moving beyond my food examples and replacing them with your own choices, and don't bother with the ones you don't like. When repeating, however, don't keep eating the same foods over and over. It's not healthy. Your body needs a balance of all foods. Remember, "too much of something and not enough of something else" = Fat, and I might add, ill health.

Once again, when selecting the weeks for your eating plan they *can be in any order that you'd like.* You will do three of my Food Formulas and then one of your own making. Well, you didn't think I was going to do it all for you, did you? Repeat the four-week cycle until month by month you happily and skinnily complete twenty-four weeks of the glorious Beverly Hills Diet Lifetime Plan maintaining.

And as your nutritional quotient soars by every possible measure vis-à-vis these frolicsome Food Formulas, hopefully your emotional quotient will too. Well, why shouldn't it. Have you ever eaten so well in your life?

Fruit Frolics

Each Food Formula week contains a fruit cleansing day, which may or may not be necessary in terms of your weight. In the early months of maintenance, until you are totally cleansed, it's a good idea to continue with at least one full day of fruit per week. Extra pounds are sometimes sneaky and don't show up for a day or two after the deed, particularly if refined sugar or salt is the villain. Part of the idea of these fruit days is to make sure there is no sugar, salt, or fat residue in your system. Your energy will be higher, and you will feel better because of them. Not incidentally, these fruit days will carry on the process of developing your skinny voice. Carry it on and make it shout!

By the end of six months you won't need my Formulas anymore, and you won't need me to tell you when to do an all-fruit day; your body will tell you. Never again will you be able to say, I can't do it. Never again will an all-fruit day be difficult to do because you will have been doing one every week for six months. These six months will help you weather every excuse. Your fruit days will be testimony to your commitment to the Beverly Hills Diet Lifetime Plan and to the golden pineapple. Your fruit days will carry on the cleansing process; emotionally as well as physically. That's fruit's magic, and the key to the BHDLP.

As time goes on, you will see that you need fewer fruit days. I rarely do them anymore, and, when I do, it's because I want to, almost never because I have to. Once your heart understands and realizes that all foods are there for you to enjoy at will, you will probably be choosing fewer extravagantly Open Meals. You will be more in tune with your body, more capable of fine-tuning without resorting to extremes.

Also, as you begin to assimilate your new perfect body, the gyrations of those early maintenance months (both mental and physical) will even out. When one famous skinny first went on maintenance, he gained weight from soy sauce. He resorted to occasional all-fruit days until his body stabilized. Now on an even keel, his body accepts the sashimi dipping without ballooning. Never abandon your fruit days altogether. They reinforce your communion with your body, and represent the essence of the Beverly Hills Diet Lifetime Plan.

Despite my formidable food imagination, the foods I have suggested in my sample meals represent only a few of the many possible combinations. I have barely tapped the surface. As you move along during the next six months, your food imagination should become as sensitized and creative as mine. I hope you will prove it to me when you send me a copy of your records. I wouldn't mind enriching my own food vocabulary.

I have the tons of miscombinations to the Food Formulas so that you will know, and experience how the different miscombinations fit into the world of Forever. As we all know, it was too many miscombinations that made us fat and unhealthy to begin with, so don't do them just to do them; make them count. If you make the exceptions exceptional, your love of them will obliterate their negative side effects. And don't you dare skimp on them during these next six months, thinking that if you don't do them, you'll be safer. Wrong. Your "skinny" needs them for self-development.

If however you're like me, and you love to indulge in heaping portions, then the more Mono Meals you do and the fewer miscombined and Open Meals you indulge in, the easier it will be to eat to your heart's content and never eat your heart out. I don't miscombine very often, and I prefer Mono Meals. Not only do they allow me to eat more, they also make me feel a lot better physically. It's all a matter of choice, and soon you will have the opportunity to experience and then decide for yourself.

Always remember, Conscious Combining is a positive. It is something you do for yourself: for your body, for your sense of well-being, for your heart, and for your soul. Never think of Conscious Combining as a punishment—a jail sentence, as something you have to do. Never think of it as a "diet" in the negative sense. It's a way of life. It is your miracle line to happiness and Forever skinny.

Tell me, how could a meal of oysters, rack of lamb, and ice cream be a misery? Can endive salad, Pasta alla Olio, and fresh, hot Italian bread and butter be deprivation? Or a breakfast of oatmeal, heavy cream, and croissants? I mean, that's not exactly torture.

So eat, experience, and enjoy. Learn how to make all those exceptions exceptional!

And now, for the weekly Food Formulas you've been waiting for! Your specific instructions for exactly what to do with them are in your Workbook to Wonderland.

Here is the key, the meal categories, repeated. Just as a reminder for you. (For the complete description of the categories, see Chapter V.)

F = Mono Fruit (one fruit)

C = Mono Carb (one carbohydrate)

P = Mono Protein (one protein)

OC = Open Carb (up to three carbs but only two of them maxi carbs)

OM = Open Miscombination (one carb and one protein)

OP = Open Protein (up to three protein foods in any combination, excluding nuts)

OD = Open Dessert (just desserts as an eating experience)

RO = Resnick Open (just drinking as an eating experience)

OH = Open Human (anything and everything, eaten with dignity and decorum)

Note: The first symbol of the Food Formula refers to the morning meal, the second to the midday meal, and the third to the evening meal. For example, F OM P translates to Fruit first, Open Miscombination midday, and a Mono Protein meal in the evening. C OC OP translates to a morning Mono Carb, an Open Carb meal at midday, and a Mono Protein meal in the evening. Easy. Right?

DOING YOUR OWN THING

I don't want to provide too much of a crutch for you. I can't carry you along indefinitely on my skinny little shoulders. Sooner or later you've got to start thinking and doing for yourself.

Maintenance means assuming responsibility for yourself. Remember, there are still fatties out there depending on me totally, who need my help every step of their "getting skinny" way.

The network of thousands of BHD skinnies will provide sustenance and support, for you, but ultimately, skinny is a product that comes from within, not without. It's your own skinny voice that will keep you perfect. It's your support system we are developing. You're skinny now, so prove it. As you develop your *own* support system, use your Rock of Gibraltar; the rules and tools of the BHD Lifetime Plan will become that foundation. You now have slim hips, and you have the ammunition to keep them that way forever.

For three consecutive weeks you will be following my Formulas, hopefully choosing some of your own foods. Every fourth week you will make up a Formula of your own. Don't be afraid. By the time we're through, you will be ready, you'll have all the knowledge you need, and you'll know how to use it.

Designing Your Own Food Formulas and Making Them Your Own

1. *Weigh yourself every day and write it down.* Never compromise your love affair with your scale, your impartial judge of skinny. Don't be afraid of it.

2. *Your "Doing Your Own Thing" week must always be scheduled in advance.* Resist the temptation to leave it open, to be spontaneous "to see what happens." You *know* what will happen. Resist that temptation to "wing it." You'll only be sorry if you do.

3. *When you begin scheduling, always plan for the possibility of added pounds.* Prepare for the worst, always schedule in the maximum Corrective Counterpart. As you develop your maintenance profile, as you begin to see what your body can handle you'll be able to ease up a little. As you learn your body, and as your body learns to respond to the Beverly Hills Diet Lifetime Plan, Conscious Combining will become automatic and you will move into the world of

Unconscious Combining. I know by experience that I can get away with eating four and a half pieces of pizza in a single night and not gain an ounce. I also know that if I eat four and a half pieces of pizza the next night in a row I will inevitably put on one and a half pounds. I've experimented with this time and time again; in fact every time I go to Chicago, I have my pizza. After years of experience and experimentation, I know my weight-gain score for all my favorite foods and even my not-so-favorite foods. Right now you only need to experiment with and experience your favorites. Why bother with the others? Remember, I had to; I was creating a universal methodology, an eating program that would include all of you.

I haven't suggested anything to you that I haven't experienced myself. Until two of my clients had proven its validity. But, always remember, the Beverly Hills Diet Lifetime Plan is experiential as well as theoretical. We Conscious Combiners know what works and what doesn't because we've tried it all.

4. *When charting your eating schedule, think first of your social and business commitments and then of your emotional needs*. First, slot your social and business eating engagements, the things you have to do. Then schedule in the foods you most want to eat, the foods that will help cement your Beverly Hills Diet loyalty. Try to combine the two, the have-to's, and the want-to's. There are only so many days in a week, you know. Next fill in the proper antidotes and precidotes. Be generous. Remember, you aren't trying to lose anymore, you're maintaining. Now tally up your nutritional quotient for the week, making sure that you have the proper amount of protein, carbs, and fats. Be sure that you are feeding your body the nutrients it needs. And do not, I repeat, *do not slight your emotional needs*. Remember, the Beverly Hills Diet Lifetime Plan is for *all* of you. It is an individualized program that must cater to the heart if it is to be Forever.

5. *How many Open Carbs versus Open Miscoms, how many Open Proteins versus Mono Proteins you'll be able to get away with in a day, a week, and a*

FOOD FORMULAS

1
F F F
F C P
P OP OP
F F OM
F F OC
C OC OC
F F OH

5
F F F
F OM P
F F OP
OP P OP
F F OH
F F F
C C OC

9
F F F
C C OH
F C OH
F OC OC
F OM P
F F OD
F F F

13
F F F
F F OM
F OH P
F F OM
F F OM
F F OC
OH P OP

17
F F F
F OD P
P P P
F F OH
F F F
F C OC
F OH P

2
F F F
F OH P
F F OC
F OM P
OP P OP
F F C
OC C OC

6
F F F
F OH P
F F OP
F C P
OM P P
F F OC
F C OP

10
F F F
OH P P
F F OC
C C OC
F F OM
F C OP
F F OC

14
F F F
OD P P
OP P P
F F OM
C OC OC
F OH P
F F OD

18
F F F
F F OD
P P P
F C OC
F OH P
F F OM
F C P

3
F F F
OM P P
F F OC
F F F
OH P OP
F F C
F OC OP

7
F F F
F C OP
OH P P
F F OC
OP OP P
F F C
OD P P

11
F F F
F OM P
F F OH
F F C
F OD P
F F OH
F F OP

15
F F F
C OM P
F F C
C OD OP
F F OM
OM P OP
F F OC

19
F F F
C C OC
F C P
OM P P
F OD P
F F OH
F F OM

4
F F F
OP P P
F F OH
F F C
C C OC
F OM P
F F OP

8
F F F
P OP OP
F OM OP
F OH P
F F F
OP P P
F F OH

12
F F F
OD P P
F F OD
F F F
OM P OP
F F OC
F OH P

16
F F F
F OH P
F OP P
P P P
F F OM
C OM OP
F F OM

20
F F F
F F OD
F F F
P OP P
F F OC
OM OP O
F F OC

month will depend entirely on you. Experience and experimentation will give you the answer, and only time will tell. Don't forget, if your OM or OH is not dinner, follow it with protein for the rest of the day. Obviously, when you're eating an Open Meal, you will have to exercise more discipline. You'll have to enlist the aid of your little skinny voice. You'll have to listen to it when it proclaims, "Enough already," because your stomach might not; that is, not if the food is still tasting good. The pizza at Due's continues to taste good to me until I literally can't fit any more in. If I'm doing an Open Carb at Matteo's and I eat roasted peppers until they don't taste great, if I eat pasta until it revolts in my stomach, if I eat garlic bread until I can't stand another bite, I'm going to chunk on the pounds, and it's not worth it. Overindulging means paying the price, pruning your pleasure and triggering the pain of guilt.

Test, taste, and try. Know your limits; *only you can set them*. Put your mind into your eating and evoke your good common sense.

At the end of two or three months you should have a fairly firm fix on just how much you can get away with, just how far you can go. *Test your limits*. Don't plan on a miscombination or an Open Human every day, but as the weeks go by, increase your pleasures and gradually increase your opens and miscombs. Now, when I say increase, I am not suggesting that each week you double your pleasure. Each week, simply schedule an additional Open Meal in any of the four categories, always keeping in mind the rules and the tools of Conscious Combining.

Mace Neufeld, the famed Hollywood producer, continued under my salubrious tutelage long into his maintenance, even after he had become slim as a reed, so that he could continue to experiment with security. Each week I gave him a new eating assignment: a deli sandwich, wine with dinner, pizza and Mexican food in the same week. We fulfilled his wildest food dreams. I was easing him into normal Conscious Combining eating, and Mace continued to maintain his weight like a champ, readily mastering the art of Conscious Combining.

Suddenly one Monday morning he emerged four pounds heavier. It was after a week's assignment of three Open Humans and two Open Miscoms. Mace chose to cram them all into a single weekend, forsaking the Three Goldens. He then appeared the following morning lugging around the weight of the consequences.

When you first start scheduling your own weeks, be gentle and ease into it. Monitor your progress each step along the way, reveling in what you can get away with and drawing the line where you must. You will find that it's a mighty skinny line that marks the difference between thin and fat, vigorous and vapid.

Something as innocuous as added salt, a diet drink, a mediocre sauce, or a handful of nuts at the wrong time can spell gained pounds.

When Jenny, a bloater of the first order, achieved maintenance, her first on-her-own experiment was several days of Deli with its multitude of salty foods. Because of the salt and because her new skinny body was still at its most vulnerable, Jenny, true to form, bloated up with extra pounds. Next time Jenny experimented, it was with a little more caution.

Experience, experiment, and enjoy. But always ease into it. Trust in the Beverly Hills Diet Lifetime Plan. It works. Every skinny BHDLP maintainer is testimony to the power of the enzyme.

In the beginning, because of your vivid fat potential, your body probably won't tolerate too many miscombinations; and more important, they won't make your body feel very well. Be aware of how you feel; it is every bit as important to maintaining as what your scale tells you. After all, feeling terrific is the bottom line, everything else relates to that: your weight, your emotions, and your world. For the next six months you will follow weekly Food Formulas that will move you into Forever. Trust your body to them, and to me, and to your skinny voice. Make skinny your own!

Special Rule Stretchers and Helpful Hints

- A maxi-carb meal can precede a protein meal with caution, but a Mono Protein meal only.
- A maxi-carb can be eaten first thing in the day following a protein dinner the night before, if that first meal of the day does not occur until you have been up and about for at least four hours.
- If you begin the day with something salty, beef (after the appropriate wait, of course) will help sop up the resultant bloat and help dispel that extra water.

Doing Your Own Thing

1. Use the *Doing Your Own Thing* charts provided for each month in the book in your Workbook to Wonderland in Chapter VIII to list your weekly choices. Begin with the occasion, then put in the category, and finally your specific food choice.

2. Think of what you want to eat and when you want to eat it. Schedule in all business and social commitments first, then your emotional ones.

3. Mark those choices on your weekly chart first, then fill in the blanks. Remember, "What you choose to eat determines what you have to eat."

A SKINNY TEST

Now test your BHDIQ. Say the following are givens:

Sunday night you are going to the movies. Monday afternoon it's a political luncheon at a hotel. On Tuesday night, you want pizza. Thursday night you are going to the Kovners' for cocktails. Friday night you'll be at the Gollers' for dinner and Saturday at noon, your perfect "bod" will shine at the Roths' wedding. Your chart at this stage would look like this:

	MORNING	MIDDAY	EVENING
Sunday			Popcorn
Monday		Banquet lunch	
Tuesday			Pizza
Wednesday			
Thursday			Kovners' cocktails
Friday			Gollers' dinner party
Saturday		Roths' wedding	

I'm not going to fill in any of the other blanks here. If you have read this book, the answers are in your head and you know exactly what to do.

To take this test: Fill in the blanks. This will be the same process you will follow when you complete your "Doing Your Own Thing" weekly charts each month.

If you are really miserable, truly unsure, or if you are smug enough, as a good BHDLP maintainer should be, and want to prove your expertise at Conscious Combining, look at the next page for my answers.

Bear in mind your answer in terms of specific food choices probably will not match mine nor would I expect it to. In correcting your test, the match should be in the *category*, not the actual food.

For instance, where I have a salad you might have stir-fried vegetables—not the same food but the same family—both carbs.

THE ANSWERS:

	MORNING	MIDDAY	EVENING
Sunday	Papaya	Mazel Salad and Sourdough Bread	Popcorn
Monday	Kiwi	Banquet Lunch Open Human	Protein
Tuesday	Papaya or Mango	Strawberries	Pizza
Wednesday	Pineapple	Pineapple	Papaya
Thursday	Apples	L-T-O	Kovner's Cocktails Vodka—Open Carb
Friday	Prunes	Strawberries	Goller's dinner party Open Human
Saturday	Kiwi	Roth's wedding Open Human	Protein

See, I told you, you had the answers. You know exactly what to do. And it wasn't nearly as hard as you thought it would be, was it? The best part of all is that it becomes easier and easier until like Conscious Combining it becomes as easy and as natural as brushing your teeth or driving a car. Soon, you'll begin to approach it as if it were a game, a game in which *you are always the winner!*

My Immovables

And now, for the whys and wherefores. In filling in my blanks, I begin with a given, that which I know is actual fact. Select a specific meal that requires a specific antidote or precidote, the pizza. I know that the day after pizza I have to eat pineapple. I always plan for the worst so I'll make *Wednesday* an all-fruit day. The pizza antidote: pineapple and papaya. *Tuesday* I have a banquet lunch so I'll schedule myself for an Open Human. The antidote: protein for dinner. Whenever I go to a party I try to prepare myself for an Open Human just in case the food is going to be worth it. Most of the time it's not, so I change on the spot to a simpler selection—Open Carb, Open Protein, or Open Miscombination. Sometimes I'll even just continue on fruit if it's available.

Thursday, I'm going to a cocktail party. I want to drink vodka so I'll schedule myself for an Open Carb; that way I'll also be able to nibble on the crudités and any of the other carb hors d'oeuvres. If I wanted to drink wine, *Thursday* would have to have been an all-fruit day. *Saturday* afternoon is another Open Human. The antidote: protein only at night. A precidote is required on *Friday*. In order to keep myself "enzymatically open" for my Open Human *Friday* night, I know that I have to eat fruit only all day. The specific fruits can be selected later, after I determine my other selections for the week. At this point, your chart should look like this:

	MORNING	MIDDAY	EVENING
Sunday			Popcorn
Monday		Open Human	Protein
Tuesday			Pizza
Wednesday	Pineapple	Pineapple	Papaya
Thursday			Kovners' Cocktails Open Carb— Vodka
Friday	Fruit	Fruit	Gollers' Dinner Party-Open Human
Saturday		Roths' Dinner Open Human	Protein

All the have-to's are now in place. Now it's time for my choices. Once again, I'll begin with a given and work around it. My thought, first and foremost—if I feed my body when I can, I can feed my heart and soul when I want to.

My Choosables

Monday I did an Open Human and a protein dinner so *Tuesday* morning I'll begin with the protein antidote: papaya or mango. Midday, I'll have strawberries, the perfect precidote for pizza. *Thursday* is actually a neutral day; no antidotes or precidotes are necessary. My oatmeal for breakfast will make a welcome change from the fruit I've been eating each morning and the cream will help fill my fat quotient. L-T-O is a good, natural diuretic to take care of all that extra salt from the pizza.

Since dried fruit, a regular part of my diet, can only follow a carb night and cannot directly precede an animal protein, *Friday* morning is the perfect opportunity for my prunes. I'll follow them with strawberries. Strawberries are the perfect counterbalance for prunes, figs, and raisins as well as an ideal precidote to an Open Meal.

Kiwi is my choice for *Saturday* morning. Their enzyme will work as an antidote and as a precidote. Likewise for *Monday* morning.

Only one day left, *Sunday*. My popcorn evening puts only two restrictions on me, no protein or desserts that day. I can either do fruit or other carbs. My morning selection of papaya was determined by my dinner the night before (Moo-river). I choose salad and bread for midday for two reasons: I schedule a couple of salads each week to meet my nutritional quotient and this was the only available occasion. Salad and bread are more filling than fruit; my evening meal of popcorn is fairly light.

The last thing I have to do is check my nutritional quotient and make any necessary adjustments. Remember, according to the Formula, at least five to six meals a week should be protein. Because there are only two straight protein meals, I will have to make sure that three of my Open Humans include protein.

Next, I check to make sure that three of my Carb meals include servings of unsaturated fat. In this example, the Mazel

Salad, the oatmeal, and the L-T-O qualify. My Carbs quotient will then take care of itself. Sunday morning I'll wake up with boundless energy, a big smile on my face, and a still skinny body because I thought about food when it didn't count so I didn't have to think about it when it did.

FOOD FORMULAS

1 FFF	**5** FFF	**9** FFF	**13** FFF
FCP	FOMP	CCOH	FFOM
POPOP	FFOP	FCOH	FOHP
FFOM	OPPOP	FOCOC	FFOM
FFOC	FFOH	FOMP	FFOM
COCOC	FFF	FFOD	FFOC
FFOH	CCOC	FFF	OHPOP

17 FFF	
FODP	
PPP	
FFOH	
FFF	
FCOC	
FOHP	

2 FFF	**6** FFF	**10** FFF	**14** FFF
FOHP	FOHP	OHPP	ODPP
FFOC	FFOP	FFOC	OPPP
FOMP	FCP	CCOC	FFOM
OPPOP	OMPP	FFOM	COCOC
FFC	FFOC	FCOP	FOHP
OCCOC	FCOP	FFOC	FFOD

18 FFF	
FFOD	
PPP	
FCOC	
FOHP	
FFOM	
FCP	

3 FFF	**7** FFF	**11** FFF	**15** FFF
OMPP	FCOP	FOMP	COMP
FFOC	OHPP	FFOH	FFC
FFF	FFOC	FFC	CODOP
OHPOP	OPOPP	FODP	FFOM
FFC	FFC	FFOH	OMPOP
FOCOP	ODPP	FFOP	FFOC

19 FFF	
CCOC	
FCP	
OMPP	
FODP	
FFOH	
FFOM	

4 FFF	**8** FFF	**12** FFF	**16** FFF
OPPP	POPOP	ODPP	FOHP
FFOH	FOMOP	FFOD	FOPP
FFC	FOHP	FFF	PPP
CCOC	FFF	OMPOP	FFOM
FOMP	OPPP	FFOC	COMOP
FFOP	FFOH	FOHP	FFOM

20 FFF	
FFOD	
FFF	
POPP	
FFOC	
OMOPOP	
FFOC	

VIII

Your Workbook to Wonderland—How to Be an All-Time Loser

This is your workbook to skinny. Use it to its max.

Please provide the appropriate pictures and information. Do not begin until you have done so. The before and after pictures are here to remind you from whence you came. As for your Forever photo, well, we'll see in six months. My educated guess is you'll look better than you do today.

```
┌─────────────────────────┐
│                         │
│                         │
│                         │
│      PASTE PHOTO        │
│        HERE             │
│                         │
│                         │
│                         │
│                         │
│                         │
│                         │
│                         │
│                         │
└─────────────────────────┘
```

Date _____

Weight _____

FAT

142

PASTE PHOTO
HERE

Date _____
Weight _____

NOW

PASTE PHOTO
HERE

Date _____
Weight _____

FOREVER

Voilà—your wondrous Workbook to the Wonderland of Skinny. Think of it as your skinny bible, jot down lots of notes, and have fun with it. It's okay to spill over into the margins, it's for you (and for me). Make your workbook a part of your life, and use it every day to guide you to Forever. The workbook is designed to connect you to Conscious Combining. It's the tool that will allow you to celebrate maintaining as a way of life. It is a concrete record of your success and as integral a part of that success as the Golden Rules. Because, to be thin always, you have to know the whys. You must understand Conscious Combining and how it works for you. The Workbook to Wonderland will cement that understanding. Promise me you'll keep it close to you and record your progress. It means happiness and success. It locks you into the reality of the Beverly Hills Diet Lifetime Plan.

Always remember, the before and after pictures are to remind you of from whence you came, to reinforce skinny. If you were fat, paste in a picture from that dread period in the space provided. Acknowledge it and admit that fat will lurk within you forever. Be smug in the knowledge that you've conquered it. If you were merely frumpy and worn, paste in a picture to remind you of those days too. See the difference between then and now for yourself: no more lifeless hair or pallid skin either.

Now, proudly paste in the today you. If you don't have a current picture that shows your perfect body to advantage, take one. You must see the difference to experience the thrill that will catapult you happily through the next six months of maintenance.

If you ever begin to waver, just gulp in those pictures and remember. After you have completed your first six months of maintenance, take another picture. You'll find subtle differences: an aura of self-assurance that was lacking in the new skinny you. Appreciate your accomplishment, wallow in its wonder, revel in its physical delights.

At the end of the six months I'll ask you to send me a copy of your records and I will welcome you into that special world of BHD Lifetime Plan maintainers with your double golden pineapple pin. Your success will be inspiration to all of us in the ever-expanding pineapple network. Each maintainer will thus be a source of strength to every other maintainer. And your records will help us prove our slimhood to the rest of the world.

TO BEGIN

1. Each week, one week at a time, fill in the number of the Food Formula you have chosen in the space provided.

2. Then, in the small box above the actual chart, fill in the Food Formula Meal Categories, OH, F, or whatever you're lucky enough to be eating.

3. Then, right on the chart itself write in the specific food or foods you've chosen to eat for each meal. Use my examples or your own choices, or a combination of both. Always record the day and the date and keep a daily record of your weight. Remember, you will be doing my Food Formulas for the first three of every four weeks.

4. The fourth week you will be "Doing Your Own Thing." On that week, because you will be making up your own Food Formula, there will not be a Food Formula number to fill in. Use the box provided to put in your formula categories and the chart itself for your actual food selections.

The Food Formula charts will become your diary to Forever; they will allow you to test and prod, experience and experiment. They will help you make Conscious Combining unconscious. You will have a permanent record of your experiments. You will know exactly what works and what doesn't, and you will get to understand your body and see the patterns in your response to foods. Seeing is believing, and you will become a believer. You will take responsibility for yourself. Gladly, fearlessly, and willingly. And as you do, Conscious Combining will truly become a way of life and the Beverly Hills Diet Lifetime Plan will become your lifestyle.

It's going to take six months of conscious, devoted effort to make the Beverly Hills Diet Lifetime Plan unconscious.

Promise me that you will make that effort. Promise me that

you will commit yourself for the next six months. Use my samples merely as samples. And make the Food Formulas your own.

Helpful Hints for Fixing the Formulas

You are absolutely not, under any circumstances, to start these Formulas on a Monday. All that will do is perpetuate your DFC, which tells you Monday is a diet day, that you should indulge on weekends and starve on Mondays. Every day is an indulging day when you live on the Beverly Hills Diet Lifetime Plan.

- Never forget the Three Golden Rules. They should be indelibly etched into your brain. Read them over and over (see pages 43–50) and refer back to them until you recite them in your dreams.
- Remember to weigh yourself and write it down every day, no matter what. Although I don't insist upon it, I do suggest that you continue the weight-loss practice of telling your weight to someone, the same person, every day.
- The tools, rules, and hints will ensure that Conscious Combining becomes Unconscious Combining; read them (see Chapter IV), study them, and make them your own.
- On days you have scheduled an Open Meal, you would be wise to select the actual foods you will be eating in advance. It lessens the possibility of blowing it. Part of making Conscious Combining unconscious involves making a commitment and sticking to it, no matter what. Also, by scheduling, you avoid the anxiety of the conflict that comes from having to make the Decision, and the ultimate frustration and disappointment that invariably follows when you choose the wrong food. Well, we never do pick the right thing, do we? Someone else's is always better. If you blow it in the middle of a week and you gain as a result, turn to the Corrective Counterparts (see pages 114–15), correct your weight gain, and then pick up where you left off and

finish out the week. Remember, only turn to the Corrective Counterparts *if you blew it and gained*.

- Whenever the Food Formulas specify Open Carb (OC) or Open Protein (OP), you can do a Mono Carb (MC) or a Mono Protein (MP) instead. If the chart says OP and all you really want is just a steak, fine. Conversely, if a Mono Meal is suggested and your scale tells you it's okay, if your weight is down and steady, then feel free to make it an Open Meal instead. You, your scale, and your environment will dictate your choice.

- If your chart reads Mono Carb (MC) and your weight is perfect, have some bagels with your salad, add rice to your vegetable plate. The Formulas are a foundation, they are like cement blocks which you can embellish upon, or diminish from. It will depend upon how you feel, the circumstances surrounding your eating experiences, and what your best friend, the scale, tells you.

    In the early months of maintenance you'd be wise not to take too many liberties with the Mono Meal, don't turn too many of them into Opens. But by the same token, if your scale is sitting on perfect, don't consistently turn your Opens into Monos. You'll feel deprived and give rise to your DFC.

- If you've followed the Food Formula and have gained weight without obvious cause, DON'T PANIC. Don't get hysterical. Don't immediately go on a fruit day or instantly fall back on Week One of the Beverly Hills Diet. Just keep on with your schedule.

    Remember, our goal as maintainers is to take life one week at a time, to weigh the same at the end of the week as we did at the beginning. There might, in fact, there probably will, be a day or two or even three when your weight is up. But don't worry, because it will all balance out over the week. I expect it, and I've planned for it; the order of the foods in each week will take care of everything. So just relax. I want to see you skinny just as much as you do!

The BHD Lifetime Plan means accepting and acknowledging yourself as you are. It means not setting yourself up for failure by expecting constancy and total perfection. Of course your weight will fluctuate slightly. When your body hovers at perfect, weight is a function of far more than food. Weather, timing, environment, and health will all cause variations. Just be courageous and know that I'm there with you, I'm holding that skinny little hand, and I won't let go. I can't wave a magic wand and fix your weight for all time. Embrace the Food Formulas and know that at the end of the week you will be fine, you will still be slim. Trust me. Didn't I help make you skinny to begin with?

NONPHYSICAL EXERCISES

The Nonphysical Exercises that precede each month in your workbook are as important as the food you will be eating. They will allow you to stand up and be counted. They will put you in touch with your reality, with your new skinny self. These are exercises for your mind. Believe me, mind maintenance is every bit as important as body maintenance. Perhaps even more so. Without it, the double pineapple will slip right through your fingers. These exercises are as vital a core to the BHDLP, to maintenance as the five Nonphysical Exercises were an integral part of the Beverly Hills Diet, to getting skinny. They will ensure your eternal slimhood.

Do not skirt these exercises because, believe me, skinny won't last if you do. They are the key to changing your thinking, they are the key to yourself. Don't think you are so sophisticated that you don't need them. Don't be afraid to confront whatever they uncover. You have to see what you are to choose what you want to be. You have to confront in order to let go.

There is a different exercise for each month and each should be practiced for at least the whole month. Hopefully, many of the exercises will become a lifetime routine for you just as they are for me. They are my tools to keeping me locked into my Forever.

Remember Conscious Combining is a way of thinking as well as a way of eating, a philosophy as well as a methodology. Your newfound waist will not change that way of thinking for itself, only you can do that by developing a new level of consciousness. By knowing and understanding yourself. By being proud.

As you do the prescribed exercise write your comments in the space provided in your book. Be honest, write down exactly how you feel about each exercise, how you respond, how you react, and how it works for you. The strength they will give you are the steel beams that will keep your support system intact, that will hold it erect so that it will never topple.

Nonphysical Exercise for MONTH One
The Skinny Proud Sheet: Part II

Let your pride and self-respect inspire sweet dreams and put you to sleep at night. Go to sleep patting yourself on the back instead of beating yourself over the head.

Place a cheerful-looking memo pad next to your bed or you can use the space provided for comments on your weekly Food Formula chart. Every night, before you go to sleep, list your accomplishments one by one. Luxuriate in the pride of your achievements. Unlike as on the weight-loss Proud Sheet, I don't want to read one word about how good you were on your diet; that's automatic (why would you be bad?). Your life is no longer about diets and dieting, it's about living. Start writing about the quality of your life, The Good Life.

Don't go to sleep without writing something on your Proud Sheet every night. I faithfully write on my Proud Sheet every day of my life, and remember I've been skinny a long time now.

WEEK **1**

FOOD FORMULA # _____

Date	Weight	MORNING	MIDDAY	EVENING

COMMENTS _____

WEEK 2

FOOD FORMULA # _____

Date	Weight	MORNING	MIDDAY	EVENING

COMMENTS _____

WEEK **3**

FOOD FORMULA # _____

Date	Weight	MORNING	MIDDAY	EVENING

OMMENTS _____

WEEK **4**
Doing Your Own Thing

Date	Weight	MORNING	MIDDAY	EVENING

COMMENTS

Nonphysical Exercise for MONTH Two
Standing Up for Skinny—Hipbone Power

Acknowledge who you are and what you are. Weight-loss Beverly Hills Dieters confronted, acknowledged, and let go of their fat person. Now you are going to recognize, acknowledge, and embrace your skinny person.

This exercise must be done with strangers.

Pick a crowded place—an elevator, a dinner party among strangers, the entrance of an "in" restaurant, a cocktail gathering of unknowns. With your hands securely anchored on those new-found hipbones, say to a stranger:

"I used to be fat. I'm not fat anymore. And I will *never* be fat again."

This nonphysical hipbone exercise achieves two marvels. First, you will openly express from whence you came—you're denying no longer, and secondly, now you have free rein to eat whatever you want. You have locked into your protruding hipbones and acknowledged their power. Skinny can proudly step out into the light instead of cowering, arms clenched, in the Shadow of Fat. This assignment is to be done with five strangers (at least) on five separate occasions.

These three statements are also to be used anytime anyone questions you about your food or your weight while you are eating. If anyone so much as whispers about your diet, if anyone is brazen enough to sneer (typically a fatty), "If you keep eating like that, you're going to get fat all over again," you simply stand up, place your hands firmly on those heavenly jutting hipbones, and tell 'em. Because you are not fat anymore, you'll never be fat again, and you have nothing to be ashamed of anymore!

WEEK **5**

FOOD FORMULA # _____

Date	Weight	MORNING	MIDDAY	EVENING

COMMENTS _____

WEEK **6**

FOOD FORMULA # _____

Date	Weight	MORNING	MIDDAY	EVENING

MMENTS _____

WEEK **7**

FOOD FORMULA # _____

Date	Weight	MORNING	MIDDAY	EVENING

COMMENTS _____

WEEK **8**
Doing Your Own Thing

Date	Weight	MORNING	MIDDAY	EVENING

MMENTS _____

Nonphysical Exercise for MONTH Three
Fine-Tuning Your Fantasy

The mouth of an Eater is like the keys of a finely tuned piano. Each little bite rings out a different note, and we're only happy when they are playing in harmony. The music goes on and on, the melody is endless. As long as the song is playing, as long as you continue to eat a variety of foods, as long as there is food in your mouth, your stomach doesn't know when it's had enough. When the mouth is on, the stomach is off.

I, like most Eaters, have an amazing capacity. As long as there is food around, as long as there are a variety of tastes and textures, and as long as it tastes good, I'll just keep eating. And when my stomach gets full, well, sometimes I'm not even aware of it. The excitement of the different tastes and textures in my mouth overrides any message my stomach might be sending. To me, one of the greatest joys in the world is sitting around a table with family or friends eating and talking, eating and laughing, eating and planning, eating, eating, eating, eating. As long as the food is there, I'll keep eating it.

It's amazing what happens when the stomach has had too much, when it has had more than it can handle; the body just stretches to accommodate it. Well, perhaps that's a bit simplified, but what do you think getting fat is all about?

When I first developed my style of eating, I discovered that the benefits of the Mono Meal were as dramatic psychologically as they were physically. I began to learn when enough is enough. While it didn't exactly transform me into a *little* eater, it did show me how to stop before I did any damage, how not to eat more than my body could handle. In other words, how to eat as much as I could without gaining an ounce.

When you are eating only one thing at a time, sooner or later it stops tasting good. No matter how fast my heart beats on the first

160

bite, no matter how violently my taste buds palpitate with that first swallow, sooner or later, even a Teuscher white chocolate truffle will stop tasting good. Sooner or later, the taste buds will get bored, you'll get bored! And even the most orgasmic taste treat will cease to be a thrill. Now, what kind of an idiot keeps eating when it stops tasting good?

Ideally it would be a lot better if my stomach said enough instead of my mouth, but it doesn't, at least not without a struggle. And quite frankly, I'm tired of fighting. I spent the first twenty-nine years of my life dealing with this overdo compulsive aspect of my personality—that part of me that says if something is good, more is better—too much is not enough.

Now, instead of fighting it, I'm accepting it. I'm living with it, and I'm making it work for me. "I surrender, I give up, I give in to thin." I eat to my heart's content and I never eat my heart out. I can satisfy my need to feel real full, I never go hungry, and I never feel deprived. Conscious Combining, and most particularly, the Mono Meal have been my salvation. It has allowed eating to bring its full potential of joy into my life.

This Nonphysical Exercise has a triple whammy. First, you become sensitized to taste. You learn just how pregnant with feeling your taste buds are. Second, you'll begin to acknowledge your stomach. You'll experience when enough is enough. And finally, you'll give up the struggle!

Schedule yourself for one specific food that means more to you than life itself, be it a chocolate soufflé, barbecued spareribs, roast duckling, or Maui potato chips. Set yourself up enzymatically to accommodate it. Arrange an appropriate setting so that you can eat your choice openly and wantonly; without guilt, without fear, with sheer pleasure and permission. And make sure you have a lot; much more than you think you'll want or would even dream of eating.

The idea is not how much you can get in, in how short a time, but how long you can make the pleasure last. Be aware of how your favorite feels when it first hits your mouth, how your taste buds perk up, what happens to your tongue. Experience the texture, the taste, the smell, how you feel, how it feels.

Experience your food fantasy bite for bite, slowly and luxuriously. Tune in to your stomach and try to identify the moment just before full. Tune in to your response and be aware. As you fill up, the food will no longer taste as wonderful as it did at first. The fuller you get, the less exciting the taste.

The first time you do this exercise, you'll probably find that you've outeaten your stomach. But don't worry, no damage has been done; on the contrary, you learn by doing, by experience. How will you ever know when enough is enough, if you don't experience it and stop while *you* have the choice?

Repeat this exercise at least three times this month with the different foods. Then, one by one, try it with all your favorites. Before you know it, every eating experience will be soul-soaring. You'll understand how food makes you feel, you'll react to being full, and overeating will be a trauma of the past.

OOD FORMULA # _____

Date	Weight	MORNING	MIDDAY	EVENING

MENTS _____

WEEK **10**

FOOD FORMULA # _____

Date	Weight	MORNING	MIDDAY	EVENING

COMMENTS _____

WEEK **11**
FOOD FORMULA # _____

Date	Weight	MORNING	MIDDAY	EVENING

MMENTS _____

WEEK 12
Doing Your Own Thing

Date	Weight	MORNING	MIDDAY	EVENING

COMMENTS _____

Nonphysical Exercise for MONTH Four
Putting the Human into the Open Human

Now is the time to prove yourself worthy of being called a skinny. A skinny can eat, enjoy, and not overindulge. Not once, not twice, but often and consistently.

Prove you are a human being. Do an Open Human, and do not gain an ounce. In fact, do three Open Humans and do not gain an ounce. You'll do this exercise in three versions.

The first time, select a "natural skinny," an "outsider," for your eating partner, someone who eats a moderate amount, and match him or her bite for bite. No more.

For the second version, eat with someone with a fat consciousness whose only concept of tomorrow is making tonight the last supper. Eat side by side with the overeater and prove you are a Beverly Hills Diet Lifetime Plan maintainer, a true skinny. Prove it by not following his lead. Remember what it was like when you ate with the "Outsider."

For the third version, and this could be the toughest, choose a fat eater who is thin. We all know and envy lots of those. The kind who pack it away, brag about it, and never gain. The kind who outate us even in our fat days, the ones about whom we always said, "Well, if they can do it, so can I." And you tried, only they stayed thin and you got fatter. Remember, you can't match them bite for bite, so don't even try. Just do your own thing and eat like a human being.

This is only the beginning for you. In fact it may be the first supper, because if you can repeatedly make it through these tests, then you have succeeded in cultivating your little skinny voice to its max.

WEEK **13**
FOOD FORMULA # _____

Date	Weight	MORNING	MIDDAY	EVENING

COMMENTS _____

FOOD FORMULA # _____

Date	Weight	MORNING	MIDDAY	EVENING

COMMENTS _____

WEEK **15**

FOOD FORMULA # _____

Date	Weight	MORNING	MIDDAY	EVENING

COMMENTS _____

WEEK **16**
Doing Your Own Thing

Date	Weight	MORNING	MIDDAY	EVENING

COMMENTS _____

Nonphysical Exercise for MONTH Five
Assertive Ordering

This is an exercise in assertiveness, practice for Forever. The life of a Beverly Hills Diet Lifetime Plan maintainer is alive with restaurants, parties, and conferences. And skinny Forever is totally unrealistic unless you are in control, not just in your home, but in your social and business world as well. A world where an abundance of meals are thrust upon you, often without your choice, often without care.

Once you have mastered this exercise, you will always be able to get exactly what you want, prepared the way you want it in almost any restaurant. I have selected pasta as the dish I want you to practice your Assertive Ordering with, because, if you are concerned with "getting salted" (see Glossary), and that is one of our chief concerns, pasta is the most difficult to do something about.

Pasta is the dish that I approached with the greatest trepidation. I had always limited my pasta excursions to a handful of places, places I knew I could trust. Typically, the noodles are cooked in advance, in salted water. (This is the biggest problem, getting them to cook the noodles in unsalted water; but don't worry, I've got that down pat and I'll show you how.) Typically, cheese is laden on top. Typically, salted butter is used in the preparation, and since most sauces are made in advance, typically they all have salt.

As I mentioned, most of my pasta experiences had been at places that knew me, so a great deal of dialogue wasn't necessary. It was at the elegant Tony's in St. Louis that I first accomplished Assertive Ordering of pasta with strangers and established an effective Conscious Combining pasta dialogue.

Pick your restaurant for this test with care. Make it easy on yourself the first time; select a restaurant that has a reputation for being accommodating. Explain to your waiter that you are on a salt-free diet and that no salt should be added to your pasta at any time, not even to the water in which it is cooked. Ask if it would be possible to cook your noodles separately, in unsalted water. You shouldn't have a problem—it's really no big deal for them to boil another pot of water—but if he hesitates or says no, be persistent. You'll get your way and your pasta. If you order an unusual noodle, the odds of your request being met are greatly improved, since it is less likely to have been cooked in advance. Try asking for vermicelli, ziti, or rigatoni.

The sauce you are going to order is also special; simple but special nevertheless, and, because of its purity, you'll be able to eat pounds of pasta without adding an ounce to your frame. Order a double order of the noodles of your choice and ask for a sauce consisting of lots of sautéed garlic and olive oil, with maybe a little fresh basil or a little parsley to give it some color and to liven it up a touch. If you like, have some vegetables added to it—mushrooms, broccoli, asparagus, for example. My favorite addition to pasta is spinach. The raw spinach wilts when it hits the hot noodles, and it's a little slice of heaven. Of course, if they are going to cook any vegetables to add to your pasta, verify that they understand "no salt." You must make it quite clear; you should repeat "no salt" and "no cheese," "no salt," "no cheese" several times in the conversation. They'll get the message, and your pasta won't get you.

Conduct this exercise at least twice and see how much easier it is the second time around. Soon, it becomes a game for those in the know, our special language of Conscious Combining. You may discover that waiters and maître d's speak the language too. Watch out, though, you're very likely to get hooked on my pasta. But feel free to indulge at will.

WEEK **17**

FOOD FORMULA # _____

Date	Weight	MORNING	MIDDAY	EVENING

COMMENTS _____

WEEK **18**

FOOD FORMULA # _____

Date	Weight	MORNING	MIDDAY	EVENING

COMMENTS _____

WEEK **19**
FOOD FORMULA # _____

Date	Weight	MORNING	MIDDAY	EVENING

COMMENTS _____

Date	Weight	MORNING	MIDDAY	EVENING

MMENTS _____

Nonphysical Exercise for MONTH Six
The Indelible Inedibles

This exercise will help erase trivial foods from your consciousness and banish unconscious eating. It will enable you to drop undesirables from your frame of reference and never even miss them. You'll never even notice they're gone, because you aren't even aware that they're there. When I look at nuts in a bowl in front of me, I simply don't see them. They have become nonentities for me. There is not one iota of temptation. I can be ravenous and sit down at a bar lined with bountiful bowls of mixed nuts, and it doesn't occur to me that they are possibilities, that they are an option. For me, roasted salted nuts simply do not exist as food. I'd like them to be the same for you.

There really is almost nothing worse than noshing on nuts (see Nuts and Seeds, page 108). As a total eating experience they're terrific, but as a nosh they're murder. Since they are constantly in our frame of reference, since our hand is constantly unconsciously in the bowl, the sooner we forget about them the better.

Experience the nuts in every sense but one—their taste. Look at them, hold them in your hand, feel them, smell them, play with them, roll them around on the table, experience the grease and the salt on your fingers and on your hands, shave them with your nails, crumble them, and smash them. Now feel and experience your fingers. Feel the grease and the salt. Now smell your fingers and then tell me you still want to eat those nuts.

If the answer is still yes, maybe you haven't played with them long enough. The idea is to put your head into your stomach right alongside your heart. So just keep experiencing them, intellectually as well as aesthetically. Your aesthetic sense will soon tell you that they aren't much fun.

Once you've said adieu to nuts, pick a few other foods, foods that are really unimportant to you but are nevertheless your unconscious nemesis. All those dumb little munching things that you don't even care about, those things that you aren't even aware of while you're eating them.

Remember, little things mean a lot. While I don't want you to give up anything that is important to you, the bottom line is, some things do have to go. If you let go of the little unimportant things, the things that don't really count, then you can get away with the biggies, the things that do count.

Eating should always feed your heart, your soul, or your body; it should never be unconscious. Once you wipe the unconscious out of your consciousness, you move out into the world of Forever, the land of Eternal Slimhood, the world of the golden pineapple. Be proud and know that you have won.

WEEK **21**

FOOD FORMULA # _____

Date	Weight	MORNING	MIDDAY	EVENING

COMMENTS _____

WEEK **22**

FOOD FORMULA # _____

Date	Weight	MORNING	MIDDAY	EVENING

COMMENTS _____

WEEK **23**

FOOD FORMULA # _____

Date	Weight	MORNING	MIDDAY	EVENING

COMMENTS _____

Date	Weight	MORNING	MIDDAY	EVENING

COMMENTS _____

IX

Open Mouth, Insert Mind—
Tying the Skinny Knot

PITFALLS AND HANG-UPS

Some of these things I've said before. But you know what? I'm going to say them again, because I want to make sure you hear me.

Fear of Getting Fat Again

We've always gotten fat in the past, despite having attained slim. That's because we've always been on a diet that excluded everything we love, where we weighed and measured everything, where maintenance was not much different than weight loss, only more so. Diet has always loomed as a suspension of our lifestyle, as something to go off of. According to statistics, you've virtually had zero chance of keeping your weight off.

Trust me, the rules and tools of the Beverly Hills Diet Lifetime Plan were not manufactured in a theoretical vacuum by natural skinnies, nor were they created on the basis of what ought to be. They were synthesized from the hard experience of hundreds of thousands of Beverly Hills Diet Lifetime Plan maintainers across the country. We know they work, because we've lived them.

Don't panic when you gain. You'll notice I didn't say "if," I said "when." It's impossible to fix your weight at a single spot once and for all and Forever. Just because you've gained a pound or two, that doesn't mean you've reentered the world of Fat, the world of the lifeless. Remember, live from week to week. If you allow yourself to experience the pleasure of food rather than the pain, the Beverly Hills Diet Lifetime Plan will work for you Forever. Look at the results; the proof is in the thousands of skinnies now populating the planet, all of us who have changed the statistics.

If we can do it, so can you!

Delusions of Grandeur

As we all know, staying thin is harder than getting thin. As a maintainer, your body doesn't embarrass you or let you down. You don't have that incessant reminder, that obvious fat for all the world to see. Any support and encouragement you were getting before has vanished with time and results. Now everyone says, "Come on, look at you, you can have one little bite." Or "You don't have to be on a diet anymore, you're so skinny." As if you're not the person you once were, as if all those little fat cells weren't poised, ready to plump back up at a moment's notice.

Now that you're thin you're tempted to eat the way noneaters do. Always remember that person lurking just inside of you. You still harbor that fat soul with a DFC just waiting to explode your body into Fat all over again. Don't delude yourself, don't fall prey to this all-too-common dastardly trap, in which well-meaning friends egg you on, holding that fork of temptation.

Move to that place where you surrender and give up. Admit you are an Eater at heart. Repeat after me, "I surrender, I give up, I'll give in to thin."

I struggled and agonized over maintenance with David. He refused to accept what fat meant to him; he repeatedly denied his fat quotient. David thought he could ultimately survive thin on limited portions. Finally I demanded, "How old are you?" "Forty-three," came the response. "And how long have you been fat?" I insisted on knowing. "Forty years," came the revealing answer. "And how many years have you tried living on limited portions?" Suddenly he saw and he accepted. You can do the same. After all, what difference does it make if you can't eat everything at once as long as you can eat whatever you want? What a tiny price when eternal slimhood is the prize.

The Deprivation Drag

Never, never deprive yourself. Many maintainers are so panicked at the thought of gaining weight that they struggle through without their favorites, diet-conscious and resentful deep within. Schedule in your favorite foods and eat them with wild abandon. They are the exceptions, so make them exceptional. If you don't consume them, they will consume you.

If you schedule your food fantasies into your life they won't turn on you. You won't revert to them illicitly or use them as an emotional stopgap. Then when you think about your mother-in-law or the crisis at work, your divorce, or the spilled trash, you won't drown your sorrows in ice cream. If you can have it in the clear light of day with permission and without fear, you are defusing a deadly emotional trigger. You are removing the guilt and the furtiveness. You are making your favorite foods pleasure givers, not pain relievers. Your favorite foods will become what they are, rather than what you want them to be.

Prepare yourself for some surprises. When you allow yourself to experience the emotional moment devoid of the food that always distracted you from it, the moment will gain clarity. Then, when you can truly experience the moment and the emotion, you will also experience the food.

You will probably find that once you are eating with your mind and heart, you won't like the way some of your "special" favorites taste or make you feel. You might not want these "forbidden fruits" anymore.

Excuses We Have Dived Into

We tend to lock into the negative for excuses to eat, and we are so willing to accept them. The Beverly Hills Diet Lifetime Plan is about banishing excuses, because it is Forever. Because it is *your* way of eating, built around *your* favorite foods, there are no legitimate excuses left; there are only manufactured ones, contrived cop-outs.

An extreme example is that of the reporter who circled me at an autograph session, criticizing, interrupting, monopolizing the conversation, harping on the negatives, and refusing to acknowledge the proof of skinny before her very eyes, the hundreds of Beverly Hills Dieters, who provide stark evidence of the success of the Beverly Hills Diet. Why was she so strident? She weighed two hundred pounds and wasn't willing to give up an ounce. She was deeply threatened by our success and had become the ultimate excuse maker.

As excuses push into your world, explore them, look beyond them to the motivation. Why are you responding? Why are you so much as listening to your DFC? That's what it is, you know, that Debilitating Fat Consciousness lurking inside, eager to squash your little skinny voice. As soon as an excuse knocks, look through the peephole first, don't just open the door. Examine the why; put your mind into the process and decide what the consequences are. If, in your judgment, the trade-off is worth it, then okay. Then you have made a conscious decision, then you have done more than react to a situation and taken advantage of an "excuse."

I suppose there will always be those of us who wallow in self-pity, the masochists who submerge themselves in fat and create the statistics of former fatties revisited. There is an excuse for every occasion, an excuse for even the most discriminating among you. Consider some of the more common excuses, and my responses to them:

1. *My lifestyle won't permit me to eat that way; it's just not accepted.* How

socially acceptable is it to be fat, or lifeless? Your social life didn't disappear while you were getting thin, and now, with your perfect body, you'll be in more demand than ever. Do you think Jaye P. Morgan flinches when she totes her pineapple and papaya around with her, when she concentrates on pasta instead of quiche? Of course not. She adores it, as a trend-setter it suits her perfectly.

2. *I was sick when I woke up, so I miscombined.* And that made you feel better?

3. *I had a business meeting at lunch.* So? A banker in St. Louis took his grapes to his lunch meeting, and his associates were jealous. Imagine how the first Conscious Combiner in Little Rock felt when she ate watermelon at her promotion dinner party. As a maintainer, the only time you will be really conspicuous is eating fruit, and you are eating it either because you need a Corrective Counterpart or you are in the midst of a three-day Fruit Fling or you just plain wanted it. Whatever the reason, always remember, *you asked for it!*

4. *I'm going to a ball game.* So eat hot dogs by scheduling them in, or do an Open Human. Miles takes his cashews to the football games; Sarah takes popcorn. You don't have to eat "diet" food anymore; you can build your eating world around your social world.

5. *I'm on vacation.* Well, that doesn't mean you stop living, does it? I hardly think you want to buy a new FAT wardrobe while you're traveling.

6. *My house was robbed.* Will a chocolate sundae miraculously make your silver tea set reappear?

7. *I stopped smoking.* All the more reason to be a Conscious Combiner—it will allow you to diffuse all that compulsiveness without gaining weight.

8. *Everyone says I'm too thin.* It should be like a cloak wrapped

around those tiny shoulders. Remember the shroud you labored under all those fat, lifeless years?

9. *I knew it wouldn't last forever.* We gain a pound or two and already it's the end of the world. We're so anxious, so willing to fail. Don't set yourself up as a loser (except in the category of weight). Is this the way you deal with the rest of your life? At some point you must begin to believe—believe in yourself and believe that you can have your cake and eat it too. Don't give up; the cake, by the way, happens to be chocolate.

10. *My daughter was mugged.* Did eating change the fact? Did eating take away the pain? Wasn't blowing it one more thing to be sorry about, a way to obliterate and divert your sorrow?

11. *I gained on pizza and peach pie, then my car broke down and I couldn't get to the market to buy my fruit.* You should have had your Corrective Counterpart in the bag before you ate such a meal. You should have been prepared. No Corrective Counterpart, no Open Human, no permission. You have permission to do anything and everything, so why are you still trying to find ways to function without it? I can't wave a magic wand and make something non-fattening when you eat it, but I can do two things that will ensure skinny Forever: (a) I can teach you how to make something less fattening by making it more digestible; and (b) I can teach you how to use the Corrective Counterpart to negate the fattening effect of anything. That's the joy of Conscious Combining.

12. *I was in Milan, and they didn't have any pineapple or papaya.* So, did that mean you had to have a café au lait and croissants every morning? Just because you can't find the correct fruit, that doesn't mean you should give up on fruit for the day. Any fruit (except melons) is better than no fruit at all.

I have an answer for every one of your excuses because I have used them all and I have abused them all. The list goes on and on.

Of course, if deep inside you want to find an excuse, you will. We Eaters are the champion excuse makers. Resist, don't succumb, don't give in. *Don't become a negative statistic.*

In the end, there is no excuse for fat. No excuse for giving up and no excuse for giving in. I surrender, I give up, I'll give in to thin. You've discovered that pie in the sky, now all you have to do is just sit back and enjoy it.

Rule-Stretching versus Rule Mutilating

Remember, besides keeping you skinny, the rules and tools perform other equally splendid miracles. They help develop and nurture your skinny consciousness. A key cog in that process is in sticking to something instinctively, making the rules as automatic as brushing your teeth and putting gas in your car.

We have a moral code that guides us in most things, our version of the "Ten Commandments." There are some things we just wouldn't do because we don't like the consequences; we don't have to think about those things, we've made our decisions once and for all. If we had to re-think everything each time we faced it, we'd be bananas—or pineapples. The rules and tools of the Beverly Hills Diet Lifetime Plan should become just as unconscious as your moral code.

Shoplifting is probably the furthest thing from your mind. Perhaps you tried it once as a kid and you got away with it. There was a certain thrill, a certain goosebumpy excitement in doing something and getting away with it. Having done it once, perhaps you tried it again; it was a lot easier the second time. It's much the same with running a yellow traffic light that's barely turned pink. Or, when you violate the rules and tools of the Beverly Hills Diet Lifetime Plan.

Once you break a rule, anything can happen, and it usually does. You say to yourself, "I did it before and got away with it." Or, "Just this once. Now that I'm thin, one bite can't hurt me."

And before you know it, zap! Your Beverly Hills lifestyle has dissipated and you've regressed to your fat yesterday. Before you know it, you've bloated back up, and your heart is sorrowful. And, along with your skinny voice and self-respect, something else will have left the planet—your newfound hipbones.

Remember that tomorrow is never more than a day away, and then you can have it all. A smile on your face, your pride, and no excuses; no "if onlys," no "I wishes," no "ifs" or "buts." So don't stretch those rules until they break; you'll only break your heart.

X

Special Cases — Aren't We All?

We maintainers move in a frenetic world. Maintenance has to be real and adaptable if it is to be Forever. A new skinny, Donna Roth from Beverly Hills, and her husband Jerry Roth, an attorney specializing in entertainment law, escaped to Hawaii just as Donna became a maintainer. I met them on the beach at the Kahala Hilton while I was there working on this book. Perhaps their experience will make the Beverly Hills Diet Lifetime Plan more real for you.

When Donna first embraced the Beverly Hills Diet, it was to "lose that fifteen pounds you can never lose." Jerry's reaction was "Oh, here we go again." "I insisted," Donna added. "Jerry, this really makes sense. Fresh foods, fruits, no chemicals, no pills, no salt or sugar." Jerry's disinterested response was a mumbled, "Sure, honey. Great."

"The more I read, the more sense it made," explains Donna. "It takes all the bad things away, and there is nothing you are eating that isn't good for you. By the end of the diet, I was the healthiest I had ever been in my life."

As Jerry confides, "I assumed it was just another diet — a good idea and a great title. I told Donna she'd last five days."

"In the old diet days," says Donna, "we'd go out to dinner and I would cut down by starving myself all the time. The thing about the BHD that I was most skeptical about was being able to eat all you want. But I loved not being hungry. I loved my high energy."

Donna talks about learning a new language, the language of Conscious Combining, and recalls her first "solid food" after beginning the BHD. "It was corn, and I devoured it. In the market, I must have looked at every ear of corn. I was going to get the best and the prettiest. I sat down to eat, and I could have eaten twenty of them. After the second, I was really getting satisfied. After the third I was totally satisfied. It was unusual. Usually when I come off a diet, I start bingeing, trying to make up for what I have been deprived of."

Jerry, an athlete who disdains food, occasionally forgets about eating, and has never been an ounce overweight in his life, started to come around. "I was a supporter because I could see the results. I didn't take much time with it. I thought Donna *wanted* to believe. But I thought maybe I'd read the book to understand what Donna was talking about. It was marked and underlined and *used*. I saw her energy level and her coloring and her figure. If it had been some doctor filling her full of shots, I wouldn't have been so supportive. Since then," Jerry adds, "I have become aware of the problem (fat) with people who truly *care* about food. One thing I sensed was that if the medical expertise were there, we would all be thin."

Donna chose a Japanese restaurant for her first Open Meal on the BHD. According to Donna, "Until you understand it and experience it, you really don't quite know how to handle it. If I went Open Protein, I could have all that raw fish and thinly sliced beef. But if I had Open Carb, the book mentioned tempura, what about the egg in the batter? I got confused. I gave up trying to figure it out and made my first meal an Open Human. I had become sensitive to salt, I felt the MSG, and I gained."

Donna persevered for the full six-week weight-loss program, and she reached her goal. She was hooked and perfect. "I had already decided it was going to be a way of life for me because I felt so good. There were no negatives. After a few days of the supplements, I felt even better. I was doing Nautilus and working out at the health club. I was getting up earlier. I was sleeping really well and had cut down on the amount of sleep I need by a full hour."

But Donna worried about maintaining. "I had to be conscious of it every day, and the decisions were troublesome. When I was dieting, all the decisions were made. Now that I was maintaining, I had to do my own deciding. When I would diet before and start eating normally again, I would gain all the weight back."

So, though hesitant but determined, Donna joined Jerry in Hawaii. First stop: the Kona Village, where the food was sumptuous, mountainous buffets in a magnificent setting that revolved around eating and drinking. Like all true Eaters, Donna really cares about food. Although she girded herself for this first tough challenge, she readily confesses that "part of me really wanted to dive in." One salvation was the abundance of glorious fruit she faithfully indulged in each and every vacation breakfast.

Jerry tells the rest of the story. "Suddenly, before a meal, Donna would be missing. She was 'working' the dining room [circling the buffet and checking out her choices, making her food decision]. She 'worked' the room for about a half hour." Although Donna would have already decided what kind of a meal she would eat, she relished the anticipation.

No doubt about it, food mattered to her. But then so did her newly perfect body. Donna wasn't going to make any mistakes, but she wasn't going to miss out on anything either.

Says Jerry, "I hadn't known that mentality. She had hidden this love of food from me. When I heard her talking, consciously thinking about food and being concerned about what she was going to eat *tomorrow* and even savoring the very thought of it, I began to understand. *My* problem," laments Jerry without a *speck* of sympathy from me, "is keeping weight on. I could do without eating. I'll miss a meal." A natural skinny in the flesh, a human who simply doesn't *care*. In truth, as you and I know, he and his brethren are missing one of life's greatest pleasures.

Donna explains her approach. "They would begin to bring the food out, and I would station myself at a vantage point where I could observe everything. Those were the highlights of my day. I'd pass on the salads, because I could get them anywhere. I'd concentrate on things like Tuna Sashimi and Mahi Mahi. Every morning I would have papaya or pineapple, usually three papaya halves or two servings of pineapple.

"Typically at lunch," Donna continues, "I'd either have a Mono something or an Open Carb, like vegetables, potatoes, and bread. Before Hawaii I had been eating fruit for lunch almost every day, so I was a little confused about what kind of a dinner to eat after an Open Carb. [Poor Donna, she didn't have this book clutched by her side!] If I gained weight," Donna went on, "I would have fruit for breakfast and lunch the next day. I really became obsessed with it.

"I found the trick was in eating enough and eating whatever I wanted. After I met you, Judy, and started eating dinner with you, that's when I really realized it. Before the BHD there were a lot of foods I really liked but never ate because I have always been so afraid of gaining weight. That's probably one reason Jerry didn't know how much I loved to eat.

"Dinner at the Kona Inn was always filled with great Open Protein choices. I knew there were going to be buffets every day. I would do either an Open Carb or just protein."

On Russian Night, Donna, who adores caviar, "fell back into my old ways." Not only did she gobble caviar and all its accoutrements, but she followed it with Mahi Mahi, a potato, and whatever else happened to be on her plate that night. Donna didn't really want anything but the caviar, but she ate out of habit. And she ate fast, reverting full-scale to her former self.

Not only did Donna miscombine, which is fine if you are doing an Open Human, but she also overate—the OH sacrilege. Donna tried to see how much caviar and everything else she could eat in the shortest period of time, instead of trying to see how long she could make the pleasure last, instead of relishing each bite. Because she was a *new* maintainer, her weight rocketed; she went up seven pounds. (The salt, on top of the miscom, on top of the overeating.) Grabbing hold of her skinny voice, aware that she teetered on the brink of disaster, Donna "got back down with fruit, fruit, and Mono Protein."

Incidentally, Donna repeated her Russian Night, only this time she specialized in the caviar. She ate it to her heart's content, and didn't gain a pound. Now she can eat caviar whenever she wants and with a clear conscience. By isolating that favorite food, she knows she can have it with pure pleasure, without guilt. From Kona they went to the Kahala Hilton on Oahu. The first day Donna arrived at the Kahala Hilton, she ate a Kahala Hamburger with everything on it, something she had been dying for. "I really enjoyed it, but I haven't even wanted another." Instead, she ate mounds of pasta and sashimi and all that spectacular fruit.

By the end of the vacation, the health-conscious Jerry was finally convinced. "I'm going to learn to combine," he says flatly. "I think it's a healthy way of eating."

"It was a first. I had never gone on vacation before without gaining five to seven pounds," Donna exults. "It was the best thing about this whole trip! I went home weighing a little less. It's far more than I had hoped for.

"Now," brags Donna, "eating has become fun. I couldn't go out and enjoy it before. Now I know I can eat everything I want. I know I'm still learning, especially to eat enough. I have never done that. I feel more comfortable eating one thing at a time because I *know* I can eat a lot and won't gain weight. I haven't even wanted to binge. Before I would binge on bread, trail mix, licorice, candy. I was totally addicted to diet drinks, too."

Now that she's back home in Beverly Hills, Conscious Combining has become far more unconscious for Donna. She no longer exists for food. Her energies are diverted elsewhere, and she has gained considerable confidence in her new way of eating.

You may think Donna's experience is extreme. But come on, think about how you panic at the thought of gaining back that weight, and fat reenveloping those hipbones. Remember, too, this was really Donna's *first* "real life" experience with Conscious Combining. She was learning, experimenting, and experiencing with the devotion and enthusiasm it deserved. At that point in Donna's life, vacationing in a bikini every day, her most important priorities were keeping that new body and that newfound energy. And, I might add, rightfully so.

If you direct your full attention to Conscious Combining in the early weeks, you can *divert* your full attention in later months.

MAKING THE EXCEPTIONS EXCEPTIONAL

You can make the BHD Lifetime Plan your own by embracing it every day of your life. Once you master the recipes in Part Three and the rules and tools, it's relatively easy to integrate Conscious Combining into your home life, into an environment that you can control. The tough part is the outside world. That's where we really use all those excuses we're so good at. Think back to how your DFC made every exception an excuse for blowing it. Think of the excuses you conjured up. Every time you ate in public, every party, dinner, business lunch, banquet, ball game, picnic, trip, theater gala, vacation (especially every vacation!) became an exception, a suspension in time. All those exceptions, all those excuses. Every outing triggered promises of "tomorrow I'll go back on my diet."

The reality, unless you live in an igloo, is that there are too many exceptions in our busy lives. If you consciously combine only at home, skinny will be a never.

No matter where I traveled, from Milwaukee to Miami Beach, from Kansas City to Boston, the question, the problem, was always the same: "I go out a lot," "I have a lot of business lunches," "I do a lot of entertaining," "How do I stay on this?" "What do I do when . . .?"

And it's true, that's what our lives are all about. How many times did you eat outside your home last week? Or the week before? Now that you are a maintainer, you're in the enviable position of being able to have your cake and eat it too. Now you'll not only enjoy the good life, you'll make it even better. There is no need to make the exceptions anything other than exceptional; this is the beauty of the BHDLP. Believe me, if the Beverly Hills elite can do it, if housewives in Muncie, Indiana, can do it, if businessmen in New York City and Topeka, Kansas, can do it, so can you.

Remember, this is a program developed for people like yourself: busy, important people, committed to living. Nobody expects you to live in a vacuum. The Beverly Hills Diet Lifetime Plan has succeeded because it works no matter how active you are or how social you are. It works because it is purely and perfectly adaptable.

I hope by this time you have exposed your little golden pineapple to the world. By now, all your friends and associates know you look more spectacular than you have ever looked, and they know why. Even the non–Beverly Hills Dieters among them are willing to overlook your little quirks because they like the new you, the you that, now thin, is much easier to get along with. They accept your bringing your pineapples along with you or ordering dessert instead of dinner.

Taking Your Pineapple Public

If you were a BHDer, you undoubtedly toted your watermelon or papaya for all to see. If so, the exercises I'm about to suggest will be easy for you. If, on the other hand, you have bricked up a sterile edifice around your eating and have never gone public, or if you are new to Conscious Combining, or if you're not yet committed to our lifestyle, this will be a little tougher. But it will hurl you over the hurdle of your pride and allow you to enjoy the "fruits of your labor." You will see that it is possible and, yes, even wise to eat fruit when the world around you is filling up on chicken fricassee and stale rolls at a banquet. You will learn that Forever is truly worth it.

As a maintainer, the times you'll have to eat fruit or bring your own are far less frequent than when you were a loser. But since they are a reality, you'd better stay in shape, literally and figuratively.

1. Choose a business lunch if you work; if not, make it a social luncheon. Bring your own fruit. Lay it on the table for all to see, and make that your lunch. The only explanations that are necessary are to the waiter or the maître d'. You will tell them you are on a special diet, ask them to serve it to you, and of course offer to pay the price of whatever their standard luncheon would cost. If you've never done it before, you'll be surprised at how simple it is, and how satisfying.

2. Bring your own fruit to a cocktail party and don't eat anything but that fruit. You may have some wine or champagne.

3. This is a two-parter, but what fun, an excuse to give two dinner parties. a) Your first assignment is to give a dinner party, and while your guests are feasting on the sumptuous banquet you have prepared, you eat only fruit. Don't feel deprived; instead, feel your hipbones. And remember, *you* prepared that meal, so you can do it again and have it anytime you want it.

b) This one will probably be more fun, eating-wise anyhow. Entertain Conscious Combining style. Give a dinner party, properly combined and saltless, of course. Don't tell your guests what you're doing until after the meal. If you're clever, the non-BHDers will never suspect, except of course by the way they feel. Terrific!

The idea is to break the conventional cycle where you simply take what comes socially. You make choices in every other part of your life. The choices you make about your body are critical, so its feeding and care should be selective, not reactive.

Consciously make the choice, whether you are on an airplane, at a ball game, or at a gourmet dinner. Chart your experiences with care. Know that nothing and everything is fattening. You don't have to eat just what's there because it's there. You have permission to eat whatever you want. You have permission to pass up that boneless breast of chicken with the weird gravy and stop at Häagen Dazs for ice cream on the way home.

If you can't go to a movie without popcorn, if a basketball game isn't a basketball game without beer, if you can't bear to watch TV without a bowl of coconut ice cream, or if you can't survive a meal at El Coyote unless it's a combination number two, *schedule it in.*

I talked a lot about socializing and travel in the original *Beverly Hills Diet,* and I urge you to review that chapter. But here are a few added thoughts for us social butterflies.

The Cocktail Crunch

Cocktail parties can foil the most stout-hearted BHDer. I always check out all the trays as they pass, but when you go to enough parties, those little goodies are all the same. Quite frankly, they're all likely to be rather mediocre. Also, I would rather socialize at a party and eat later, when I can concentrate on eating and, I might add, relax and enjoy it. I usually pass completely on the cocktail munchies; after all, how socially attractive am I when my mouth and hands are loaded with food? Are you likely to seek out the person with sauce dripping down his chin or the slim conversationalist in the center of the room who is free to shake your hand and clasp your slim shoulders? Are you at that party to socialize or to eat?

The cocktail party is the nibbler's nemesis. Practice the following exercises and remove yourself from the clutches of your DFC:

- Do not aim straight for the food table as soon as you walk through the door. Check your watch when you arrive and ignore the food for at least fifteen minutes.
- Break the habit of having "just one" of everything that is passed. Stop and think about those little tidbits first. Try to recall just how many of those "just ones" you remember after the fact. How many were really worth it?
- If you do decide to eat, choose consciously, moving to and away from the food. Break the hover habit. Deprogram that demonic hand-to-mouth cycle.
- Eat only what you choose to eat.
- Remind yourself that this is a *social* occasion, not exclusively an eating occasion. Focus on your priorities, and realize that there will be a trillion cocktail parties in your future.

Restaurant Romance

Know the type of meal—Open Protein, Open Carb, Open Human, or Wide Open—that you are going to have, and think about what you want to eat before you so much as glance at the menu. Unless the sky falls in, stick with your premeditated choice. Part of making Conscious Combining unconscious is making a commitment and sticking to it no matter what. Remember, you can always come back again. Unleash your skinny soul and let *it* take charge.

And remember, just because you're at a restaurant it doesn't mean you have to have an Open Human. Besides, how boring! Remember, the staff are there to serve you, to cater to your every whim, so let them. You can pick and choose, mix and match to your heart's content: three appetizers, two desserts, two entrees and an appetizer, just vegetables, or even just fruit. Have what you want and have fun. Remember, the restaurant is in business to give you what you want to eat, that's all, no other reason. Intimidation has no place in any eatery. *You* are the customer, so ask for foods you want, cooked the way you want them, in the order you would like them. Don't demand, just ask. Be gentle, but be firm.

We Beverly Hills Dieters are in restaurants and other people's homes constantly, and the bottom line is, we just can't indulge our every whim and take everything that comes without ballooning up and out of skinny. Not that Conscious Combining menus are exactly hard to take: Lobster dripping with butter is not the end of the world. Just don't get zapped by the "I'll do it tomorrow" mind set. Understand that there is no tomorrow, that tomorrow is here.

Travel

When I travel, I usually want to eat someplace wonderful when I arrive. So I eat *very carefully* en route. I know there's not much else to do when you're ensconced in a plane, but really, do you have to eat their food? When you can have your choice of anything in the world, why would you choose airline food? Even when you are traveling first-class, the food is still microwaved, it's been sitting around for umpteen hours, and no matter what it is, it's still not as good as the food when you get there.

When I went to Hawaii, they served rack of lamb on the plane. It was very tempting, and I decided to try it. The reality: Sure it was great for airline food, but do you notice how I qualified it? *"Great for airline food."* It certainly didn't even compare to rack of lamb I've had anywhere else. *Don't eat it just because it's there.*

Take your own food, dried fruit or Tupperwared fresh fruits, or take them whole and cut them en route. Snacks like popcorn or unsalted chips are great. And how about cold chicken? All of them are easy to tuck into your tote bag. I've taken bagels from the Stage Deli in New York, pasta from Tony's in Houston. That's right, I've taken restaurant food on flights with me and eaten it in lieu of the airline food. While I was on tour, I spent a portion of almost every day (usually the dinner hour) on an airplane. We (Cindy, my secretary, and I) never had a chance to actually sit down and eat during the day, and the first chance we would have to eat at night was usually not until at least 10:30 or 11:30 P.M. So, on our way to the airport we would stop someplace terrific, order something to go (anything from roast duck to french fries), take it along, and eat it when everyone else was eating. Maybe it wasn't piping hot by the time we got to eat it, but it was always a lot better than what was being served. For instance, when I was in Houston, I stopped at Brenner's and got a steak to go. Now, I knew I could get steak on the plane, but it wouldn't have even compared to one from Brenner's. Now why would I ever eat something second best when I can have the best? Sure, the steak on the plane was free; it came along with the ride; but, you know, there is no free food; it always costs us something. If it's not in terms of dollars and cents, then it's in the disappointment or in having to give up something else later on.

You will probably want to, and will eat again when you arrive at your destination. If you eat airline chow (sorry, but it's hardly worthy of being called food), you will end up doing both and having to pay the consequences on the first day of your trip, probably a day you were most looking forward to a special Open Human meal.

Now that your weight is perfect, there are lots of foods you can take with you that will keep you "enzymatically open" for whatever is coming. Use your imagination; and don't forget the three-hour waiting period between foods. On longer flights prepare for a couple of eating experiences. Flying to Columbus, Ohio, I had blueberries at takeoff, bagels at touchdown, and baked potatoes and salad after my last radio show.

Now if you're still not convinced, if you're still opposed to bringing your own, then at least order a salt-free meal. Despite my undying efforts, despite my throwing my weight around (maybe I just don't weigh enough), I've not been successful in ordering and receiving a vegetable plate without cheese, or a salad without either sesame seeds or cheese. Besides, the salads they've given me are so small, they would barely fill a snail's stomach; they're like giving someone a Band-Aid for a broken neck or like taking a dog for a walk on a string. And please forgo the fruit plate—two mean apples, oranges, and cottage cheese.

You'll feel much better physically and mentally if you eat your own food; and your body will surely say thank you.

Once you're there, ah, now that's a different matter. The beauty of maintaining is that you can do it all, anything you want if you just follow the rules.

Look at us, Cindy and I. We did it. Despite four months of traveling, a different city and a different great restaurant every night, we didn't gain an ounce. And believe me, we didn't eat fruit every night. *Au contraire*. The first question we would ask when we would arrive at a new city was "What's the best restaurant" and our first telephone call would be to make arrangements for our late dinner.

See for yourself, when you travel on the BHDLP, stick to your weekly plan, follow the rules, and you won't gain weight. Need I remind you that an Open Carb or Open Protein meal does not represent sacrifice, nor does a Mono Meal? Far from it. Pasta, as you recall, is a Mono Meal; so is steak or caviar. Look back to the sample meals if you were about to whimper about any imagined deprivations of combining. Your first trip could well be the happiest trip of your life, just like Donna's. You will be able to eat all the foods you love, yet you will be able to eternalize your perfect body. Experiment, enjoy, and indulge. But keep those Corrective Counterparts on hand just in case you momentarily lapse back into old habits.

A FINAL WORD TO
YOUR SOCIAL ANIMAL

Our natural inclination, our *habit*, is to overdramatize each meal. Although we *know* everything will still be here for us to enjoy tomorrow, we still haven't *internalized* and accepted that fact.

Again and again, keep telling yourself that tomorrow means a choice; what you forgo today, you can fill up on tomorrow.

Practice it until it's easy, and follow through with it until it becomes unconscious. Think in terms of weeks, not in terms of wisps of time. Just as life is a composite of seconds and minutes—past, present, and future—nutrition is just as much a product of the meal before and the meal after as it is of the meal before you. Don't allow yourself to be a victim of each singular experience. Don't be a martyr every time food confronts you. Think back over the last week. How many meals do you remember? How many bites? What exactly did you eat? Now think ahead to the next week and think about what you really want to eat.

All those negative food thoughts should be banished, thoughts such as "I shouldn't eat that," "It's fattening," "Maybe just one bite." Now that you have plugged your energy drain, now that you have erased the guilt that sapped your energy, you will probably become the social butterfly of the BHD set. Now you can put all that energy into the pure enjoyment of it all. You have left the Valley of the Shadow of Fat and have entered the Land of Eternal Slimhood, a land where the double golden pineapple will always shine upon you.

PART THREE

RECIPES TO FOREVER— FROM OUR KITCHEN TO YOURS

XI

Making It Our Way

INTRODUCTION

I'm a Conscious Combiner, a BHDer who also happens to love to cook and to eat, and who, I'm proud to reveal, enjoys a superb reputation for turning out fine haute cuisine. I do this not only for my own dinner parties, but also for others, catering specialty items from pâtés to Pithiviers. I also teach classes in the techniques required for making foods that are both delicate and delicious. The most fun of all is teaching "Cuisine for Kids." The youngsters joyfully come to make gingerbread houses, chocolate Easter bunnies, pizza, pasta, and French fruit tarts. Six months ago, however, I decided to put all this hedonism aside when I discovered that I could rid myself of the bread and chocolate that sat upon my hips by eating pineapples and pasta.

Ergo, the challenge when Judy Mazel telephoned me to declare that "man does not live by papaya alone." Could I turn my culinary talents with food and pastries into something to BHD by for the rest of our lives by adapting and creating recipes for Conscious Combiners? Could I do it with gourmet food? Could I create recipes à la Conscious Combining that were exciting and delicious?

Before my eyes flashed my years as fashion director of *Seventeen* magazine, covering the collections in Europe to bring home the

209

fashion news, secretly adoring dining at the sensational Parisian restaurants, peeking in the windows at Fauchon, and observing demonstrations in haute cuisine at the Cordon Bleu cooking school. Surely the aesthetics of creating beautiful fashions were closely allied to creating beautiful food. There must be balance, proportion, and beauty as well as exquisite taste in both areas. Judy's challenge would offer me the opportunity to share my experience and knowledge with others for the purpose of looking magnificent while eating magnificently.

The results of my efforts follow: recipes, tips, and techniques for creating the ultimate in elegant cuisine for the Conscious Combiner. There are basic sauces and those that are just a bit more complex. Become familiar with them and then learn how to combine them to beautify all that you eat, from the simplest vegetables to the most elaborate of puff-pastry extravaganzas.

Essential to your success will be your willingness to experiment. You can adapt your favorite recipes simply by separating carbohydrates from proteins. Don't flour meats to be sautéed, pat them dry and they'll brown in hot butter and oil. You don't need flour to thicken sauces and pan juices—simply add a bit of butter, some demi-glacé, and some heavy cream, turn up the flame and whisk until thickened. Enhance the flavors of all your dishes by discovering the wonders of herbs—there are literally hundreds, many of which will thrive in pots on your kitchen windowsill. You will find that no one will ever again ask you to "pass the salt" when you've remembered that pinch of thyme or tarragon. Vegetables are glorious when you take a moment to purée a lowly turnip with butter and cream or steam a humble carrot with ginger and thyme.

Use the techniques I serve up here and let your imagination run wild. For this is just the beginning. As you try each of these recipes, you will come to internalize the aesthetics of beautiful food consciously combined. The effects of your new adventure in eating will be as far-reaching in your house as they have been in ours. For this year when our daughter Marisa reminded us to leave cookies and milk for Santa, her sister Amanda insisted that if they left a pineapple instead, the truth about Santa's identity would finally be known!

NANCY H. MARCANTONIO

Beurre Blanc
(White Butter Sauce)

Serve as a sauce with vegetables or alongside Puff-Pastry Tourtes with vegetable filling (see p. 254). Delicious also with fish or shellfish.

(see p. 254)

4 Tbs. finely minced shallots	1 Tbs. tepid water
2 Tbs. rice vinegar (substitute stock or water when using with protein)	4 ounces (1 stick) unsalted butter, cut in 4 pieces (at room temperature)
2 Tbs. water	

Place the shallots, vinegar, and water in a small heavy-bottomed saucepan, and simmer over a low flame until all the moisture evaporates and the shallots are soft.

Remove from the heat, add the additional tablespoon of water, and begin whisking in the soft butter. This is done off the heat so that the butter does not melt but begins to emulsify into a fluffy mass with the shallots. When completed, the sauce should have the appearance of a thick cream.

YIELD   1 cup.

Crème à l'Eschalote
(Shallot Cream)

Delicious over poached fish, chicken, or eggs.

2 Tbs. unsalted butter
4 Tbs. minced shallots
½ cup chicken or veal stock
  (see pp. 235–36)
2 cups heavy cream

1 egg yolk
1 Tbs. tarragon (or another
  herb appropriate to the use
  of the sauce; fennel or anise
  are wonderful complements
  to fish)

Melt the butter in a small heavy-bottomed saucepan.

Add the shallots and sauté until shallots wilt and are lightly browned.

Drain off butter and add chicken or veal stock; raise the heat and reduce by half.

Add the cream and over medium to high heat reduce the sauce by about one-quarter, whisking as it cooks.

Remove from heat and immediately add egg yolk and herbs while whisking briskly. Serve warm.

YIELD   2 cups.

Mazel Dressing

¼ cup rice vinegar
1 cup sesame oil
Chopped garlic to taste*
   (1–2 small cloves)

Chopped or grated ginger to
   taste*
Freshly ground pepper

Combine all ingredients.

YIELD   1¼ cups.

*From clove to clove and root to root, garlic and ginger may differ in intensity. If they are left to steep in dressing, their flavors will intensify. Therefore, depending on when you make the dressing, on the strength of the garlic and ginger, and, of course, on personal taste, the amounts used may differ. Start with one clove garlic and 6 or 7 gratings of ginger and increase to 3 times that amount if desired.

Hollandaise

Hollandaise is a simple sauce to make. Once you get the hang of it, it should take you only about 3 to 5 minutes to do. Since it's categorized as a fat, it can be used to embellish either carbs or proteins. Try it over vegetables, as well as over fish or eggs.

This recipe will make enough Hollandaise to serve 6. Should you wish to reduce or increase the amount of sauce, the basic proportions are 1 egg yolk to 1 tablespoon of water to 1 stick of unsalted butter.

2 egg yolks	Freshly ground white pepper
2 Tbs. water	(optional)
8 ounces (2 sticks) unsalted	Pinch of cayenne pepper
butter, melted and cooled	(optional)
slightly	Chives, parsley, tarragon
	(optional)

Place the egg yolks and water in a heavy-bottomed saucepan, and begin whisking over a low flame. This will gently poach the egg in the water. You will feel it start to thicken as you whisk. When it has thickened, but before it begins to curdle or come apart, remove from heat.

Off heat, begin to dribble in the melted butter and whisk constantly. Still whisking, slowly add the rest of the butter, taking care to omit the milky residue on the bottom. Whisk quickly so the sauce stays warm. The sauce should be thickened and fluffy. Season with a twist of white pepper and herbs, if desired.

You can try to warm the sauce very lightly over warm water for 1 or 2 minutes, but beware of too much heat or the sauce will separate. If you have to hold the sauce, you may keep it over *tepid* water for a short while.

YIELD   2 cups.

Béarnaise

Béarnaise is made by following the same simple technique used to make a Hollandaise. It is, however, herb-based, creating flavors that are more intense.

2 Tbs. minced shallots
1 Tbs. Fresh tarragon
   (or 2 tsp. dried)
2 tsp. dried chervil
2 Tbs. rice vinegar, or 2 Tbs.
   water or stock when using
   sauce with protein

2 Tbs. water
Freshly ground white pepper
2 egg yolks
2 Tbs. water or stock
8 ounces (2 sticks) unsalted
   butter

Place the shallots, tarragon, chervil, vinegar, water and pepper in a small heavy-bottomed saucepan. Place over high heat and reduce until only 1 to 2 tsps. of liquid remain. Add yolks and water to reduction. Whisk over low heat until thick and fluffy. Remove from heat.

Proceed as for Hollandaise Sauce, dribbling in the melted butter and whisking constantly.

YIELD   2 cups.

Crème au Raifort
(Horseradish Cream)

Quick to make and gives great zip to all simply cooked beef dishes, from potted brisket to standing rib roast.

1 cup heavy cream
¼ cup freshly grated
    horseradish
Freshly ground white pepper

Pinch cayenne pepper
1 Tbs. green peppercorns

Beat cream in a chilled bowl until stiff.

With the back of a spoon, press horseradish against a fine sieve to remove moisture.

Combine horseradish with two gratings of white pepper and a tiny pinch of cayenne.

Fold into whipped cream.

With a mortar and pestle, or simply with the bottom of a glass on a flat surface, crush the peppercorns and fold them into the whipped cream mixture.

Refrigerate until ready to serve.

YIELD   approx. 1½ cups.

Béchamel

A béchamel is a simple sauce to make, but a versatile one, with many uses. It can be a thickener or liaison (see Glossary, p. 329) for pureed vegetables and can be used as a base for creamed soups and sauces. It is traditionally made by combining scalded milk with a roux of unsalted butter and flour, but Conscious-Combining recipes call for making it with a thin roux and then completing it with heavy sweet cream.

2 cups heavy cream

1 bay leaf

Twist of freshly ground white pepper

Grating of fresh nutmeg

2 Tbs. unsalted butter

2 Tbs. flour

Heat the cream in a heavy saucepan until it begins to bubble lightly at the edges. Remove from heat.

Add the bay leaf, white pepper, and nutmeg, cover, and set aside to steep.

Melt the butter in a heavy-bottomed saucepan until it bubbles. Whisk in the flour, making sure to incorporate all the flour in the butter, and cook until it foams. Remove from heat until cooled somewhat.

Pour the cream mixture over the roux and whisk constantly, placing the saucepan back on a medium flame. Continue whisking until the sauce thickens. Cook over a low flame for 5 or 6 minutes, whisking occasionally. Remove bay leaf.

If not used immediately, remove from heat and place a piece of plastic wrap directly on the sauce to prevent a skin from forming.

YIELD   approx. 2 cups.

VARIATION   A velouté is the sister of a béchamel and is made exactly the same way except that vegetable stock is substituted for the cream, the butter and flour are increased to 3 tablespoons each to make the roux, herbs are added, if desired, and the cooking is increased to 20 minutes. Skim off fats or impurities as it cooks. Lighter and less rich than a béchamel, a velouté is also used in purees, soups, and as a sauce base.

Mayonnaise

Make mayonnaise in a food processor or blender. It takes 2 to 3 minutes to do, but once you get into the habit you will enjoy having fresh mayonnaise at hand for any number of uses and variations.

Carb Mayonnaise	Protein Mayonnaise
2 egg yolks	1 whole egg
2 tsp. rice vinegar	1 Tbs. stock or water
Freshly ground white pepper	Freshly ground white pepper
¼ tsp. dry mustard	¼ tsp. dry mustard
Pinch of cayenne	Pinch of cayenne
1¼ cups sesame or safflower oil or a combination of both	1½ cups sesame or safflower oil or a combination of both

In the bowl of the processor or blender, place the egg yolks (or whole egg) and add the liquid, pepper, mustard, and cayenne. Process for 2 minutes.

With processor running, begin to dribble the oil through the feed tube. Proceed very slowly, adding only the smallest amount of oil until you see that the egg has begun to absorb the oil and a mayonnaise is forming. Then you may begin to add the oil in a thin steady stream.

Taste for seasonings. You may prefer to add more pepper.

YIELD   1½ cups.

VARIATION 1   *Sauce Verte* (Green Mayonnaise): Puree in a food processor or chop very fine: 1 bunch watercress (leaves only), 2 tablespoons chopped parsley, 1 tablespoon fresh chopped dill or tarragon. Fold into mayonnaise.

VARIATION 2   *Mayonnaise aux Tomates (Tomato Mayonnaise):* Prepare 3 tomatoes by plunging into boiling water for 10 seconds, peeling and chopping. Puree by pushing through a fine sieve to remove seeds. Fold puree into mayonnaise for a thick tomato dressing.

VARIATION 3   *Mayonnaise au Moutarde (Mustard Mayonnaise):* Make a paste of 1 teaspoon dry mustard, 1 tablespoon mayonnaise, and 1 tablespoon crushed green peppercorns. Fold paste into 1 cup mayonnaise.

VARIATION 4   *Aïoli (Garlic Mayonnaise):* Place 5 cloves of minced garlic and ¼ cup mayonnaise in processor. Process until garlic is pureed into mayonnaise. Add a pinch of cayenne and fold into 1 cup mayonnaise.

Pesto

Make pesto in the summer when fresh basil is plentiful. Freeze to enjoy it all winter long.

2 cups fresh basil leaves, Olive oil
    tightly packed
4 cloves garlic, minced

Wash and dry the basil leaves thoroughly. Place leaves in bowl of food processor. Add garlic and process until basil and garlic are chopped and combined.

Dribble olive oil through feed tube. Take care to add only enough to make pesto thick and pasty. Store in small jars in freezer.

YIELD   ¾ cup.

Marinara Sauce

Make marinara in the summer when the tomatoes are luscious. Freeze for use all winter long.

7 Tbs. olive oil
2 onions, chopped
4 cloves garlic, minced
4 lbs. tomatoes, seeded and
    chopped

10 fresh basil leaves and a sprig
    each of fresh oregano and
    thyme
Freshly ground black pepper, to
    taste

Heat the oil in a large, heavy-bottomed saucepan. Add onion and cook slowly until wilted (about 15 minutes), but do not brown. Add garlic and chopped tomatoes and toss with oil and onion in pan. Add herbs and spices, cover, and cook until tomatoes are soft and flavors are blended, approximately ½ hour. Cool for 5 minutes.

Place sauce in the bowl of food processor or in a blender jar, and, with on/off chopping motion, lightly puree the sauce. Freeze unused portion.

YIELD   6 to 8 cups, depending on variety of tomatoes.

Mazel Ketchup

1 lb. plum tomatoes	1 small onion, minced
¼ tsp. cayenne	1 tsp. oregano
1 clove garlic	Freshly ground black pepper, to taste

In a large pot of boiling water, cook the tomatoes for 3 minutes, just until softened. Drain immediately and plunge into a bowl of cold water.

Peel, seed, and chop the tomatoes into small dice.

Place the diced tomatoes, the onion, and the seasoning in the bowl of a food processor or in a blender jar. Puree.

YIELD   approximately 1 cup.

SPECIAL SEASONINGS

Once you become committed to Conscious Combining with the ultimate in elegant foods, your search will begin for delicious and exciting new ways to season your carbs and proteins.

Discover the glories of herbs and spices: tarragon, thyme, oregano, sage, basil, summer savory, ginger, marjoram, cardamom, dill, fennel and anise, coriander, sorrel, cayenne, and peppercorns—black, white, or the newer green. All will impart wonderful flavors to your cooking. Try growing your own herbs in summer. They flourish easily—the bugs don't like them as much as you will! Dry or freeze them to use all winter long. Use them to make herb vinegars, piquant mustards, or herb butters.

HERB VINEGARS Bring 2 cups of rice vinegar to the boil. Pour over a bunch of fresh herbs (for example, tarragon, oregano, garlic, rosemary, or thyme) which you have placed in a glass jar. Cover and allow to steep in a warm spot for at least two weeks. Strain to remove herbs, replace with a fresh sprig, cover and label. Use in salads and sauces.

MUSTARDS Turn dry mustard into a delicious condiment. Combine 1 tablespoon rice vinegar or 1 tablespoon water or stock (rice vinegar for carb, stock for protein), 1 tablespoon minced herbs of your choice, 1 clove garlic, minced, 2 teaspoons shallots, minced, and a twist of fresh pepper (or crushed green peppercorns), into ¼ cup dry mustard. Should approximate the consistency of ordinary mustard.

HERB BUTTERS Soften ½ cup butter and whisk in 2 to 3 tablespoons minced herbs (parsley, chives, dill, tarragon, thyme, or summer savory), and a pinch of cayenne or freshly ground black pepper, if desired. Use to top grilled or poached fish, chicken, beef, or lamb. Use over vegetables. Spread under skin of chicken or fish when grilling, or use as a final enrichment in soups. *Garlic Butter*: Peel and mash 3 garlic cloves, beat into ½ cup softened butter, cover and refrigerate, allowing several hours for flavor to develop. Use over grilled steak or chops. *Pimento Butter*: Char, peel, seed, and chop a red pepper and mash into a smooth paste. Beat in ½ cup softened butter and use on pasta or with fresh vegetables.

MEL'S SECRET SEASONING Char, peel, seed, and chop 1 hot green pepper. Sauté in pan with 2 tablespoons olive oil. Store in a jar and use when you want to add real zing to any sauce or vegetable.

SALADS

Mazel Salad

2 bunches spinach, thoroughly
washed
2 bunches watercress
2 small heads Belgian endive
1–2 bunches mustard greens
3 carrots, grated
2 raw beets, grated

1 Daikon radish, grated
25 mushrooms, cleaned and
sliced
1 bunch chopped parsley
3 leeks, cut diagonally into
¼-inch pieces
Mazel Dressing (p. 214)

Be sure all vegetables are clean and thoroughly dry. Tear spinach, watercress, endive, and mustard greens into large, bite-sized pieces. Add remaining ingredients. Toss with Mazel Dressing.

YIELD 2 servings.

The L-T-O

1 large, firm head iceberg
lettuce
4 tomatoes
1–2 cucumbers, peeled

1 large red, or Spanish, onion,
peeled
Mazel Dressing (p. 214) or olive
oil

With a sharp knife, cut all vegetables into good-sized chunks. Toss with dressing or oil.

YIELD 2 servings.

Sweet 'n' Sour Salad

A great combination of sweet basil and tangy watercress leaves.

2 cups basil leaves, washed, dried, and chopped

2 bunches watercress, leaves and tender tops of stems, washed, dried, and chopped

3 large tomatoes (or 4 medium), chopped into large chunks

2 cups chopped onions

3 cloves garlic, chopped

½ cup olive oil

In a large salad bowl, combine the basil leaves, watercress, tomatoes, and onions.

Sprinkle the chopped garlic over all and toss with olive oil. (Use only enough oil to lightly coat the salad. Do not saturate or the salad will wilt.)

YIELD   2 servings.

SOUPS ON THE CARB SIDE

Vegetable Stock

6 onions
2 carrots
4 leeks
10 celery stalks with leaves
3 parsnips
1 large bunch parsley

3 tomatoes
10 mushrooms
5 scallions
1 Tbs. unsalted butter
Include scraps from any other
  vegetables that you've
  accumulated over the week

Preheat oven to 350°.

Wash and slice vegetables. Melt butter and combine with the vegetables. Turn into large casserole.

Bake, uncovered, for 30 minutes. Add 5 quarts of water to casserole, partially cover, and simmer on top of stove for 4 hours. Strain and refrigerate. Can be frozen.

YIELD   4 quarts.

Potage Crème de Légume
(Cream of Vegetable Soup)

Start with a Béchamel base (p. 218), add a pureed vegetable, herbs, and spices, and any number of creamed vegetable soups are possible.

YIELD   4 servings.

227

VARIATION 1 *Potage Crème de Choux Broccoli (Cream of Broccoli Soup)*: Wash and cut 1 large bunch of broccoli into large dice. Cook in boiling water until fork tender. Drain and puree in processor or blender. Add puree to 2 cups heated velouté, whisking to combine thoroughly. Season with freshly ground pepper, nutmeg, and a large pinch of oregano and thyme to taste. Thin to desired consistency with heavy cream.

VARIATION 2 *Potage Crème de Céleris (Cream of Celery Soup)*: Wash and cut into large dice 1 head of celery, including leaves. Cook in boiling water until tender. Drain and puree in processor or blender. Season with freshly ground white pepper, nutmeg, a pinch of cayenne, marjoram, and sage to taste. Combine puree with 2 cups velouté, whisking thoroughly. Heat through and thin with ½ cup heavy cream if desired.

VARIATION 3 *Potage Crème Nivernaise (Cream of Carrot Soup)*: Wash, peel, and slice 1 pound of carrots into ¼-inch rounds. Boil until fork tender, drain, and puree as described above. Season with pepper, nutmeg, 2 tablespoons thyme, and pinch cayenne. Stir into 2 cups velouté. Thin with heavy cream to desired consistency.

VARIATION 4 *Potage à la Florentine (Cream of Spinach Soup)*: Follow instructions for cream of broccoli soup, but puree spinach with 1 clove of minced garlic, if desired, and season with dill, nutmeg, and pepper.

VARIATION 5 *Potage aux Navets (Cream of Turnip)*: Follow instructions for cream of carrot soup.

Potage Parmentier
(Leek and Potato Soup)

4 medium leeks
2 Tbs. unsalted butter
2 Tbs. flour
6 cups water
6 boiling potatoes
    (about 1½ lbs.)

Freshly ground white pepper, to
    taste
Sprig of fresh thyme
Sour cream (optional)
½ cup heavy cream

Trim the leeks to within an inch of the white part and discard the green. Cut a shallow cross in the stem end and wash leeks thoroughly under a strong steam of cold water, making sure to get all the sand out. Slice the leeks into thin rounds.

Melt the butter in a saucepan, stir in the leeks, and cook over a low flame until the leeks are wilted. Do not brown them. While leeks are cooking, wash and peel the potatoes and slice them thinly.

Whisk the flour into the leeks and butter, and cook until absorbed, but not browned.

Boil the water. Add it slowly to the leek mixture, whisking to be certain the flour is absorbed. Add the potatoes and season with pepper and thyme. Cover and cook at the simmer just until potatoes are tender.

Puree in a food processor or put through a food mill, reheat, and add ½ cup of heavy cream.

Spoon into serving bowls and, if desired, garnish with a dollop of sour cream.

YIELD   6 servings.

Corn Chowder

3 Tbs. unsalted butter
1 onion, peeled and sliced
2 boiling potatoes, peeled and
    cubed
2½ cups water
Bouquet garni of parsley, bay
    leaf, thyme, and celery stalk
    with leaves, tied together
    with string or wrapped in a
    square of cheesecloth

2 cups fresh corn kernels (you
    may substitute frozen if
    fresh is unavailable)
2 Tbs. flour
¼ cup water
1 cup heavy cream
2 egg yolks

Melt the butter in a large saucepan. Wilt the onion in the butter, add the potatoes, water, and bouquet garni. Cover and simmer gently for 15 minutes.

Add the corn to the soup mixture and cook until vegetables are fork tender.

Blend the flour into the ¼ cup water with a small whisk. Add to the soup mixture and stir to dissolve. Whisk in the cream and simmer over medium heat until soup thickens.

In a small bowl, whisk the egg yolks until thickened and sticky. By spoonfuls, beat about ¾ cup of the soup into the yolks.

Remove bouquet garni from soup pot, stir liaison of egg yolks and soup back into larger pot. Do not allow to boil or egg will curdle. Serve immediately.

YIELD   4 servings.

Borscht

8 small to medium beets (the
    smaller the beet, the more
    intense the color and taste)
1 carrot, cut into large chunks
1 turnip, cut into large chunks
5 cups vegetable stock (p. 227)

2 Tbs. rice vinegar
2 large baking potatoes
½ cup sour cream
2 Tbs. chopped dill (for
    garnish)

Scrub the vegetables to remove surface dirt. Place vegetable stock in a large pot, bring to the boil, add the beets, carrot, and turnip, and boil until they are easily pierced with a fork. Test carrot and turnip after 15 minutes. Remove them from the pot. The beets may take half an hour more before they are tender. Continue cooking the beets until done. Total cooking time should be about 1 hour.

Rinse carrot and turnip under cold water and peel. When beets are tender, remove from stock, rinse and peel. Cut beets, carrot, and turnip into thin julienne. Return vegetables to stock and add 2 tablespoons of vinegar, or to taste.

Meanwhile, boil the potatoes until fork tender and cut into 3 or 4 pieces.

To serve, put borscht into bowls, add 1 or 2 pieces of potato, a dollop of sour cream, and a sprinkling of dill.

YIELD   4 servings.

Zuppa di Pomodori con Pesto
(Tomato Soup with Pesto)

2 Tbs. unsalted butter
3 onions, diced
3 cloves garlic, minced
1 stalk of fennel, diced
3 lbs. tomatoes, seeded and
    cubed
4 sprigs parsley

3 sprigs fresh thyme (or 2 tsp.
    dried)
Freshly ground white pepper, to
    taste
2 cups water or vegetable stock
1 cup heavy cream
¾ cup pesto sauce (p. 220)

In a large saucepan, melt the butter until foaming. Add the diced onion, garlic, and fennel, and cook until wilted, about 15 minutes.

Add the tomatoes, parsley, thyme, and pepper, and cook 5 minutes more, stirring gently. Stir in the water or stock, bring to the boil, and simmer for 30 minutes, or until tomatoes are tender.

Puree in a food processor or put through a food mill, reheat, add cream, and sour cream and serve with a dollop of pesto sauce in the center of each serving.

YIELD   3–4 servings.

Soupe au Pistou
(Vegetable Soup with Basil Sauce)

Pistou is the French version of pesto and is an equally delicious concoction.

4–5 leeks (depending on size)
1 celery root, minced
7 carrots, sliced into thin
    rounds
2 ounces (½ stick) unsalted
    butter
3 qts. boiling water

1 cauliflower, in florets
½ lb. potatoes, washed, boiled,
    peeled, and cut into chunks
Freshly ground white pepper, to
    taste
½ cup heavy cream (optional
    for extra enrichment)

Pistou:

½ cup fresh basil leaves,
    tightly packed

3 cloves garlic
Olive oil

Wash vegetables. (Cut leeks in half lengthwise, from the white through the green, and make sure to wash out all the sand.)

Melt the butter in a large saucepan. Cut leeks into tiny mince and sauté them until softened and wilted. Add minced celery root and carrots. Stir until coated with butter.

Add the 3 quarts of boiling water, the cauliflower, and the potatoes, bring to the boil, and simmer until all the vegetables are tender.

Drain vegetables, reserving stock, and pass through food processor or food mill, pureeing them to a heavy creamy consistency. Whisk puree into stock.

Make the pistou by placing basil and garlic in the bowl of a food processor. Process by pulsing for 1 minute. Then, with processor running, dribble in the olive oil, using only enough to form a thick paste.

Reheat soup, season with pepper, and whisk in cream at the last minute. Serve Provençal style with a dollop of pistou in the center of each serving.

YIELD   6 servings.

Potage Germiny
(Sorrel Soup)

A soup with the deliciously tart taste of this wild herb.

1 leek	5 cups vegetable stock
4 Tbs. unsalted butter	(see p. 227)
1 lb. sorrel leaves	3 egg yolks
4 Tbs. flour	¾ cup heavy cream
	Freshly ground white pepper

Trim the leek, leaving about 1 inch of green above the bulb, cut in half lengthwise, and wash in running cold water until free of sand. Shake dry. Mince very finely.

In a large saucepan, melt the butter until foaming. Add the minced leek and sauté until wilted but not brown.

Strip the sorrel leaves from stems and wash and dry them. Mince leaves finely.

Stir the sorrel leaves into the leeks, and cook until wilted. Sprinkle the flour over the mixture, and stir until combined. Bring the stock to the boil. Remove the pot from the heat and pour in the stock, whisking constantly as you pour so that the flour does not lump.

Return the pot to the stove and, whisking occasionally, simmer soup until heated through and thickened.

Meanwhile, in a medium bowl, beat the egg yolks with the cream until thickened. Tablespoon by tablespoon, whisk in 1 cup of the soup. Return this egg-soup mixture to the soup pot and whisk it all together over very low heat. (Do not let the soup boil now or the eggs will curdle.) Season with white pepper to taste.

Serve immediately.

YIELD   4—5 servings.

Fonds de Volaille
(Chicken Stock)

2 4-lb. chickens, cut into
pieces, plus the necks,
gizzards, hearts, and
chicken feet if possible (do
not include liver)
3 large or 5 small shallots, cut
in quarters
10 cloves
5 garlic cloves, crushed in the
husk

10 peppercorns
10 sprigs fresh thyme (or 2 Tbs.
dried), and a small bunch of
fresh dill (or 2 Tbs. dried)
10 sprigs fresh parsley (the flat
Italian variety is the most
flavorful)
4 bay leaves
8 quarts cold water

Place all ingredients in cold water, bring to the boil, and skim
off impurities that rise to surface.

Lower heat and simmer for 2 hours. Strain through a fine mesh
strainer into a large bowl. Cool uncovered.

Remove all the fat from the stock and use quart containers to
freeze whatever portion of the stock not used immediately.

YIELD   6–7 quarts.

235

Fonds Brun
(Brown Veal Stock)

5 lbs. veal bones
4 large or 7 small shallots, cut
    in quarters
10 cloves
½ cup minced chives
5 garlic cloves, crushed in the
    husk

10 peppercorns
10 sprigs fresh thyme (or 2 Tbs.
    dried)
10 sprigs fresh parsley (the flat
    Italian variety is the most
    flavorful)
4 bay leaves

Preheat oven to 475°.

Place the veal bones in a large roasting pan and brown in preheated oven for 30 minutes. Remove bones to a large stock pot, cover with cold water to about 2 or 3 inches above bones, bring to the boil, and skim off impurities that rise to the surface while cooking. Lower heat and simmer until the water appears clear and nothing further rises to the surface.

Add the shallots, cloves, chives, garlic, peppercorns, thyme, parsley, and bay leaves.

Return to stove and bring to the boil. Reduce heat and allow to simmer over a very low flame for 24 hours. From time to time skim the fat off the top of the stock.

Strain finished stock into a large bowl through a fine mesh strainer. Let stand uncovered until cool, remove any fat that accumulates on the top, and return to clean stock pot. Boil and reduce by at least ⅓ to intensify flavor.

YIELD   approx. 6 quarts.

Demi-Glace

A demi-glace is a reduced stock used to enrich a sauce or pan juices. It is whisked in, the heat is raised, and the sauce or pan juices are reduced by boiling at the end of the cooking time.

In a heavy-bottomed saucepan, place 4 cups of chicken or veal stock, raise heat to high, and boil until stock is reduced by half. You can freeze demi-glace in small containers until needed.

Glace de Volaille or Glace de Viande

An even more intense enrichment of a stock, actually made from a demi-glace, which is further reduced. Use to flavor sauces or pan juices by stirring in during final cooking period, raising heat, and enriching at the last moment with some heavy cream.

In a heavy-bottomed saucepan, reduce demi-glace over high heat until all that remains is a heavy, syrupy glaze. Freeze in ice-cube trays. When frozen, place cubes in a plastic bag, where they will always be available to enrich the flavors of sauces used with protein dishes.

Fumet de Poisson
(Fish Stock)

Because the making of stock is time-consuming, it is wise to prepare it in large quantities—as in the following recipe—and store in pint or quart containers in the freezer. In this way, it is always at hand when needed.

4 lbs. fish bones and heads from any fresh, white-fleshed fish such as sole or flounder. It must be fish of a nonoily variety.

6 shallots, quartered

6 sprigs Italian parsley

3 bay leaves

4 sprigs fresh thyme (or 1 Tbs. dried)

10 black peppercorns, lightly crushed

2 Tbs. fennel seeds, crushed

Several hours or the night before preparing fumet, cover the fish bones with ice water and refrigerate. This will disgorge the blood from the bones.

If using fish heads, remove the gills, which can impart a bitter flavor.

In a large casserole or stock pot, place the fish bones and heads, the shallots, parsley, bay leaves, thyme, peppercorns, and fennel seeds. Add water to cover, bring to the boil, reduce heat, and simmer 30 minutes.

Strain through a fine sieve.

YIELD   6 quarts.

Court Bouillon

A court bouillon is an aromatic liquid commonly used to poach a whole fish, a fish steak, or a fish fillet. Here is a variation using clam juice.

1 cup clam juice (make your own by steaming clams and reserving their cooking broth)
4 shallots, peeled and quartered
10 peppercorns
3 garlic cloves, mashed with the flat side of a cleaver
5 sprigs Italian parsley
2 bay leaves
4 sprigs thyme (or 1 Tbs. dried)
2 Tbs. fennel seeds, crushed
1 Tbs. dried red pepper flakes
Freshly ground white pepper

Combine all the above ingredients plus 6 quarts of water in a fish poacher or a pot large enough to hold the fish to be poached. (A large roasting pan will serve perfectly well.)

Bring to the boil and barely simmer for 30 minutes, until all the flavors are gently blended.

Allow court bouillon to cool before using it to poach your fish.

YIELD   6 quarts.

Bouillabaisse

A Provençal shellfish and seafood stew fragrant with the essence of garlic.

20 cups of Fumet de Poisson (p. 238)
2 Tbs. fennel seeds, crushed
6 Tbs. chopped garlic
5 sprigs fresh thyme (or 1½ Tbs. dried)
4 sprigs fresh parsley
2 tsp. paprika
Freshly ground black pepper
½ tsp. cayenne pepper
¾ tsp. saffron threads, crushed

2 large live lobsters (1½ to 2 lbs. each), cracked and cut apart at joints
2 lbs. each of 3 different kinds of firm, white-fleshed fish of a nonoily variety (bass, cod, tilefish, halibut, sea trout), cut into chunks
1 lb. littleneck clams
1 lb. mussels
2 lbs. sea scallops, cut in quarters

Place the Fumet de Poisson in a large stock pot. Add the fennel, garlic, thyme, parsley, paprika, black pepper, cayenne, and saffron, bring to the boil, and cook for 30 minutes.

Add the lobster pieces, simmer for 5 minutes; add the cubed fish and simmer for an additional 5 minutes. Then add the clams, mussels, and scallops, and cook 5 minutes longer.

Serve the Bouillabaisse with a bowl of Sauce Rouille passed around the table for your guests to help themselves.

YIELD   4 servings.

Sauce Rouille

1 egg yolk	¼ tsp. paprika
2 Tbs. chopped garlic	Freshly ground black pepper
½ tsp. fish stock	1 cup olive oil
¼ tsp. cayenne pepper	

Place all the ingredients, excluding the oil, in the bowl of the food processor and process for 1 minute. Dribble the oil into the yolk mixture through the feed tube until the sauce is thickened.

Pass with the soup. Each diner should place a dollop of rouille in the center of his or her bowl.

YIELD   4 servings.

Clam Soup

48 littleneck clams	1 cup water or fish stock
3 sprigs parsley	(p. 238)
2 cloves garlic, minced	2 eggs yolks
2 shallots, minced	1 cup heavy cream
1 bay leaf	½ tsp. saffron
½ tsp. dried red pepper flakes	2 Tbs. minced parsley

Scrub the clam shells and soak them in cold water. This will encourage the clams to open and disgorge their sand. Change the water a few times until all traces of sand disappear.

Place the parsley, garlic, shallots, bay leaf, and red pepper flakes in a large saucepan. Add the clams and the water or stock, cover, and, over medium heat, bring to the boil. Steam the clams just until they open. This should take no longer than about 5 minutes. Overcooked clams become tough, so be careful to remove the clams with a skimmer as they open. Shell clams, mince, and set aside.

Set the remaining broth on a high flame and reduce by about ¼ to ½.

Remove 4 tablespoons of the broth from the pot, beat the egg yolks in a small bowl, and whisk in the 4 tablespoons of broth. Set aside.

Add the cream and saffron to the clam broth reduction, raise heat, and boil until thickened slightly. Off heat, stir in egg liaison. Distribute minced clams equally among soup bowls, and pour soup over. Serve garnished with minced parsley.

YIELD   4 servings.

Mouclades
(Breton Mussel Soup with Cream and Saffron)

4 qts. mussels
2 cloves garlic, minced
½ cup shallots, minced
1 bay leaf
3 or 4 sprigs fresh thyme (or 1 Tbs. dried)
3 or 4 sprigs fresh parsley, coarsely chopped
Freshly ground black pepper, to taste

1 cup fish stock (p. 238)
1 cup heavy cream
1 egg yolk
Pinch of saffron
Pinch of ground star anise (or 2 Tbs. fennel seeds, crushed)

Scrub and beard the mussels. Discard any open ones. Soak in cold water to cover for several hours.

In a large, heavy-bottomed saucepan, or small stock pot, place the drained, rinsed mussels, garlic, shallots, bay leaf, thyme, parsley, black pepper, and fish stock. Cover with a tight-fitting lid and, over a medium to high flame, steam the mussels until they open. Remove from the broth with a skimmer, set them aside, and keep warm.

Strain the mussel broth through a fine sieve, return to the saucepan, place over high heat, and reduce the broth by about ¼. Add the heavy cream, raise heat, and whisk until broth begins to thicken a bit.

Beat egg yolk. Off heat, remove ½ cup of broth to a small bowl and whisk it into the egg yolk by tablespoons. Add the pinch of saffron and pinch of star anise, or fennel. Return this mixture to pot of broth, and reheat, stirring constantly, but do not allow to boil or egg will curdle.

Divide mussels among individual soup bowls, pour the soup over them, and serve immediately.

YIELD   4 servings.

Soupe de Poisson
(Fish Soup)

1 qt. mussels
1 qt. littleneck clams
¼ cup olive oil
1 cup shallots, minced
3 Tbs. minced garlic
1 tsp. saffron threads
3–4 cups Fumet de Poisson
   (p. 238)
1 bay leaf

1 Tbs. thyme
Pinch of cayenne
2 star anise pods
Freshly ground white pepper, to
   taste
1 lb. fish fillets, without skin
½ cup heavy cream
2 Tbs. fennel seeds, crushed
Sauce Rouille (p. 241)

Beard, scrub, and soak the mussels in cold water to cover, for several hours. Also scrub and soak the clams, keeping them separate from the mussels.

Heat the olive oil in a large heavy-bottomed saucepan or casserole. Add the shallots and garlic and sauté gently until wilted. Rub the saffron gently between your fingers and add to the shallots and garlic.

Add the fumet, bay leaf, thyme, cayenne, star anise pods, and white pepper, and bring to the boil. Simmer for 10 minutes. Add the fish fillets. Cook 5 minutes longer, keeping the water at a gentle simmer.

Place the mussels in a medium saucepan with ¼ cup water and steam until opened (about 5 minutes). Reserve cooking liquid.

Repeat this procedure with the clams, again reserving cooking liquid.

Add the mussels, clams, and their cooking liquid to the soup. Bring to the boil, lower flame, stir in the cream, and heat through.

Serve in individual soup bowls topped with a sprinkling of crushed fennel seed. Pass a Sauce Rouille (see p. 241) with the Soupe de Poisson.

YIELD   4 servings.

PASTA WITH PLEASURE

Pasta constitutes the ultimate in eating pleasure. No longer are your choices limited to spaghetti in a garlic butter sauce or a fettuccine Alfredo as they were when you were losing weight. Consider the glorious delights of a fettuccine or fettuccelle tossed in a white truffle sauce or a delicate herb pasta in a light béchamel, thinned with heavy cream. Try tiny shells (conchigliette) or little bow ties (farfalle) in olive oil and garlic with lightly sautéed crunchy garden vegetables. To find out just how varied "pasta with pleasure" can be, buy one of the many books now available that deal exclusively with pasta and its sauces. These books will jog your imagination and start your creative, as well as digestive, juices flowing. Visit your nearest gourmet store, and if it's not already there, you will more than likely soon have a large selection of fresh and frozen pastas to choose from—everything from the finest capelli d'angelo (angel's hair) to a hearty dark-green spinach lasagna.

Insalata di Pasta
(Pasta Salad)

3 Tbs. olive oil

1 lb. small shells, bow ties, or rotelle (corkscrew-shaped pasta)

½ bunch broccoli

½ head cauliflower

10 asparagus tips

½ lb. snow peas

2 sweet red peppers

1 green pepper

⅓ cup heavy cream

1 cup homemade mayonnaise, either aïoli or mixed with ½ cup pesto sauce (p. 220)

Herbs of your choice: thyme, basil (preferably fresh)

Freshly ground black pepper, to taste

In a large pot of boiling water, add 1 tablespoon olive oil, and cook the noodles until just al dente. Drain immediately. Rinse in cold water. Toss with 2 tablespoons olive oil in a large bowl. Set aside to cool.

Cut the broccoli and cauliflower into florets and parboil. You want them to remain crisp, so be careful not to overcook them. Two to 3 minutes should be sufficient if the florets are small enough. Drain and refresh under cold water. Cook the asparagus tips the same way. Refresh. The snow peas will need only about 15 seconds of cooking. Refresh immediately.

Place the red and green peppers under the broiler, char them on all sides, and peel off the skin. Cut into strips.

Bit by bit, whisk the heavy cream into the mayonnaise to thin it sufficiently so that it will coat the pasta. You may not need all the cream, depending on the consistency of your mayonnaise.

Combine the pasta with the vegetables. Toss to coat with the mayonnaise cream. Add herbs, either fresh or dried, grind black pepper over all, and toss. Chill and serve.

YIELD   4 servings.

Fettuccine with White Truffles

---

1 oz. white truffles
1 Tbs. olive oil
1 lb. fettuccine

5 Tbs. unsalted butter
Freshly ground white pepper

Slice truffles paper-thin and reserve any juice. (It is best to use a special truffle slicer for this purpose, which will enable you to shave the truffles paper-thin for the fullest taste.)

In a large pot of boiling water to which you have added 1 tablespoon of oil, add fettuccine and cook while stirring, just until pasta is al dente. (If fettuccine is fresh, this will be less than 1

minute after pasta is added and water returns to the boil. Dried
fettuccine will take about 8 to 10 minutes at a full rolling boil.)

Immediately add 1 cup cold water to the boiling pasta to stop
the cooking. Drain.

In a large sauté pan, melt the butter. Add the drained pasta and
toss. Top with freshly ground white pepper, the white truffles, and
any reserved truffle juice.

Serve immediately.

YIELD   4 servings.

Trenette con Funghi
(Narrow Noodles with
Wild Mushrooms)

---

4 Tbs. unsalted butter
5 Tbs. olive oil
¼ cup onion, minced
2 Tbs. shallots, minced
3 cloves garlic, minced
¼ cup tomato paste
2–3 cups vegetable stock
3 bay leaves
1 tsp. fresh rosemary (or ½ tsp.
   dried)

1½ ounces dried wild
   mushrooms (use porcini,
   morels, chanterelles, or a
   combination of varieties)
Freshly ground white pepper, to
   taste
½ cup heavy cream
1 lb. trenette (narrow, flat
   ribbon noodles)

Heat butter and oil in a sauté pan until melted. Add onion,
shallots, and garlic, and sauté until lightly colored. Add tomato
paste. Whisk together.

Add 2 cups stock, bay leaves, and rosemary. Simmer on low
flame until thickened, about 45 minutes to 1 hour. (Add additional
stock to thin sauce, if necessary.)

Meanwhile, soak the dried mushrooms in 1 cup water for about ½ hour. Drain and dry. Cut into bite-sized chunks.

Start heating large pot of water. While waiting for it to boil, stir mushrooms into sauce. Add pepper and heavy cream. Cook the trenette until just al dente. (If the trenette are fresh, start testing for doneness about 5 seconds after water returns to boil). Meanwhile, heat sauce just to boiling.

Drain trenette, sauce, and serve.

YIELD   4 servings.

Pasta Rosa alla Panna
(Red Pasta in a Butter and
Cream Sauce)

Try to find pasta rosa for this recipe. It's a fresh pasta dough made with pureed beets, giving it a luscious deep red color that's lovely to see when tossed with the delicate white cream sauce.

1 Tbs. olive oil

1 lb. pasta rosa (spinach
    fettuccine can be
    substituted)

8 Tbs. unsalted butter
    (approximately)

4 egg yolks

½ cup heavy cream

Bring a large pot of water to the boil. Add oil and cook the pasta until al dente.

While the pasta is boiling, melt 2 tablespoons butter in a sauté pan.

In a small bowl, whisk the yolks together until thickened. Then whisk in the heavy cream and set aside.

When the pasta is ready, drain it thoroughly. Run under cool water, drain again and add it to the sauté pan. Add 4 to 6 more tablespoons butter and toss. Pour on the egg yolk and cream sauce, and toss very quickly. Heat through but do not allow to cook or the egg will coagulate.

Serve immediately.

YIELD   4 servings.

Gnocchi with Sage Butter

You will also enjoy gnocchi served with a marinara sauce.

1½ lbs. boiling potatoes,   ½ Tbs. oil
   unpeeled
1½ cups flour

Sage Butter:

½ cup unsalted butter   2 cloves garlic, minced
4 Tbs. fresh sage leaves, finely
   chopped (or 2 Tbs. dried)

Make Sage Butter: Melt butter and add sage leaves and garlic. Cook over gentle heat for 5 minutes. Let butter stand for about 1 hour to develop flavor.

Boil potatoes until tender when pierced with a fork. Drain and peel them, and purée in processor or put through ricer while still warm.

Place puréed potatoes in bowl and slowly add flour until mixture is smooth and homogeneous, but still sticky.

Shape dough by rolling into long and narrow sausage shapes, about the diameter of a nickel. Keep work area lightly floured. Then, with a sharp knife, cut on the diagonal into pieces about 1 inch long.

Shape into small crescent shapes.

Cook gnocchi in 5 quarts of rapidly boiling water to which you have added the oil to prevent sticking. Stir.

When gnocchi rise to surface, allow to cook 1 more minute, then remove with slotted spoon and drain.

Serve gnocchi with warm sage butter poured over them.

YIELD   4 servings.

Risotto alla Milanese
(Rice in the Style of Milan)

In a perfectly cooked risotto, each grain of rice is creamy but still distinct and al dente, a balance of qualities best achieved with Arborio, a particularly plump, pearly, short-grained rice from Italy. Capable of absorbing an uncommon amount of cooking liquid while still retaining a nugget of resistance, Arborio is the rice of choice for this famous dish.

3 Tbs. unsalted butter	Pinch of thyme
1 Tbs. minced onion	Freshly ground white pepper, to
1 clove garlic, minced	taste
1 cup Arborio rice	1 pinch saffron threads
4 cups water or vegetable stock	½ cup heavy cream, at room
Pinch of oregano	temperature

In a covered, 4- to 6-quart heavy pot, melt 2 tablespoons of the butter until bubbling gently. Add the minced onion and garlic, and sauté over a low flame until the onion is softened.

Stir in the rice, coat it completely with the butter and onion, and keep stirring for several minutes. Then begin to add the water or stock a cup at a time, mixing well after each addition and stirring until the liquid is absorbed.

Stir in the oregano, thyme, and pepper. Rub the saffron threads between your thumb and forefinger and dissolve in a cup of stock. Add to rice and stir gently until all the moisture is absorbed. Continue in this manner—adding stock and stir-cooking—until the rice is tender but still chewy. (It may not be necessary to use all the liquid called for in the list of ingredients.)

Fold in the remaining tablespoon of softened butter and the heavy cream. Serve immediately.

YIELD   4 servings.

Risotto con Asparagi
(Rice with Asparagus)

---

1 lb. fresh young asparagus,
    washed and lightly peeled*
3 Tbs. butter
1 Tbs. minced onion or shallot
1 clove garlic, minced
1 cup Arborio rice (see Risotto
    alla Milanese, p. 250)

Freshly ground pepper, to taste
4 cups water or vegetable stock
1 cup heavy cream
2 Tbs. fresh summer savory or
    thyme (or 1 Tbs. dried)

Slice asparagus into ½-inch lengths cut on the diagonal.

Make risotto as described in recipe for Risotto alla Milanese, but add the sliced asparagus to the sauté of onions, garlic, and rice. If using dried herbs, add at this time.

When the risotto is ready, fold in fresh herbs and serve.

YIELD   4 servings.

*Almost any other vegetable can be substituted for the asparagus.

Pâte Feuilletée Fine
(Puff Pastry)

4½ cups unbleached flour (use
    dry measuring cups, dipped
    and leveled)
1⅓ cups water

10½ Tbs. unsalted butter,
    melted
1 lb. (4 sticks) unsalted butter

Make the détrempe: Place flour in a large bowl. Form a well in the center. Add the water and the melted butter to the well. Starting at the center of the well, use your fingers to begin mixing the flour into the liquid center, beginning with a small amount and gradually adding more and more flour to the liquid. Form this mass into a ball, knead once or twice, form into a 1½-inch-high square, wrap in plastic wrap, and refrigerate for 30 minutes.

Lightly flour 1 pound of butter. Place the long way between 2 sheets of wax paper, and begin flattening and elongating the butter by tapping it with a heavy rolling pin. When the butter is approximately 5 inches by 12 inches, fold it in 3 by scraping it up and turning it over onto itself as you would a business letter. Make a ¼ turn of the butter and repeat the above procedure. Flour the surface on both top and bottom, place between two sheets of wax paper, and begin tapping it out to elongate it.

N.B.: The butter must remain cold or it will begin to stick to the paper and will necessitate the use of too much flour to roll it and elongate it. So work quickly and press it out as evenly as possible, continuing this procedure 4 or 5 times until the butter is an elongated rectangle of approximately 5 inches by 14 inches between 2 pieces of wax paper. Refrigerate for 15 minutes.

It is essential that both the détrempe and the butter be at approximately the same temperature because they will now be folded together, and the butter must not under any circumstances bleed through the flour détrempe.

On a pastry marble (which will maintain the cold temperature of the pastry for the longest period of time), roll out the détrempe to a size approximately 4 or so inches longer and wider than the butter. This will allow enough room to enclose the butter when it is laid over the détrempe. Place the rectangle of butter in the center of the détrempe, fold the edges up over the butter so they meet, and press the pastry together to seal the butter inside. Now, with a heavy rolling pin, roll the pastry into a somewhat larger rectangle, approximately 20 inches long. From the bottom up, fold the pastry into thirds as you would a business letter, give the pastry a ¼ turn clockwise, and repeat the rolling/folding procedure one more time. You have now given the pastry 2 turns. Wrap in plastic wrap and refrigerate to rest the dough and relax the gluten in the flour so that the dough will not shrink back when rolled.

After a rest of about 1 hour, place the pastry on the floured work surface and begin the rolling and folding for 2 more turns. Refrigerate, wrapped in plastic wrap, for 2 more hours.

Make 2 more turns, so that you've completed 6 in all. The pastry is now ready to use. Keep it chilled until ready to roll it.

Puff-Pastry Tourte with Leek and Mushroom Filling

---

2 lbs. leeks
6 Tbs. unsalted butter
1½ Tbs. flour
¾ cup heavy cream
Freshly ground white pepper, to
  taste
Pinch cayenne
2 tsp. fresh thyme (or 1 tsp.
  dried)

Freshly ground or grated
  nutmeg
¾ lb. mushrooms, sliced
1 recipe for puff pastry (keep
  pastry cold until ready to
  roll and fill)
1 egg yolk beaten with 1 Tbs.
  water to make a glaze

Preheat oven to 475°.

Prepare the filling. Make 2 long, crosswise slices down through the green of the leeks and a little way into the white. Wash carefully under cold running water to make sure you've removed all the sand. Slice the leeks into very thin rounds. Melt 2 tablespoons butter in a heavy sauté pan and cook the leeks over moderate heat, stirring occasionally, until they begin to wilt but not brown. Add 2 more tablespoons butter, cover, and slowly steam the leeks in the butter. Uncover, stir in 1½ tablespoons flour, blend in well, cook for 3 or 4 more minutes, and set aside.

Place the cream in a small heavy-bottomed saucepan and reduce over high heat by about half. Stir the cream into the leeks and add pepper, cayenne, thyme, and nutmeg. Reheat, stirring until thickened.

Melt 2 tablespoons butter in a sauté pan and add mushrooms. Sauté until mushrooms are lightly browned and all their moisture has evaporated. Stir into leek mixture and set aside.

You will need only ⅔ of the puff pastry for this recipe. Cut in

3; reserve 2 sections and freeze the third. On a floured marble or pastry board, roll out 1 piece of pastry until it is ⅛-inch thick. Using a 9-inch vol-au-vent cutter or a 9-inch pot cover, cut out a circle of pastry. Place circle on a buttered cookie sheet which has been sprinkled with cold water. Place leek and mushroom mixture in a mound in the center of the pastry. With a pastry brush and water, paint a circle around the mound of filling, taking care not to allow it to drip off the edge of the dough circle. (This would cause the layers of dough to stick together and inhibit the rising of the pastry.) Roll top half or cover of tourte 1/16-inch thicker than the bottom. Cut as you did the top and place over the bottom layer and the filling, gently pressing all around the outside of the circle of filling to join the two circles of pastry. Poke a steam hole in the top of the tourte.

Using the dull side of a small paring knife, scallop the outside edge of the tourte by pressing in the edges of the pastry at 1½-inch intervals. Decorate the top with the sharp side of the knife—draw curving lines from the center to the outside edge.

With egg yolk and water glaze, paint the top of the tourte, taking care not to allow the glaze to drip over the edges of the tourte.

Bake in a 475° oven for 20 minutes, reduce temperature to 400°, and bake for 35 minutes longer, until golden brown and cooked through. If you feel the top or part of the top is browning too quickly toward the end of the cooking time, cover that part loosely with aluminum foil.

Serve immediately.

YIELD   6–8 servings.

VARIATION   *Spinach-Dill Tourte:* Substitute 2 lbs. chopped spinach and 2 Tbs. chopped dill for the leeks.

Feuilletées
(Individual Puff-Pastry Shells)

Individual feuilletées can be prepared in advance, frozen raw, and then simply popped into the oven and baked just before serving.

1 recipe for puff pastry
1 Tbs. water

1 egg yolk beaten with 1 Tbs. water to make a glaze

Preheat oven to 475°.

It is easiest to work with and cut the feuilletées if the puff pastry is divided in 3 before rolling. Using a large, sharp, floured knife, cut the pastry crosswise into 3 equal pieces. Refrigerate 2 of them while working on the other. Flour the work surface and roll the pastry into a square approximately ⅛-inch thick. Using a ruler, cut pastry into squares of about 5 inches. Cut off ½-inch strips all around and place the squares on a pastry sheet rinsed with cold water.

Brush the top outside edges of the squares with water, taking care not to let water run down the sides of the pastry shell or it will not rise properly. Now gently place the strips all around the edges of the pastry squares overlapping at the corners, and press down lightly. (You are creating a little box which, when it rises, will serve to encase any vegetable filling.) With the blunt side of a small paring knife, lightly press a ¼-inch scallop pattern around the outside edge of the pastry shell. Glaze the borders of this box with egg/water mixture (again being careful not to let the liquid run down the sides). Prick the center of the box with a fork so that it will not rise as high as the outside.

Bake in 475° oven for 5 minutes, reduce temperature to 400°, and bake 8 to 10 minutes longer.

Remove to a rack and cool. Carefully scoop out center of square to allow room for the filling.

Fill with any vegetable puree or any fresh-cooked vegetables in sauce, for example, fresh asparagus tips with Hollandaise Sauce (see p. 00) over all.

For feuilletées with spinach and dill, simply make the filling for the spinach/dill tourte, pile into the feuilletées, and serve piping hot.

YIELD   6 servings.

Pâte Brisée

Short-crust pastry for vegetable tarts or tart shells for vegetable purees:

1¼ cups unbleached flour
½ cup whole wheat pastry flour or unbleached stone-ground pastry flour (available in health food stores)
12 Tbs. (1½ sticks) unsalted butter

¼–⅓ cup ice water (Flour, even the same brand, will react differently every time you use it. Its moisture content varies considerably and that, and weather conditions, which also affect how much liquid it can absorb, will determine how much water you use.)

Combine the unbleached and whole wheat pastry flours in the bowl of the food processor and process for 2 or 3 seconds to blend.

Cut the frozen butter into 12 equal parts and place in bowl of processor.

Process on and off (pulse) 10 or 12 times or until the butter is combined with the flour and is broken up into small pea-sized pieces. N.B.: Do not overprocess, or pastry will be tough.

With the machine running, add the ice water, being sure to add only as much as is needed to make the dough begin to stick together. It will start to gather in a ball on top of the blade.

Remove the dough immediately and smear out on the work surface to give a final blending to the flour and butter. Shape into a ball and refrigerate for at least 1 hour before rolling. This will give the gluten in the flour the opportunity to relax before rolling.

(This dough can be made in a large bowl if you prefer. Combine the flour, make a well in the center, add the cold-but-not-frozen butter, using your fingertips, 2 knives, or a pastry blender, blend with flour until small morsels are formed, add the water, mix, and form into a ball. Refrigerate.)

To roll, form, and bake: Preheat oven to 450°. Generously butter a 9-inch tart tin (with removable bottom). (A 9-inch pie tin is acceptable.) On a floured work surface (a pastry marble is the best, but a board will do), roll the dough into a circle approximately 11 to 12 inches in diameter. Roll the dough back onto the rolling pin and unroll gently onto the tart tin. Carefully ease the dough into the tin, pressing into the grooves with your thumb. Roll the rolling pin over the top to remove the excess dough. Refrigerate to set or freeze for 5 minutes, then proceed. Place a piece of buttered aluminum foil over the dough and gently mold it into the shell. Fill with metal baking beans (if unavailable, rice or dried beans will do), and bake at 450° for 13–14 minutes. Remove foil and beans and bake for 3 minutes more. You now have a partially baked tart shell baked blind, which can be used for any vegetable filling.

YIELD   1 9-inch or 10-inch tart shell.

Tarte Provençale

2 lbs. tomatoes, preferably
   Italian plum variety
4 Tbs. olive oil
4 medium or 5 small zucchini
Freshly ground black pepper, to
   taste
2 or 3 cloves garlic (to taste),
   minced

½ cup fresh bread crumbs
2 Tbs. chopped Italian parsley
1 8- or 9-inch pâte brisée tart
   shell, baked blind (see
   Glossary) for 15 minutes or
   until set
5 leaves fresh basil, minced

Preheat oven to 400°.

Plunge the tomatoes in boiling water for 10 seconds. Peel, slice, and seed them. Cut into dice.

Sauté tomatoes in 1 tablespoon of olive oil until just softened and still a bit firm. Remove from pan and set aside.

Cut zucchini into about the same size dice as the tomatoes, and sauté in 1 tablespoon olive oil until tender but crunchy. Set alongside the tomatoes, and grind fresh pepper over both.

Sauté half the garlic in 1 tablespoon olive oil until softened, add the bread crumbs and chopped parsley, and sauté just until fully moistened.

In the precooked pastry shell, assemble the cooked zucchini and tomatoes, and top with minced basil, the remaining minced garlic, and the sautéed bread-crumb mixture. Dribble remaining tablespoon of olive oil over all and bake in preheated 400° oven for 20 minutes. Serve immediately.

YIELD   6–7 servings.

Zucchini Pancakes

You can substitute carrot for the zucchini.

2 lbs. zucchini
1 onion, minced very fine
3 egg yolks, lightly beaten
1 cup whole wheat pastry flour
   (or 1 cup unbleached flour)
1 tsp. double-acting baking
   powder (the low-sodium
   variety available at the
   health food store)

Freshly ground black pepper, to
   taste
Freshly ground or grated
   nutmeg
1 Tbs. minced fresh basil
   (or ½ Tbs. dried)
4 Tbs. olive oil
Safflower oil for frying
Sour cream (optional)

Wash and grate the zucchini. Combine with minced onion. Stir in egg yolks, flour, baking powder, pepper, nutmeg, and basil. Stir in olive oil and allow batter to rest for 15 minutes.

Film a large frying pan with safflower oil. Drop batter into hot oil and flatten into pancakes. Brown, and turn to brown other side. Drain on paper towels and keep warm.

Continue with the rest of the batter, adding oil as necessary. Serve with sour cream. (They are also delicious served plain.)

YIELD   4–5 servings.

Asparagus in Garlic-Herb Bread Crumbs

Almost any other vegetable can be substituted for asparagus.

1 bunch asparagus, about 2
    dozen
7 Tbs. butter
1 cup bread crumbs (make them
    from your own homemade
    day-old French bread)

1 tsp. dried thyme (or 2 tsp.
    fresh)
1 tsp. fresh basil, minced
1 tsp. oregano
1 tsp. Italian parsley
Small pinch ginger (optional)
3 cloves garlic, minced

Select firm, fresh asparagus. The tips should be tight and closed.

Wash asparagus, cut off the woody ends of the stalks, and trim spears to equal length.

Tie together in 2 bunches and cook in boiling water to cover for about 10 minutes, or until just fork tender. Drain and set aside.

In a sauté pan, melt the butter and add the bread crumbs, sautéing until lightly colored. Add the herbs and garlic, stirring gently to combine. Pour over the asparagus and serve.

YIELD   4 servings.

Duxelles
(Mushroom Stuffing)

Use duxelles to fill mushroom caps, fill a puff-pastry casing, or simply as a delicious vegetable dish all by itself.

4 Tbs. unsalted butter
1 onion, minced
2 shallots, minced
1 lb. mushrooms, minced
    (include stems)

Freshly ground pepper, to taste
Fresh herbs (1 tsp. thyme,
    oregano, or tarragon)
    (optional)

In a medium sauté pan, melt the butter, add the onions and shallots, and sauté gently until wilted. Do not brown.

Add the mushrooms, raise the flame, and cook the mushrooms over high heat to evaporate all the moisture in them. As they are cooking, shake the pan back and forth over the flame so that the mixture does not stick and the heat is evenly distributed. When the moisture has evaporated, the duxelles is ready to serve.

Season with pepper and fresh herbs, if desired.

YIELD   approx. 1 cup.

Vegetarian Antipasto

When you buy the vegetables for this dish, choose them with particular care, for freshness and appearance are very important here.

1 lb. carrots

1 large bunch broccoli, over
   1 lb.

1 large cauliflower

½ small, tight head of red
   cabbage

3 large artichokes

4 small red peppers (the long,
   spicy variety of red Italian
   peppers)

1 lb. fresh mushrooms

2 firm, small zucchini

1 bulb fennel (if unavailable,
   use fennel seeds)

4 tomatoes

1 large red onion

¼ cup rice vinegar

2 cloves garlic, minced

2 Tbs. shallots, minced

Freshly ground black pepper, to
   taste

½ cup olive oil

Wash and scrape the carrots and cut into 3-inch-long julienne, break the broccoli and cauliflower into bite-sized florets and wash them, shred the cabbage, and cut the outside leaves and the large stem from the artichokes.

Place the artichokes in a large pot of boiling water and simmer until still firm but tender when pierced at the bottom. Drain, remove all the leaves and the choke, and cut the bottoms into large chunks.

The carrots, broccoli, and cauliflower should be separately cooked in simmering water until just tender but still firm when pierced with a fork. Shred the cabbage, place in a bowl, and pour boiling water over it. Drain after 3 minutes. Refresh all the vegetables with cold water immediately after cooking them. This will help them retain their bright color.

Char the peppers over an open flame, cool them, and peel off the skin, seed, and cut into thin strips.

Remove the stems from the mushrooms and slice the caps paper-thin.

Peel and slice the zucchini into julienne.

Pull apart the fennel bulb and slice into long, thin strips. (Discard the stalks, or use to flavor soup.)

Slice the tomatoes into wedges and remove the seeds.

Slice the red onion into thin rounds.

Prepare the antipasto platter, arranging the vegetables in a circular pattern and working from the outside toward the center, with the larger pieces on the outside. Be sure to contrast the colors as well as the sizes. Sprinkle the mushrooms over all.

Sprinkle the vinegar over the antipasto, season with garlic, shallots, and pepper, toss lightly. Then drizzle with oil and serve.

YIELD   4 servings.

Potato Salad

3 lbs. small new potatoes (the red-skinned ones make the prettiest salad)
¼ tsp. dry mustard
Freshly ground white pepper
2 Tbs. rice vinegar
¼–⅓ cup oil (olive, or sesame and olive mixed)

2 Tbs. fresh tarragon, minced (or 1½ tsp. dried)
½ cup shallots, minced
1 Tbs. chervil, minced (or 1½ tsp. dried)
3 cloves garlic, minced
2 Tbs. Italian parsley, minced

Wash the potatoes and place in a large saucepan with cold water to cover. Bring to the boil and simmer until just fork tender (15 to 20 minutes at the most). Drain and let cool just a bit.

While potatoes are boiling, make a vinaigrette. Combine the mustard, pepper, and vinegar. Then whisk in the oil until dressing thickens. Add the tarragon, shallots, chervil, and garlic.

Place the vinaigrette in a large bowl and top with the potatoes. Toss. Sprinkle with minced parsley and serve warm.

YIELD   4 servings.

Champignons Sauvage aux Herbes
à la Crème
(Wild Mushrooms with Herbs
and Cream)

There are many varieties of wild mushrooms available today. If you are unable to find them at a local gourmet shop, many of the food catalogues and mail-order houses have them available. Or watch for advertisements in the backs of the home and food magazines.

1 lb. fresh wild mushrooms (choose one variety or combine cèpes, morels, chanterelles, or porcini) (or 3–4 ounces dried)
4 Tbs. unsalted butter
4 Tbs. minced shallots
1 clove garlic, minced

2 Tbs. tarragon (or 1 tsp. dried)
2 Tbs. chervil (or 1 tsp. dried)
2 Tbs. thyme (or 1 tsp. dried)
2 Tbs. Italian parsley
Freshly ground black pepper, to taste
6 Tbs. heavy cream
1 pâte feuilletée "fleuron" for each serving (see below and p. 252)

If mushrooms are dried, soak until softened, drain, and wipe dry. They will approximately double their size.

Cut mushrooms into quarters or large bite-sized chunks.

Melt the butter in a large sauté pan. Add the shallots and cook until wilted. Add the garlic and sauté briefly.

Place the mushrooms in the sauté pan and cook quickly, 2 or 3 minutes, just until heated through. If exposed to too much heat, they will begin to wilt and lose their moisture.

Sprinkle on the herbs and pepper, and add the cream. Toss all together until well combined, remove from flame, and serve immediately.

Garnish each plate with a fleuron. A fleuron is a small crescent, about 3 inches in length, made from puff-pastry scraps (keep them in the freezer, never discard them!). Roll out dough, cut crescent shape with cookie or pastry cutter, paint with glaze of 1 egg yolk beaten with 1 Tbs. water, place on cookie sheet, and bake at 475° for 5 minutes. Lower heat to 400° and bake 8 to 10 minutes longer until puffed and golden.

YIELD   4 servings.

Pizza con Cipolle
(Pizza with Onions)

A Sicilian-style pizza with onions, garlic, and herbs—delicious!

Dough:

1 cake fresh yeast (or 1 pkg. active dry yeast)
⅓ cup tepid water
1½ cups tepid water

2 cups whole wheat flour
2 cups bread flour or unbleached flour

Filling:

6 Tbs. unsalted butter
½ cup olive oil
8 onions, sliced paper-thin
8 garlic cloves, minced
1 cup bread crumbs (p. 292)

½ cup chopped Italian parsley
3 Tbs. oregano
Freshly ground black pepper, to taste

Make the Dough: Place yeast in ⅓ cup tepid water (90° to 100°). Stir to dissolve. Place in bowl of food processor, process 10 seconds. Add 1½ cups tepid water and again process 10 seconds. Then, by level cupfuls, add the flours to processor, running for 30 seconds after each addition, until absorbed. When adding final cup, do not put in full amount at once. (Flour absorbs moisture differently at different times. Add it gradually until you achieve the texture described below.) Knead the dough in the processor for about 1 minute until it begins to ball up and accumulate on the top of the blade and is a somewhat sticky, homogeneous mass. Flour your hands, remove the dough to a floured surface, and knead for a minute or so by hand.

Form into a large fat pancake shape, place on a lightly floured plate, sprinkle the top with flour, and cover with plastic wrap. Refrigerate for about 6 hours before making pizza.

Make the Filling: In a large sauté pan or skillet, melt 3 tablespoons butter with ¼ cup olive oil. When heated, add the onion slices and half the minced garlic. Over a low flame, allow to cook until onions are completely wilted, but not brown (20 to 25 minutes). In a smaller sauté pan, melt the remaining 3 tablespoons butter, add the bread crumbs, and sauté until golden in color. Add the remaining garlic, the chopped parsley, and the oregano to the bread crumbs, mix thoroughly, and cook until flavors are blended. Grind black pepper over all, mix, and set aside until ready to assemble pizza.

Preheat oven to 450°. Remove dough from refrigerator and allow to rest at room temperature for 15 minutes. Meanwhile, grease a large jelly-roll pan (11 inches by 18 inches), preferably the heavy black variety, with 1 tablespoon olive oil. Using a rolling pin on a floured work surface, roll the dough into a rectangle approximately the same size as the pan. Place the dough in the pan and with your hands work it into the corners of the pan, making it higher at the sides than in the middle. Bake in a 450° oven for 15 to 20 minutes, until risen and lightly browned.

Remove from oven. Spread onions over the pizza, top with bread-crumb mixture, sprinkle with remaining olive oil, return to oven, and bake 10 to 15 minutes longer, until browned and cooked through. Cut in large squares and serve.

YIELD   5–6 servings.

To make Dough by Hand: Place the yeast in ⅓ cup tepid water and stir to dissolve. In a large bowl, place the 2 cups of whole wheat and 2 cups of white flour and combine. Make a well in the center, add the dissolved yeast and the 1½ cups additional water. Using your index finger, begin stirring the flour into the liquid. Work the mixture together well, turn out onto a floured work surface, and begin kneading, pushing, and turning the dough exactly as you would if you were making bread. If the dough becomes sticky as you knead, sprinkle on a bit more flour. The dough is ready when it becomes smooth and elastic. Kneading to this point should take approximately 10 minutes. Proceed with recipe as above.

Tabbouleh

2 tomatoes
2 small beets
1 cup bulgur (bulgur is cracked
    wheat; found at health food
    stores)
¼ cup minced scallion
¼ cup thinly sliced mushrooms
¼ cup finely minced carrots

4 or 5 minced fresh mint leaves,
    if available (or 2 tsp. dried
    dill weed)
Pinch of thyme
½ cup white rice vinegar
½ cup sesame oil or safflower
    oil
Boston or romaine lettuce
    leaves

Plunge the tomatoes in boiling water for 10 seconds. Then peel, seed, and dice.

Parboil the beets, let cool, peel, and mince.

Wash bulgur under cold water and then steep in cold water to cover for 15 to 20 minutes.

After soaking, drain bulgur, squeeze it to extract as much

moisture as possible, and wrap in a kitchen towel to dry it still further.

Put bulgur in a large bowl and toss with the raw vegetables and herbs.

Combine the vinegar and oil and toss with mixture.

Serve on salad plates atop the lettuce leaves.

YIELD   4 servings.

Cornmeal Pancakes with Sour Cream

1¼ cups stone-ground
    cornmeal
¼ cup unbleached flour
1 tsp. baking soda
1 cup heavy cream (additional
    ½ cup, if necessary)
¾ cup sour cream

4 Tbs. unsalted butter, melted
3 egg yolks, beaten lightly
4 Tbs. unsalted butter
Additional sour cream to serve
    with pancakes

Combine dry ingredients in mixing bowl.

Beat heavy cream into sour cream, add melted butter and egg yolks, whisking gently, then fold into dry ingredients. Do not overbeat. If batter becomes too thick, add additional ½ cup heavy cream.

Melt 2 tablespoons butter in a skillet. When foaming, spoon batter in, making pancakes about 4 inches in diameter. Turn pancakes when bubbles appear on the surface, and brown on other side. Remove from pan and keep warm. Replenish the butter in the skillet as necessary, until all the batter is used.

Pass pancakes with sour cream on the side.

YIELD   4 servings.

Sloppy Sue, or BHD Chili

2 Tbs. olive oil
1 onion, sliced very thin
2 tomatoes, seeded and
    chopped
¼ lb. mushrooms, minced

Dash of Mel's Secret Seasoning
    (p. 224)
½ lb. green peas
1 small onion pita or 1 slice of
    rye bread

In a small sauté pan, heat the olive oil. Add the sliced onion and cook over low heat until wilted, about 20 minutes.

Add the tomatoes, the minced mushrooms, and Mel's Secret, raise the heat, and sauté until all ingredients are well combined.

Meanwhile, bring 6 cups of water to the boil, add the peas, and cook for 4 to 5 minutes, just until crisp/tender. Drain and add to onion/tomato mixture. Cook until all vegetables are tender.

Open the pocket in the pita bread, fill with Sloppy Sue mixture, and serve. Or serve open-faced on rye bread, or on its own with garlic rounds (p. 291) on the side.

YIELD   1 serving.

Hamburger with Everything Without

3 Tbs. sesame oil
1 medium onion, thinly sliced
1 buttered hamburger bun
1 Spanish onion, sliced

Lettuce
1 medium-sized tomato, sliced
2 Tbs. mayonnaise (p. 219)
1 Tbs. Mazel ketchup (p. 222)

In a medium sauté pan, heat the oil and sauté the regular onion until lightly browned. Press the hamburger bun into the pan as the onions finish browning. It will absorb the flavors of the onion, as well as the oil.

On the bun, place the grilled onions, the raw onion slices, the lettuce, and the sliced tomato. Top with mayonnaise and ketchup.

YIELD 1 serving.

Eggless Benedict

Pure carb all the way!

1 English muffin
2 slices of tomato

2 slices of giant mushroom cap
½ cup Hollandaise Sauce
(p. 214)

Preheat oven to 350°.

Toast and butter the muffin. On each half of the muffin, make an open-faced sandwich of a slice of tomato and a slice of mushroom cap. Place on heatproof dish, put in oven, and warm through (about 10 minutes).

Remove from oven and top with warm Hollandaise Sauce. Serve immediately.

YIELD 1 serving.

BEEFING IT UP

Carpaccio

Carpaccio is raw beef sliced paper-thin and served with a piquant sauce. It is a more refined and rather elegant substitute for the better-known steak tartare. It is also the perfect hors d'oeuvre for an Open Protein supper. (The eye of the prime rib is the most tender and flavorful cut for this dish.)

¼ lb. beef per serving   Freshly ground black pepper, to
                                           taste

Sauce:
Delicious with either aïoli (p. 220), pesto (p. 220), a mustard-based mayonnaise (p. 220), or horseradish cream (p. 217).

Trim the meat of all fat and cut into paper-thin slices.
Arrange on a serving platter and serve with one of the sauces suggested above.

YIELD   1 serving.

Butterflied Leg of Lamb

¼ cup Dijon-style salt-free
mustard (or 2 Tbs. dried
mustard mixed with 2 tsp.
Fonds Brun—p. 236)
2 cloves garlic, mashed
1 tsp. fresh ginger, grated
1 Tbs. dried rosemary, crushed
(use a mortar and pestle or a
rolling pin)

Freshly ground black pepper, to
taste
2 Tbs. olive oil
1 leg of lamb, boned and
butterflied (ask your
butcher to do this for you)

In a small mixing bowl, combine the mustard, garlic, ginger, rosemary, and pepper. Drop by drop, whisk in the oil until marinade has a mayonnaise consistency.

Spread the marinade on the lamb and allow to marinate all day if possible.

Preheat broiler until hot. Broil 7 minutes on each side for rare. Increase time accordingly for better-done meat.

You may grill, on an open barbecue, about 10 minutes on each side for rare. Increase time accordingly for a greater degree of doneness.

YIELD   6 servings.

Steak au Poivre

2 Tbs. black or green
  peppercorns, crushed
4 1½-inch-thick shell steaks,
  boned and trimmed

3 Tbs. oil
1 cup heavy cream

Scatter the peppercorns on a large plate and coat the steaks on both sides by pressing them into the peppercorns.

In a large sauté pan, heat the oil until nearly smoking. Add the steaks and sauté over medium to high heat until rare (about 5 minutes on each side). Set aside to keep warm.

Pour off the fat in the pan, add the cream, raise the heat to high, and boil the cream until it thickens somewhat. Pour over the steaks, and serve.

YIELD   4 servings.

Veau Poêlé à la Moutarde (Casserole-Roasted Veal with Mustard)

2 lbs. boned shoulder of veal
3 garlic cloves, minced
1 tsp. rosemary, crushed (use a mortar and pestle or a rolling pin)
2 tsp. dried thyme
Freshly ground black pepper, to taste

2 Tbs. olive oil
3 Tbs. butter
⅔ cup veal stock (additional ½ to ¾ cups if needed)
2 Tbs. shallots
¼ cup Dijon-style salt-free mustard
½ cup heavy cream

Open roast and lay flat. Sprinkle on the minced garlic, rosemary, thyme, and pepper. Roll and tie roast with kitchen twine.

In a large, heavy-bottomed, covered saucepan or casserole, heat the oil and 2 tablespoons of the butter until foaming. Brown the meat well on all sides, pour the stock over the roast, reduce the heat, cover, and cook until fork tender. During the cooking, turn the meat to make sure it roasts evenly. Add more stock if the pan juices dry up during the cooking. The roast should take anywhere from 1½ hours to 2 hours to cook. It is done when the juices run clear when veal is pierced.

Remove roast from pan and set aside to keep warm. If no pan juices remain, stir in about ½ cup veal stock, raise heat, and scrape up the bits at the bottom of the roasting pan with a wooden spoon. Add the remaining butter, melt, add shallots, and cook until wilted (4 to 5 minutes). Whisk in the mustard, raise flame, pour in the cream, and heat until bubbling and thickened slightly. Pour over roast and serve.

YIELD   4–6 servings.

Sole en Papillote, Crème à l'Eschalote
(Sole in an "Envelope,"
Shallot Cream)

Cooked in aluminum foil or parchment paper, the fish steams in its own juices. The flavor is fresh and intense.

6 sprigs Italian parsley
3 shallots, minced
2 cloves garlic, minced
1½ lbs. lemon sole, divided
    into 4 servings

4 Tbs. unsalted butter
Freshly ground white pepper, to
    taste
2 cups Crème à l'Eschalote
    (p. 238; substitute fish
    stock for chicken stock)

Preheat oven to 500°.

Cut the aluminum foil in large heart shapes of approximately 15 inches in width and height. Oil the entire piece of foil, fold in half along the center seam of the heart, and open again.

Place the ingredients on ½ of each heart: Divide the parsley and distribute equally. Cover parsley with shallots and garlic. Top with a portion of the sole, a tablespoon of butter, and freshly ground pepper.

Place the baking dish in which the papillotes will cook in the oven to preheat.

Now fold over the other half of the heart so its edges match those of the first half. Starting at the bottom point, begin folding foil over on itself so that bit by bit you make a ½-inch border all the way to the top. Pinch the edges tightly to make sure you have an airtight packet of foil in which the fish can steam. Repeat with the other hearts.

Place the foil envelopes in the preheated baking dish. Bake for 5 minutes.

Serve the fish still enclosed in the foil, permitting each person to cut open his or her own papillote and enjoy the wonderful aroma that will arise from it.

Serve with Crème à l'Eschalote.

YIELD   4 servings.

Filets de Saumon à l'Oseille
(Salmon Fillets with Sorrel)

---

4 cups sorrel leaves, tightly
    packed (approx. 1 lb.)
4 Tbs. unsalted butter
2 shallots, minced
2 large fillets of fresh salmon
    (approx. 3–4 lbs. in all)

Freshly ground white pepper, to
    taste
1 qt., approximately, of court
    bouillon (p. 239)
1½ cups heavy cream

Wash, dry, and remove the heavy stems from the sorrel, and cut leaves into long, thin strips.

Preheat oven to 375°.

Choose a large, low-sided gratin dish, or use an enameled-iron roasting pan, to poach the fillets in the oven. The dish must be flameproof.

Grease the dish with 1 tablespoon of butter, sprinkle in the shallots, and add the fillets. Season with white pepper and add just enough court bouillon to nearly cover the fillets.

Place a piece of buttered wax paper over the fillets, buttered side down, and bring to a low simmer on top of the stove.

Place in the oven and cook for 10 to 12 minutes, or until fish is still moist but separates easily when poked with a fork.

Drain fillets and place the poaching liquid in a heavy-bottomed saucepan on top of the stove. Keep fish warm while preparing the sauce.

Bring fish-poaching liquid to the boil and reduce by about ⅓. Add the cream and, still over high heat, continue to reduce until thickened. Remove from heat, add the sorrel, then cook for just 1 minute more. Remove from heat and stir in remaining butter.

Pour the sauce over the poached salmon fillets and serve.

YIELD   4 servings.

Moules à la Marinière
(Steamed Mussels)

---

4 qts. fresh mussels, beards removed, soaked, and scrubbed clean

3 cloves garlic with husks left on, crushed with the flat side of a cleaver

½ cup chopped shallots

1 bay leaf

4 sprigs fresh thyme (or 2 tsp. dried)

4 sprigs fresh Italian parsley

Freshly ground black pepper, to taste

¼ tsp. hot red pepper flakes

1 cup fish stock (p. 238) (or ¾ cup water mixed with ¼ cup clam juice)

2 Tbs. fresh minced Italian parsley

Place the mussels, garlic, shallots, bay leaf, thyme, parsley, black pepper, and red pepper flakes in a large, heavy-bottomed saucepan. Pour in the fish stock, cover, and bring to the boil.

Steam the mussels over medium heat until they open (5 to 6 minutes). If any do not open, discard them.

Place the mussels in soup bowls, pour the cooking liquid over them, top with minced parsley, and serve.

YIELD   4 servings.

Moules Farcies à la Crème à l'Anis et au Thym (Stuffed Mussels with Cream, Anise, and Thyme)

---

4 qts. mussels, steamed open as
   in Moules à la Marinière
   (p. 278)
2 Tbs. unsalted butter
2 cloves garlic, minced

2 shallots, minced
½ cup heavy cream
Pinch thyme
Pinch star anise

Steam mussels for approximately 5 minutes until opened. Remove mussels from shells. Reserve half the shells to stuff.

Place mussels on work surface and chop into small pieces.

Melt 2 tablespoons of butter in sauté pan and add minced garlic and shallots. Cook until wilted. Add chopped mussels, cream, thyme and anise. Raise flame and reduce mixture quickly to about half.

Fill mussel shells with mixture, place on cookie sheet, and brown for 3 minutes under broiler. Serve immediately.

YIELD 3–4 servings.

Cold Seafood Salad

You will need about 3½ lbs. of seafood (weighed in the shell except for the scallops). Choose any combination of shrimp, scallops, crab, or lobster.

2½ Tbs. unsalted butter
¼ cup minced shallots
1 lb. shrimp, washed, peeled, and vein removed
½ lb. sea scallops (remove small tendon), washed and cut in half

½ cup court bouillon (p. 239)
1 live 1-lb. lobster
1 1-lb. crab or about 1 lb. of crab's legs
1 cup mayonnaise (protein variation, p. 219)
3 Tbs. fresh minced tarragon (or 1½ Tbs. dried)

Melt 2 tablespoons butter in a medium sauté pan. Sprinkle shallots over bottom of pan. Place the shrimp and the scallops over the shallots and add ½ cup court bouillon. With remaining ½ tablespoon butter, butter a sheet of waxed paper, lay it buttered side down over ingredients in pan. Put lid on pan and place over low heat. Cook 10 to 15 minutes, or until bouillon comes to a slow simmer. Strain, cool, and refrigerate.

Place 3 cups of water in a large saucepan or steamer, and bring to a boil. Add live lobster and crab, cover, and steam over medium heat for about 12 to 15 minutes, depending on their size. Drain, cool, and refrigerate.

To assemble the salad: Crack the lobster and crab, removing the meat in chunks and cutting it into 1-inch cubes. Place in large bowl. Add the shrimps and scallops.

Whisk the tarragon into the mayonnaise and toss with seafood. Refrigerate until ready to serve.

YIELD   4 servings.

Broiled Chicken with Herbal Mustard Coating

2 Tbs. dry mustard
2 Tbs. chicken stock (p. 235)
2 Tbs. fresh tarragon (or 1 Tbs. dried) *or* 1 Tbs. fresh rosemary (or 1½ tsp. dried)
1 tsp. freshly grated ginger
Freshly ground white pepper, to taste
Freshly ground or grated nutmeg, to taste
1 broiling chicken, cut into serving pieces

In a small bowl combine the dry mustard and the chicken stock. Add the herbs, ginger, pepper, and nutmeg and mix to a paste.

Coat the chicken pieces with the herbal mustard mixture. Allow to marinate for 1 hour.

Preheat oven to 350°.

Bake chicken for 30 minutes. Transfer to broiler, skin side up, and broil for 8 to 10 minutes until nicely browned. Serve immediately.

YIELD   3—4 servings.

Coq à l'Ail
(Chicken with Garlic)

Until you try this, you will never believe how sweet the garlic tastes when spread on the chicken before eating. It's sensational.

4–6 Tbs. oil

2 large roasting chickens, about 4 lbs. each, cut into serving pieces

4 Tbs. unsalted butter

1 cup minced shallots

2 Tbs. tarragon

2 large heads of garlic (or 3 small), separated into cloves, husks left on. There should be at least 30 fair-sized cloves.

Freshly ground black pepper, to taste

10 sprigs Italian parsley

1 cup chicken stock (p. 235)

Preheat oven to 375°.

In a large cast-iron or heavy-bottomed casserole, heat 4 tablespoons of the oil until very hot. Meanwhile, wipe the chicken parts with paper towels until they are completely dry. Brown the chicken in the oil, skin side first, and turn to brown on other side. When the pieces are brown, remove them and set aside. Continue until all the pieces are browned, adding more oil if necessary. When the browning is completed, discard the remaining fat.

Melt the butter in the casserole. Add shallots, the browned chicken, tarragon, garlic, pepper, and parsley. Pour the chicken stock over all.

Cover the casserole with a tight-fitting lid, and place in preheated oven for 1 hour and 15 minutes.

When chicken is ready, remove to a serving platter. Strain the pan juices to serve alongside. Remove the garlic cloves from the strained-out herbs and scatter them over the chicken. When you serve, distribute some to each person. The softened garlic is to be eaten slipped from the husk and spread on the chicken.

YIELD   4 servings.

Suprêmes de Volaille à l'Estragon
(Chicken Breasts with Tarragon)

---

3 Tbs. unsalted butter
6 chicken breast halves,
  skinned, boned
¼ cup minced shallots
¾ cup chicken stock (p. 235)
2 Tbs. minced fresh tarragon
  (or 1 Tbs. dried)

Freshly ground white pepper, to
  taste
½ cup heavy cream
A few sprigs of fresh tarragon

Melt the butter in a large sauté pan. Add the breasts and over a low to medium flame sauté on both sides, just until they whiten and lose their raw pink color.

Sprinkle the shallots over the breasts, pour in the stock, add the tarragon and freshly ground pepper, cover, and gently poach for 5 minutes.

Remove cover and raise flame to high. Scraping bottom of pan with wooden spoon, begin reducing the stock until only about ¼ cup remains. Pour in the cream and, over a high flame, continue reducing sauce until thickened.

Remove the chicken to a warm serving platter, pour the sauce over it, garnish with a few tarragon sprigs, and serve immediately.

YIELD   4 servings.

Quenelles de Volaille
(Chicken Quenelles)

Light as air and delicious as they are, or topped with a sauce, or served in a flavorful chicken consommé.

1 lb. chicken breasts, skinned, boned
1½ cups heavy cream
Freshly ground white pepper, to taste
Freshly ground or grated nutmeg, to taste
1 egg yolk

Place the breasts and the cream in the freezer for about 15 minutes, until well chilled.

Cut chicken into cubes and place in the bowl of a food processor. Add pepper and nutmeg. Process for 30 seconds.

Add the egg yolk and gently blend it with the chicken. Process for 5 seconds.

With the machine running, add the heavy cream in a thin stream.

Transfer mixture to a bowl and refrigerate for 1 hour.

Butter an oval gratin dish large enough to accommodate all the quenelles in a single layer.

Shape the quenelles with two large soup spoons: Scoop up a spoonful of the mixture in one spoon, and round and shape it with another spoon dipped first into very hot water. As you complete each one, gently place it in the gratin dish. Continue until you have used up all the quenelle mixture.

Bring approximately 7 cups of water to the boil. Ladle gently over the quenelles just to cover, then place a piece of buttered wax paper that has been cut to the shape of the dish over the quenelles. (Place the buttered side down.) You are ready to poach the quenelles.

Bring to the simmer on top of the stove and simmer very gently for 5 minutes. Turn gently, replace the wax paper, and continue poaching for another 5 minutes. Remove and drain on paper towels.

Serve in chicken broth, or with Crème à l'Eschalote (p. 276), or with an herb or butter sauce.

YIELD   4 servings.

Pâté de Foies de Volaille
(Chicken Liver Pâté)

---

2 Tbs. minced shallots
1 Tbs. minced garlic
2 Tbs. unsalted butter
1 lb. chicken livers
¼ cup chicken stock (p. 235) or veal stock (p. 236)
¼ cup heavy cream

Generous grating of fresh nutmeg
2 tsp. fresh thyme (or 1 tsp. dried)
Freshly ground white pepper, to taste
½ cup unsalted butter, melted

Sauté the shallots and garlic in the butter until wilted. While shallots and garlic are cooking, pick over livers to remove membranes.

Add livers to pan and brown quickly on outside, but do not cook through.

Remove from pan and set aside to cool slightly.

Add stock to pan. Raise heat and reduce by half.

Place sautéed livers and stock in bowl of food processor, add cream and seasonings, and process until pureed and smooth.

Add melted butter and process for 5 more seconds.

Distribute among individual ramekins and chill.

YIELD   4–6 servings.

Chicken Salad with Sweetbreads

A delicate and delicious combination of flavors and textures.

1 lb. sweetbreads	1 bay leaf
2 Tbs. unsalted butter	10 black peppercorns
½ cup minced shallots	½ cup tarragon butter (p. 223)
8 sprigs Italian parsley	¼ cup heavy cream
3 chicken breasts, bone in, skin on	1 sprig fresh tarragon

Soak the sweetbreads in cold water and leave overnight in the refrigerator.

In a sauté pan, melt the butter, add the shallots, and cook 3 or 4 minutes until softened. Drain and dry the sweetbreads and place in pan. Place 4 or 5 sprigs of parsley over them, add ½ cup water, cover, and braise for 45 minutes.

While sweetbreads are braising, place the chicken breasts in a large pot, cover with cold water, add remaining parsley, bay leaf, and peppercorns to pot, and bring to the boil. Simmer for 12 minutes. Remove from heat and set chicken aside to cool slightly in the broth.

At the end of 45 minutes, remove sweetbreads from pan. Pick over them to remove membranes and veins, wrap in a kitchen towel, and weight them with a heavy pot to flatten them.

When cooled, remove chicken and pick over to remove skin and bones. Cut into ½-inch dice and set aside.

Take the weight off the sweetbreads and slice into ½-inch-thick dice. The pieces of chicken and sweetbreads should be of equivalent size.

Soften the tarragon butter and beat the heavy cream into it until it has the consistency of mayonnaise. Put the chicken and sweetbreads in a bowl, toss with the tarragon dressing, and top with a sprig of fresh tarragon. Serve chilled.

YIELD   4 servings.

Terrine de Volaille
(Terrine of Chicken)

A good dish for entertaining, as it should be made 2 days ahead of time to allow the flavors to develop.

2 lbs. boneless chicken breasts
5 egg whites
Freshly ground white pepper, to taste
Freshly ground or grated nutmeg
¼ tsp. powdered sage
⅛ tsp. ground cloves
3 Tbs. fresh tarragon (or 1½–2 Tbs. dried)
1½ cups heavy cream, ice cold

Preheat oven to 350°.

Place half of the chicken breasts in bowl of food processor. Process until chicken becomes a gummy paste. With processor running, slowly add half of the egg whites. Add half the herbs and spices. With processor running, slowly pour in half the cream.

Remove mixture from processor and repeat with remaining half of ingredients. Combine both halves in a large bowl and mix thoroughly.

Butter a 1½-quart terrine and fill with the chicken mixture. Cover terrine with aluminum foil and place in a bain-marie (see Glossary), making certain that the boiling water comes ⅔ of the way up the sides of the terrine.

Bake for 45 minutes to 1 hour. Terrine is done when a knife inserted near the center comes out clean. Cool and refrigerate.

YIELD   4–6 servings.

Eggs Benedictless
---

2 eggs
2 Tbs. unsalted butter
2 thick-cut slices of Canadian
  bacon

¾ cup Hollandaise Sauce
  (p. 214)
Pinch of cayenne

In a small saucepan, poach 2 eggs for 3 minutes.

While the eggs are poaching, melt the butter in a small sauté pan. When it foams, add the Canadian bacon and cook until lightly browned on one side; turn and finish browning.

Place the Canadian bacon on a warmed platter, top each slice with a poached egg, and top with the Hollandaise Sauce.

Add a pinch of cayenne, and serve immediately.

YIELD   1 serving.

BREAD

Salt-free breads are simple to bake. The primary purpose salt serves in bread-baking is to retard the action of the yeast. Unsalted bread dough may tend to rise excessively. Therefore, experiment. Bake these breads, or any other that you may want to try without adding salt, but cut down either on the yeast or the rising time. Be particularly careful about the final rise. If permitted to go on too long, the bread may explode when the yeast is activated by the warmth of the oven!

French Bread
(The Baguette, a Long, Thin Loaf, and Pain de Campagne, a Round Peasant Loaf)

Anyone who has ever been to France and eaten the bread can never forget the delicious crustiness of a real French baguette. The twofold secret of baking such good bread at home is to bake it on a rack lined with terra cotta tiles and to spray it with water to create humidity as it bakes. These two simple procedures will be your way to a sensational "French" loaf of bread.

⅓ cup warm water
1 package active dry yeast
   (or 1 cake compressed
   fresh yeast)

4 cups of bread flour (or 3 cups
   bread flour and 1 cup whole
   wheat flour)
1½ cups tepid water

In an 8-ounce glass measuring cup, put ⅓ cup warm water. Be certain the water is not above 115° for dry yeast or 95° for fresh. Higher temperatures will kill the yeast. Stir the yeast into the water until smooth and set aside.

Place the flour in a large work bowl. Make a well in the center and pour the 1½ cups tepid water into it. Add the yeast and water mixture, and begin scooping the flour into the liquid, mixing quickly with your fingers until the dough sticks together in a single mass.

Place the dough on a floured work surface and begin to knead. This is a soft dough with a lovely texture that is easy to handle. If dough becomes sticky, merely flour your hands and the work surface, and continue kneading. As you work the dough, it will become smooth and elastic and should spring back when poked. The dough is then ready for its first rising. (Up to this point, you may also make the dough in the food processor. Follow instructions for pizza dough, p. 266.)

Place the dough in a buttered bowl, turn to coat the entire mass of dough with the butter, cover with a kitchen towel, and set aside to rise. The rising time will depend upon the warmth of the kitchen. The dough should double in size in about 2 hours. Punch down, turn dough in bowl to grease it again, and allow it to rise again until doubled. The second rise should take a somewhat shorter time. If, however, you wish to retard the rise, refrigerating the dough will slow it up. Simply remove it from the refrigerator whenever you're ready, and let the dough double in size.

Punch down again and remove to a floured work surface. Flatten the dough and with a large knife cut into 3 pieces, much longer than they are wide. To form the dough into a baguette, roll it with your hands from the center to the ends, your hands working in opposite directions. Repeat until you have made 3 long, skinny loaves. As they are formed, place either on a floured cookie sheet for final rise, or in a lightly floured French baguette-baking tin. Cover with a kitchen towel and allow to rise for no more than ½ hour. The final rise happens rather quickly in salt-free bread.

Meanwhile, line the oven rack with terra cotta tiles. These are available, in a 6-inch-square size, from any ceramic tile store.

Preheat the oven to 425° and prepare a spray bottle, which you have filled with fresh water. Flour the tiles.

With a quick jerking motion, roll the bread directly onto the preheated tiles, or place the baguette tin on the tiles, spray lightly with water 2 or 3 times, and close the oven. In 10 more minutes, spray again. Bake for 30 minutes or until the bread is brown and sounds hollow when tapped on the bottom.

To make a loaf of pain de campagne: Do not cut in 3 when shaping loaves for the final rise. Simply roll the dough into a ball shape, place on floured cookie sheet to rise, and cover with a towel. Bake directly on the tiles, and spray as above.

YIELD   3 baguettes or 1 large round loaf.

Garlic Rounds

5 cloves garlic, unpeeled   3–4 Tbs. unsalted butter
1 baguette (as skinny as you can
   make)

Place the garlic cloves, still in their husks, in boiling water to cover, and simmer until soft.

Slice the bread into rounds approximately ¼ inch thick.

In a large sauté pan, heat the butter until it foams. While the butter is melting, squeeze the garlic cloves from their husks and mash in a bowl. Stir the mashed garlic into the butter.

Sauté the bread rounds in the garlic-butter mixture. Brown on both sides. The rounds should be as crisp as a garlic cracker.

When completely cool, store in tins until ready to use.

YIELD   about 4 crackers.

Bread Crumbs

To make bread crumbs, use day-old French bread, preferably your own. Cut into large cubes, place in bowl of food processor or blender jar, and process until reduced to tiny crumbs. You may add dried herbs to the bread crumbs; for example, parsley, oregano, basil, or thyme. Store in an airtight container until ready to use.

Sage and Ginger Bread

This bread makes delicious toast topped with sweet butter. To save time, I make it in my food processor. Should you prefer to knead by hand, the proportions are the same.

1 package active dry yeast
   (or 1 cake compressed
   fresh yeast)
⅓ cup warm water
1½ cups tepid water
1 tsp. ginger, freshly grated
   (more if you like the zing)

2 Tbs. fresh sage (or 1 Tbs.
   dried)
2 Tbs. fresh oregano (or 1 Tbs.
   dried)
2 Tbs. sesame oil
2 cups unbleached white or
   bread flour
2 cups whole wheat flour

Dissolve the yeast in ⅓ cup tepid water (not above 115° for dry yeast or 95° for fresh). Place in bowl of processor or electric mixer equipped with a dough hook. Add the 1½ cups of additional water, the ginger, sage, oregano, and oil. Process or beat for 30 seconds. Add 1 cup of the flours at a time, making sure it is all incorporated before adding the next cup. If the dough appears very moist, additional flour may be necessary. Process until the dough forms a ball.

Flour your hands and work surface, remove the dough from the processor or mixer, and knead for 1 minute or so, until you have a smooth, malleable mass.

Place in a greased bowl and allow to rise until doubled in bulk (approximately 2 hours). Punch down, and allow to rise until doubled again (about 1 hour). Punch down again. Remove from bowl to floured work surface, and divide in 2. Roll and shape into 2 loaves. Place in greased bread pans or make them round and free-form, peasant style. Cover with a towel and allow to rise for 1 hour, or until nearly doubled in size.

Bake in a preheated 350° oven for about 45 minutes, or until nearly doubled in size.

YIELD   2 loaves.

Rye Bread

Serve this flavorsome bread with lots of sweet butter.

2 Tbs. unsalted butter
½ cup heavy cream
½ cup water
1 package active dry yeast
    (or 1 cake compressed
    fresh yeast)
1 cup warm water
3 cups unbleached white or
    bread flour
1¼ cups finely minced onion

3 Tbs. and 1 pinch caraway
    seeds
3 Tbs. chopped fresh dill
    (or 1½ Tbs. dried)
½ tsp. ground cardamom
1½ cups rye flour
1 Tbs. cornmeal
1 Tbs. water

In a saucepan, melt the butter. Add the cream and water to the same pan. Heat just until tepid and remove from flame.

Dissolve the yeast in the cup of warm water (115° if using dry yeast, 95° if using fresh), and combine with the cream and butter mixture. Place in a large mixing bowl and stir in the unbleached or bread flour. Stir in the chopped onion, 3 tablespoons caraway seeds, dill, and cardamom. Add 1 cup rye flour and beat to combine.

Turn out onto a floured work surface and knead until smooth and elastic, about 10 minutes. As the dough becomes more moist during kneading, add the extra ½ cup rye flour, and work it into the dough.

Grease a large bowl with butter, place the dough in the bowl, and turn it to coat the entire mass of dough with the butter. Cover with plastic wrap and let rise until doubled in bulk (1 to 2 hours, depending on the temperature of your kitchen).

When fully risen, punch down. Allow to rise again until doubled in bulk.

Again punch down and turn out onto a floured work surface.

Press dough into a rectangle of about 9 inches by 6 inches. With a large knife dipped in flour, cut dough into 2 equal pieces. Begin working 1 piece of the dough into a ball, pinching it in at the bottom and pulling to round out the top. Repeat with the other piece.

Sprinkle the cornmeal on a cookie sheet. Place both loaves on it and brush the dough with water. Sprinkle a pinch of caraway seeds on the loaf tops, cover with a kitchen towel, and set aside to rise for about 35 to 45 minutes.

Preheat oven to 350°.

Place loaves in oven and bake for 1 hour or until they are brown and sound hollow when rapped on the bottom. Set aside to cool.

YIELD   2 round loaves.

XII
Making Their Way
Our Way

INTRODUCTION

The following recipes represent a sampling from four of the glorious restaurants I dined in while on tour. I include both versions to show you how simple it is to adapt your own favorites. When you see how easy it is to make your recipes BHD safe, when you realize how little the taste is affected, you will use these examples to adapt each and every cookbook on your shelves.

JUDY MAZEL

Cape Cod Scallops, Sauté au Citron from The Blue Fox, San Francisco

---

2 lbs. bay scallops	Chopped parsley
Flour	½ tsp. Worcestershire sauce
1 cup oil	Salt and pepper
¼ lb. butter	6 slices of toast
2 large lemons	Lemon wedges for garnish

Wash and drain 2 pounds fresh Cape Cod scallops and dry well in a kitchen towel. Dredge in flour and shake vigorously to remove all excess flour. In heavy skillet, heat cooking oil ¼-inch deep. When oil is very hot, add the scallops, let them brown very lightly for about 1 minute. Pour off all fat, and add ¼ pound butter. Sauté scallops until butter is light brown. Remove from stove and add the juice from 2 large lemons and 2 teaspoons finely chopped parsley, ½ teaspoon Worcestershire sauce, salt and pepper to taste. Serve on slices of toast. Garnish with lemon wedges and parsley.

YIELD   6 servings.

Scallops Provençale à la Conscious Combining

2 lbs. bay scallops, tendons removed
8 Tbs. butter

½ cup minced shallots
4 cloves garlic, minced
4 Tbs. minced parsley

Wash and dry the scallops on paper toweling.

In a large sauté pan, heat the butter until it foams. Add the minced shallots and garlic and sauté until very lightly browned.

Add the scallops, raise the heat, and sauté very quickly. As they cook, take hold of the handle and jerk the pan sharply every few seconds to keep the scallops tossing and turning. This ensures that they will cook evenly. The entire cooking time should be no more than 4 or 5 minutes.

Arrange on a serving platter and top with minced parsley.

YIELD   4 servings.

Note: Soft shell crabs can be sautéed in the same manner. Simply increase the cooking time to 5 minutes on each side.

Chicken Paillard with Rosemary Butter from Mortimer's, New York City

1 chicken breast, 4 to 5 ounces,   1 Tbs. melted butter
   skinned and boned   Salt and pepper to taste
                       Grilled tomato halves and
                         watercress for garnish

Place the chicken breast, fillet side up, between 2 sheets of clear plastic. Beat the surface gently with a mallet until the meat is evenly spread and is about ⅛ inch thick. Brush with the butter, and season. Cook quickly over a very hot charcoal grill (or at home in a very hot, well-oiled iron skillet). Garnish with grilled tomato halves and watercress. Serve with a slice or 2 of Rosemary Butter.

YIELD   1 serving.

Rosemary Butter:

2 sticks sweet butter   1 tsp. dried rosemary, coarsely
⅓ cup Dijon mustard   chopped
                       1 tsp. marjoram

Cream the butter and mustard, add herbs. Wrap in foil and shape into a roll. Freeze. Cut into ¼-inch slices and serve with chicken.

YIELD   4 servings.

Chicken Paillard with Rosemary Butter à la Conscious Combining

Simply eliminate the salt in the recipe. When making the Rosemary Butter, substitute dry mustard made into a paste with chicken broth, or use the low-sodium variety of Dijon mustard available in health food stores.

YIELD   1 serving.

Steak Tartare
from Cricket's, Los Angeles

2 anchovies
Capers
1 tsp. olive oil
1 egg yolk
1 tsp. Lea and Perrins sauce

1 tsp. Dijon mustard
1 Tbs. chopped onions
1 oz. ground top round
1 tsp. chopped parsley
Ground pepper, to taste

In a salad bowl, mash the anchovies into a puree. Then mash the capers. Add 1 teaspoon olive oil, then egg yolk, Lea and Perrins sauce and Dijon mustard. Mix together and add the chopped onions. Add the ground meat and mix together. Serve on a cold plate with toast.

YIELD   1 serving.

Steak Tartare Mazel

1 lb. ground sirloin
2 cloves garlic, finely minced
Freshly ground black pepper, to
  taste

⅛ tsp. Mel's Secret Seasoning
  (p. 224)
1 egg yolk
Seeds of 1 papaya, washed and
  dried

In a large bowl, combine the ground sirloin with the garlic and pepper. Add the Mel's Secret Seasoning.

Shape into a large patty, make a depression, and drop 1 raw egg yolk into the center. Scatter papaya seeds over all, and serve.

YIELD   1 serving.

Terrine de Légumes
from Le Cirque, New York City

9 oz. artichoke bottoms
6 oz. snow peas
6 oz. broccoli
6 oz. shredded carrots
7 oz. shredded knob celery

5 oz. red pepper (skinless)
4 oz. green asparagus tips
Salt and pepper
8 sheets of plain gelatin
4 oz. carrot juice

Boil artichoke bottoms for 12 minutes. Steam remaining vegetables for 5 minutes. Add salt and pepper. Set vegetables aside to cool.

Presoak 8 sheets of plain gelatin in cold water, then mix with carrot juice. Heat for 10 seconds.

In a 4-pound mold pan, alternate layers of vegetables and gelatin. Refrigerate for 6 hours.

Serve with a vinaigrette sauce.

YIELD   20 slices.

Terrine de Légumes à la Conscious Combining

The secret of a beautiful vegetable terrine is that all the vegetables be of uniform size, both in width and in length. In this way, the presentation of the terrine is a delight to the eye as well as the palate.

½ lb. string beans, washed and ends snipped off
¾ lb. carrots (select carrots as near the same size and as straight as possible)
6 artichokes
1 large cauliflower
2 Tbs. unsalted butter
2 Tbs. flour
½ cup heavy cream

2 egg yolks
1 tsp. fresh tarragon (or ½ tsp. dried)
¼ tsp. cayenne
Freshly ground or grated nutmeg
Freshly ground white pepper, to taste
Mayonnaise (p. 219)

Cook the string beans in a large pot of boiling water for 5 minutes, or until crisp/tender. Refresh under cold water.

Scrape the carrots and boil them whole for 7 or 8 minutes, depending on width. Plunge into cold water. Slice into long, thin julienne strips.

Trim the tops of the artichokes. Cook trimmed artichokes in boiling water for 30 minutes. Drain, remove the choke, and trim the leaves until you are left with just the bottom, which is to be trimmed as evenly as possible.

Wash the cauliflower, cut into small florets, and cook in boiling water until tender when pierced with a fork. Drain thoroughly. Puree in a processor or food mill.

Melt 2 tablespoons of butter in a small saucepan, add flour, and whisk until foamy. Off the heat, add the cream, and whisking constantly, return saucepan to stove and cook at a low boil until the béchamel thickens. (This béchamel is a form of panade and will hold the terrine together.) When it has thickened, add the cauliflower puree and stir until well blended. Beat in the egg yolks.

Season mixture with tarragon, cayenne, nutmeg, and pepper.

Butter a 1½-quart loaf pan or terrine. Cut 1 green bean into tiny strips, and cut small carrot rounds into flowers. Decorate the bottom of the terrine with these tiny flower carrots on long green-bean stems. Refrigerate terrine to harden butter and to set flowers.

Remove terrine from refrigerator. Pour the first ½-inch layer of the cauliflower mixture into the terrine. Then add the artichoke hearts set close together, another layer of cauliflower, a flat row of green beans, more cauliflower, the carrots placed side by side as tightly as possible, cauliflower, green beans, and finally cauliflower.

Bake in a bain-marie (see Glossary) in a 350° oven for 25 minutes, or until a knife inserted in the center comes out clean. Cool and refrigerate until ready to serve. You may serve from the terrine or invert onto a serving platter. Pass with a flavored mayonnaise (p. 219). Can also be served warm with Beurre Blanc (p. 212).

YIELD   6–8 servings.

PART FOUR
UNFINISHED BUSINESS

XIII

The Answers
You've Been Waiting For—
Answers for You All

THE HEALTHFULNESS OF IT ALL

What makes you such an authority? You're not even a doctor.

That's absolutely true. I'm not a doctor or a scientist, and I don't have a degree in nutrition nor do I hold myself out as a technical authority. I had a *personal* stake in it. My credentials: I was fat and now I'm thin; I was unhealthy and now I'm healthy.

I didn't start out to change the world or the eating habits of humanity. I don't see myself as a messiah. My revolutionary discoveries are the result of a desperate search to make myself thin and healthy. I was a fatty and an Eater combined in one body pushed to the brink of disaster. I had tried it all, and nothing worked. No one had the answer for me, so I tried to find it for myself.

At my fattest I weighed 170 pounds and had been diagnosed as having a nonfunctioning thyroid, an almost nonfunction pituitary, and an adrenal system that was shot. I was taking ten grains of a thyroid medication, four Lasix (a diuretic), laxatives, diet pills, mood equalizers, and tranquilizers—all to maintain the weight of 130, a weight I had achieved by starving myself from Monday to Friday and eating anything that wasn't nailed down from Friday night through Sunday night. I fluctuated; on Fridays I would weigh 130, and by Monday morning it was usually between 140 and 145.

I began studying nutrition, the role that food plays in the health of the human body, and started experimenting on myself. I began using food instead of drugs; I went to the refrigerator instead of the medicine cabinet to resolve a problem that had been my nemesis, a physical condition that had been an affliction for twenty years. The result of my experiments was a 102-pound healthy, pill-free body. Nutrition entered my life at the age of twenty-nine, and along with it, my cure for fat.

Friends who experienced the new me sought my advice and I responded. Well, you can't keep slimhood a secret. Word quickly spread, and I agreed to disclose my findings to the outside world, to those who cared and needed my help. Before I knew it, I was conducting group classes as well as private sessions. Within three years I had personally supervised weight-loss programs for about a thousand people.

I've never pretended to be a doctor or an academically trained expert, but I have read and studied and synthesized the works of many doctors and scientists in developing the Beverly Hills Diet and the Beverly Hills Diet Lifetime Plan.

I have been honest and in response to surging demands, I have shared what worked for me in a book. I've tried to explain the BHD in my own way, in an uncomplicated, easy to understand, and easy to visualize fashion, so that people all over, not just those in Beverly Hills, could experience the supreme joy of slimhood.

Why is there such rivalry among the developers of different diets?

Frankly, I don't understand all the competition. There are 222 million people in this country, and one out of three of them is overweight. Certainly there is enough fat to go around. The irony of it all is that, according to Dr. Myron Winick, head of Columbia University Medical School's Institute of Human Nutrition, half of the adult population of the United States is malnourished.

I really feel that all the arguing that's going on takes away from what should be our single-minded goal: making the world thin. We've all been fortunate enough to have found ways of losing weight that work. Instead of wasting our energies on spats among ourselves, what we should be doing is sharing those methods with as many people as possible.

Just as there are Fords, Chevrolets, and Cadillacs, so it is with diets. Some work better for certain people than others, some fit people's lifestyles better than others. No single diet is likely to fit everyone's need; and the need is vast.

My doctor has prescribed medication. Will it interfere with my maintenance?
Possibly. But do whatever your doctor tells you to do.

Is diarrhea really a problem?
It's not even a consideration on the Beverly Hills Diet Lifetime Plan, but should it develop discontinue the plan until you consult your doctor.

I'm constipated. Help!
Increase your bran to three tablespoons in the morning and your sesame seeds to three tablespoons at night. Also use more oil. Constipation is generally resolved by an increase in fiber and/or oil.

I seem to get tired after eating protein. Is that reasonable?
Absolutely. Protein is difficult to digest. Now, don't take that the wrong way; it's not bad for you, it's just complicated for your system to break down. You get tired because of the energy required to digest it. Also, trytophane, an essential amino acid present in animal protein, is a sleep-inducing agent.

Is it true that your way of eating encourages one to eat a lot of high-cholesterol foods?
While the percentage of cholesterol may be greater in a single eating experience than it is in some other diets, if you were to match, ounce for ounce, bite for bite, the amount of cholesterol-

laden foods you ate in your former life to what you're eating now, you would see that your total cholesterol consumption is far lower overall on the Beverly Hills Diet Lifetime Plan.

I have just had surgery. Can I continue on maintenance?

As always, you must consult your physician. Most authorities agree that your protein needs are much greater before and after surgery than at other times of your life. Your cells need those building blocks for healing.

I just found out I'm pregnant. I'm a loyal Conscious Combiner. Now what?

Follow your doctor's advice about a diet tailored for pregnancy. Your OB/GYN knows best what you should be eating now because you have very specific nutritional needs.

How can bread and pasta be nutritious?

It is the proper balance of all foods that will keep you slim and healthy. Eliminating bread and pasta and other grains from your diet is every bit as unhealthy as eliminating animal protein or oil or vegetables or any other natural foods. An overweight condition means you are getting too much of something and not enough of something else. Among the "something else's" are probably the grain foods, which includes bread and pasta. No doubt, they were the first things you eliminated when you tried to lose weight. Think back to the way you used to eat, think back to the low energy, that drawn and tired look. Think back to the protein, protein, protein. God forbid you should eat carbohydrates, they're so fattening; or so you thought! Carbohydrates are essential for proper protein metabolism. The way your body uses protein depends on the proper balance of carbohydrates.

Think back to how you felt on your high-protein diet and compare it to how you feel now. Think back to how you looked then and see how you look now, now that you are a follower of the BHD Lifetime Plan. Your state of being should indicate the quality of your health, which is a direct product of what you eat.

Is there a certain number of days I should do protein or carbs in a row?

Your nutritional quotient, your scale, and your heart are your guides. There are no limits to the number of days you should concentrate on any one food. Remember, though, it's the week as a unit that counts. I recommend having a mix throughout the week. The Food Formulas are balanced accordingly, and as long as you follow their lead, then you are eating the proper nutritional mix over a week's period. When you begin "Doing Your Own Thing," you can schedule proteins and carbs as you wish, making sure, however, you fill your nutritional quotient. Remember, though, a weight gain means your body did not properly process what it was given, probably too much of something and not enough of something else. If you should experience a weight gain, check the balance and if you are eating more of one thing than another make the necessary adjustments.

Ultimately, only you have the answer to this question. Your experience and experiments are the key. If there were a set answer to questions like this, the BHD Lifetime Plan wouldn't be *your* eating plan, it would be mine.

How nutritious is it to go out and have a meal of desserts and nothing else?

Not very, but then, how nutritious is it to eat just sugary cereal or doughnuts for breakfast? How nutritious is it to stop for an ice cream cone at 3:00 P.M.? You're going to eat dessert any-way, and it isn't any healthier to pile it all in at once, on top of everything else. In fact, that's probably worse. At least this way, on its own, you are giving your body a chance to process it properly. Besides, Open Dessert is not a regular eating experience for a Conscious Combiner, only a special occasion, hardly often enough to be really unhealthy for you. It's the weekly balance of your nutritional quotient that really matters. It's those desserts nutritionally combined with everything else eaten over the week's period that count.

One last word: Consider the drastic decrease in your sugar

consumption now that you are a Beverly Hills Dieter. Do you still really question the healthfulness of an Open Dessert?

If I eat something I know isn't so great nutritionally, how can I compensate?

At this stage you are so far ahead of the nutritional game, so much better off than when you were a "normal" eater, that you probably have nothing to worry about nutritionally. Because you are feeding your body when you can, your heart and soul can get a nonnutritional nibble now and then without any damage. Look at yourself, have you ever felt better or looked better in your life? If you consciously combine faithfully, good nutrition will be automatic.

Can the supplements be taken in any other form?

Sorry. I have found no effective substitutes. But they are a far less bitter pill to swallow than fat. You'll develop a taste for the yeast, and the bran will stop tasting like sawdust. You couldn't possibly be complaining about your crunchy bedtime snack, the sesame seeds, could you? Believe me, if there were an easier form, I'd tell you; I want you to be happy!

What do I do if I gain my weight back?

Why should you? You will only gain your weight back if you have forsaken the Beverly Hills Diet Lifetime Plan and everything it means to your skinny little soul.

If, horror of horrors, you've done just that, then pick yourself up, dust yourself off, get back in touch with your skinny voice, and start all over again on the Beverly Hills Diet. Begin with Week One only if you have been totally away from Conscious Combining for at least six months, only if fruit has totally and irrevocably left your realm of reasoning. Otherwise, begin your Beverly Hills Diet weight-loss program at Week Two and proceed accordingly.

Don't kid yourself into thinking that you're never going to gain some weight back, especially in the beginning. You have to test your outer parameters, the framework of your fat potential. It's all part and parcel of being a thin person. You have to know just how far you'll let yourself go, how fat you'll let yourself get. In order to reaffirm what you don't want to be, you sometimes have to return to it—to see it and reexperience it. It doesn't matter how long you've been skinny. The fear of fat hovers until you test it. I was put through the test as recently as two years ago. What a relief when I discovered that at 115 I had had it; there was no way I could've weighed any more and lived with myself. When I saw 115 on the scale, it squelched my uncontrollable appetite of the previous month; I just wasn't hungry anymore. That brief period was the only time in all the years that I've been skinny that my weight has fluctuated by more than three pounds from its ideal.

If you never really acknowledged and confronted your weight in the beginning of weight loss, you may need to go back now and do so. If you never really saw who you were, how could you ever choose not to be it? Once you do, once you see what you don't want to be, then you can make the conscious choice to be perfect. And sadly, sometimes we have to go back almost to the starting point we came from to say, "I don't want to be there anymore!"

Why can some people eat more than others?

No two bodies handle food in exactly the same way—physically or emotionally. Your former nutritional condition and your past emotional state are critical to the way you process food. Of one thing you can be sure: the more you relax, the more you let go of your food fears, the more you can get away with and the more you will probably be able to eat. Unfortunately, it's usually the people who don't care about food who can get away with the most. It doesn't seem fair, does it?

I am finding that certain foods are unpredictable. I eat exactly the same thing and sometimes I gain weight, while other times I don't. Why?

Your state of mind, your state of being, your hormones, the moon, what you ate before, what you ate afterward, all are factors in your weight equation. If there is no consistent pattern, assume that the weight gain is temporary. And continue to experiment with the food that could be the culprit. The proof and the answers lie in *your* experiments. You are learning what works and what doesn't and how to get away with the things that don't. How to include them in your life. Remember, as a maintainer, think in terms of *weekly* maintenance, rather than daily fluctuations.

Will I ever be able to eat like a "normal" person?

Probably not, so stop trying. Remember David. It's not important anymore. If portion control and time limits and a multitude of nevers were easy for you, if you were happy with three meals a day, you would have been thin long before now.

Count your blessings for the pasta and other food fantasies you now have permission to eat. Say to yourself, "If I can have my cake and eat it, what difference does it make if I eat it one piece at a time?"

Do you ever gain weight?

Sure! I'm human, too, you know. But I also lose any weight gain right away. That immediate loss is the crux of the Beverly Hills Diet Lifetime Plan.

What if I continue to lose on maintenance?

Lucky you. It's quite common; though, it's a fringe benefit of perfection, of living the BHDLP. It comes with giving up the struggle. Diets and dieting, losing weight, keeping it off, that's probably one of the biggest, if not the biggest struggle in our lives. At least it was. Combining properly means the absence of fat. Forever. If you lose more than you wish, joy of joys, the obvious solution would be to eat more Open Humans. However, you will probably choose not to miscombine too often, not because you can't, because you're afraid you'll gain weight, but because it doesn't feel good. Avoid too many Mono Meals. Do more Open Carbs or Open Proteins instead. Try two or even three meals a day; you're probably one of the lucky ones who can handle it!

People say I should curb my compulsiveness, that I'm like an alcoholic, and that the Beverly Hills Diet Lifetime Plan feeds that compulsiveness. Is this true?

I really resent people comparing being an Eater to being an alcoholic, almost as much as I resent people telling me to change my behavior. I am what I am, you are what you are, and that's perfectly okay. I refuse to *give up* anything, that's painful. Now, if I should happen to *let go* of something, that's different. There's joy in letting go. If some of your "food craziness" dissipates, terrific, but I don't want to force your hand. The reality is, it will happen naturally and organically, because once you have acknowledged and accepted your compulsiveness, you tend not to be compulsive anymore. By encouraging you to fulfill your food fantasies in the cold light of day, without fear and without guilt, the BHD Lifetime Plan erases those compulsions. It obliterates bingeing because bingeing and compulsiveness are no longer necessary.

A music lover can put on earphones and bliss out over Wagner. Something happens to his ears that allows him to alter his state of consciousness. An art lover can get lost at the Metropolitan Museum of Art. For someone tuned in to taste, to being an Eater, it is food that matters most, food that provides the escape. Every sensitive person responds with passion to his or her senses. It is the guilt we associate with eating that compels us to overeat and get fat. But once food is acknowledged for what it is, it ceases to become a threat. And compulsions slip away. On the Beverly Hills Diet Lifetime Plan you acknowledge all foods—not just the notoriously nonfattening but the infamous as well. When you acknowledge all those heretofore considered nos, all those foods you used to hide behind, you can let it go. I don't deny that for many of us food is a diversion and a refuge. However, it is only when you deny its existence, when you refuse to accept its place in your world, that it creates havoc.

Now that I'm thin, the social pressure to eat "normally" is almost overwhelming. How do I handle it?

Don't succumb. Giving in to social pressure is a sign of insecurity. Now, I know fat people are insecure, but you are not fat anymore. What do you have to be insecure about?

Don't you miss having a regular meal?

Sometimes, so then I have one. But for the most part I find them rather boring, unsatisfying, and I don't feel so terrific after I eat one.

Is it okay to eat more than one fruit at a time, as in a fruit salad?

Not really. Your stomach won't be very happy. Remember, fruits pack the most potent enzymes, and it's best not to mix their might. Each fruit performs its unique miracles. If you do combine fruit, if you simply cannot pass up a fruit salad, it is best to choose fruits that don't clash too harshly, fruits that are related. Select your combo from within their little family units. For guidelines, see the Burn, Feed, and Wash listings on page 114.

What do I do if a fruit is out of season?

Papayas and pineapples grow year-round in Hawaii. Grapes are also available year-round. Watermelons left over from the summer are kept in cold storage, and the new-season Mexican variety starts arriving in January. Strawberries are imported from Australia and New Zealand when the American varieties are not readily available. So what's left? Blueberries and mangoes—no big deal; those you can do without. Besides, by this time you've made friends with your grocer and he'll get you anything you want. You know, until you came along he probably didn't even know what a mango was, and now he's selling them by the gross. Believe me, your produce man wants to show a profit as much as you want to show a loss, he wants to make money just as much as you want to stay thin. You'll see, your enzymatic fruits will be happily lined up alongside the radishes and turnips just when you need and want them most.

Think about it. How much of what you eat is "in season" and grown locally? Do you think they grow lettuce in Cleveland in the winter? Do you think it's any more difficult to fly papaya to Houston than it is to fly apples? Ask and ye shall receive. It's really that simple.

How important is it to stick with watermelon and grapes once I've begun eating them on a particular day?

Very. Their action is unique and specific, and if it is interrupted by anything else, you will not only not lose, you will probably gain.

Can I really eat as much as I want every day?

Not only can you, you should. One way I convince my reluctant new skinnies is to go out to eat with them. They only have to experience a meal with me once they see how much I eat, to be reassured. This program is designed to feed your body, not starve it. Eating is what made you thin, and it is eating that will keep you thin.

Are there any tricks that will help me get away with more Open Meals?

The best one of all is eliminating salt as much as possible. It's so easy to ask for it without, so easy not to add any.

The second hint that will help you multiply your Opens is to insert your mind into the process. Eat slowly, bite for bite for bite. Remember, it's not how much you eat in how short a time, it's how long you can make the pleasure last.

What about drinking? I heard that wine is good for digestion.

Wine is good for digestion simply because it has a tendency to relax you, to put you in the proper frame of mind to process your food. It really doesn't work well digestively, however, unless you have it with fruit. If you have it as a miscombination, though, be sure to pick and choose your occasions and make them count. I often have vodka with protein, and it hasn't exactly been my demise. But take a look at the people around you who are drinking wine. They gulp it, like a glass of water. Since when is wine a thirst quencher? Do they really enjoy what they're drinking? The only thing I ask is for you to appreciate it, to hold it sacred, just like all the things you ingest. Use it, don't abuse it.

Ideally, what should I drink?

Water, coffee, or tea. I have recently discovered Fauchon mango tea, and it has completely replaced my morning coffee.

What about juices?

Drinking fruit juice is the same as eating fruit. If you drink it, follow the fruit rules. If you drink vegetable juice, follow the carb rules. Juice contains overly concentrated calories while lacking its original and essential fiber. It is a food out of its natural balance, and I don't recommend it.

What about decaffeinated coffee?

I would recommend the decaf coffee that is made by a water-soluble process that is available at most gourmet markets and coffee stores. Unfortunately, most commercially decaffeinated coffees and most instant coffees are oozing with added chemicals.

I am a vegetarian. What do I do?

If you are a true vegetarian, meaning you eat nothing from animal sources, eat raw nuts and seeds instead of animal protein. If you are a lacto vegetarian and dairy has become the protein mainstay of your diet, I would prefer that you cut down somewhat on the dairy and augment your diet with nuts and seeds. If you are going to continue with a lot of dairy products try and get "Raw." The lecithin will still be present hence they will be more easily digested. Also, if you are going to continue eating a lot of cheese it should not only be raw, but also low sodium. Something I don't insist upon for the occasional cheese eater.

The "experts" are saying your enzyme theory is a lot of bunk.

What most of them actually say, if you listen as carefully as I do, is that there is no scientific evidence that *proves* my theory. What is not mentioned is that there is no scientific evidence to DISPROVE it either. Regardless of the why's the bottom line is,

The Beverly Hills Diet and The Beverly Hills Diet Lifetime Plan work. The pounds permanently lost are the incontrovertible truth.

I happen to believe it's the enzymes. But I invite, in fact I would be overjoyed, if those "experts" would join me so that together we could explore the whys of the BHD and the BHDLP and answer the riddle of why it works once and for all.

XIV

The Good Life Is Yours—
Welcome to Forever

You did it, you found that pot of gold at the end of the rainbow. Eternal slimhood is yours. You've earned it, so be proud of yourself, because I'm proud of you. You have entered the good life, the land of plenty: plenty of food, plenty of fun, and plenty of time to enjoy it. You have created a life for yourself that is a dream come true. And now you know for sure, now you really believe that you can be as thin as you'd like for the rest of your life without giving up anything, without *ever* being deprived. You know, because you've done it. You are experiencing the wonders of the good life, a life that includes everything you have ever wanted. Food is now *your* slave and you are the master; it works for you, not against you.

All the shame and degradation, the heartache and hunger, the diet and deprivation are banished. They no longer exist. They are gone Forever. You've smashed that miserable, debilitating fat cycle, you erased the tape. Your fat consciousness has been pushed aside by your skinny voice. You're not fat anymore and you'll never be fat again.

Six months ago I told you there were three things you were going to have to give up if you wanted skinny to become a Forever reality. And as you gave up your fat, as you gave up your guilt, and as, one by one, you let go of all your preconceived ideas about fat and fattening, diets and dieting, you replaced them with a pride and self-confidence you never knew you possessed. You've taken control of the essence of your life and put it to work for you. You have learned to exploit the synergy of your mind and body. You are powerful. And your hipbones and cheekbones are the joyful testimony to your success.

You have spent the last six months understanding, accepting, and internalizing the concept of tomorrow, the heart of the Beverly Hills Diet Lifetime Plan, the concept of Forever that will keep you thin. A tomorrow that only existed in your wildest fantasies is here, a tomorrow that is now a reality, a tomorrow free from fear.

You're a skinny today, and so will you be tomorrow. And every tomorrow thereafter. Being skinny means having it all, a perfect body and the freedom to enjoy it. You've embraced the secrets of the Beverly Hills Diet Lifetime Plan, and in making them your own, you have found YOUR CURE FOR FAT.

The Three Golden Rules that are now embedded in your consciousness have become as much a part of you and have become as sacred as any other aspect in your moral code. Your support system is secure; you don't need anyone else, because now you have you. You have learned not to depend on anyone or anything but yourself. You can now even shed your dependence on me. You are all you need; you are an entity unto yourself, a self-contained skinny for all to see.

You're finding that living the tools and rules you've spent six months practicing have become easy; you don't even have to think about them anymore, they just happen, they're automatic. The Advanced Non-Physical Exercises have also become automatic, not something apart but a part of your life, a regular activity. With each exercise your skinny soul gained momentum and strength until finally it silenced your fat voice completely. Now they keep it quiet. The Beverly Hills Diet Lifetime Plan has entered your consciousness and altered it immeasurably and Forever.

You have learned to listen and respond to your body. You

experience food, and you understand that how it makes you feel is far more important than how it tastes. Because you now understand the totality of food, you realize that you are a product of what you eat, nothing more, nothing less. You have learned to love the foods that make you feel good and to love the foods that merely taste good less. Your heart understands and agrees.

Eating is no longer just a function of your emotions, a reaction, a habit. It is now a pleasure. It is nourishment. It is a positive.

And you never doubted me once, did you? Well, maybe just once. Like that time you ate seven pieces of pizza and gained four pounds. But when you saw it come off with pineapple the very next day, you became a believer all over again. You wanted to kill me when you got on the scale, but you knew I wouldn't let you down. In your heart you always trusted me, but more than that, you trusted yourself. And, in that trust, you reached in and touched your little skinny person, and that meant Forever.

Once you learned the tools and the rules and put them to work, you had no more excuses for being fat, no rational reason to be anything less than vital and alive. Oh sure, you still have a few problems left; being thin didn't make them all disappear. But the biggest problem you had is gone—you! That's right, you against you. Well, now that you're thin, doesn't life happen *your* way, aren't *you* making it happen *your* way now? Before this, your Debilitating Fat Consciousness tainted your world. No matter how separate, how isolated, how cleverly you compartmentalized it, your fat permeated your life and all it encompassed. You were coming from a core of imperfection, a base of Fat. Being fat mattered, just as skinny does—vitally. Now your positive energy nourishes your every focus, it frees you for living.

Your slimhood frees you from your dependence on me, too. When you maintained your weight "by the book," you were protected, you were supported by my Food Formulas and the reassuring structure of the charts. I held your hand through the agonies of equalizing and leveling, those dreaded, fearsome post-weight-loss gyrations. Now that you're there, now that you can go it alone, you know that the Golden Pineapple Network will sustain you always. Your support system is cemented in place, it is secure.

In becoming a thin person, you became a thin person. You confronted, acknowledged, and let go of the fat person. You discarded your cloak of secrecy; now everyone knows who you are and what you are. They know that you're an Eater, and you aren't ashamed of it. Well, why should you be, you're no longer wearing the negative side effects, the fat! You don't have to pretend to be someone you're not; you don't have to conjure up excuses, you can openly enjoy eating; you can unleash your wildest fantasies and food fetishes. When you detail the raptures of a mango, bask in the delights of a meal eaten yesterday, or eagerly anticipate an eating experience three days away, you don't worry: You don't care what other people think. You have permission to experience food and make it an experience. You have all the security and power of a thin person, a true Beverly Hills Diet Lifetime Plan skinny, a person no longer ashamed of who you are. With your new food security blanket, you can have whatever you want, whenever you want; you can eat a chocolate soufflé instead of lunch, you can have popcorn for breakfast or sunny-side-up eggs for dinner. When it comes to food, you can have it your way.

You are experiencing how food energizes your body instead of draining it. You have pioneered the ultimate transformation: Instead of eating to bring yourself down, as a refuge from misery, you eat for the pluses—the pleasure and the power. For the first time in your life you are satisfied; you will never be hungry again—not for food, not for anything. You have achieved the most difficult goal in your life and now that you've done that, now that you're skinny, you can do and have anything. Your skinny person is in control, and it is all-powerful.

Your scale has indeed become your best friend, it has become an integral part of your life, it is your point of reference, your foundation with reality. Your weight is no longer your measure of good and bad, but rather a guidepost to what works and what doesn't. It is a barometer that tallies your state of being, not a noose around your conscience. And every time you get on that scale and celebrate not having to lose one more pound, each time you leap on that scale and experience the high of saying, "I'm perfect," you've cemented one more maintenance block in place, and you can put fat that much further behind you. Now that you can luxuriate in your perfect weight, you can let your fantasies run free. Now you have summoned Forever!

And time has become another barometer. Each week that passes is another notch toward Forever. A day is insignificant in the total scheme of things. You think in terms of weeks, nutritionally, physically, and mentally. A pound doesn't catapult you into frenetic frenzies, because you can indulge in the security of a sure cure.

If you can maintain for six months, you can be skinny Forever. The first months are the scourge of the golden pineapple, the nemesis of the good life, mentally, emotionally, and physically. It is during these first treacherous six months, as the cleansing process continues, while your body is stabilizing in spurts and sputters and your brain is absorbing, assimilating, and adjusting, that you are moving from the negative to the positive, that you are discarding your fat consciousness and replacing it with skinny. Fixing the golden pineapple forever in your heart.

While the faces of fat are ever poised to attack, there is a balance. Your friends have finally stopped expecting you to "go off," to gain it back. They've stopped pressuring you to "cheat." You're finding that you're not alone, that the world is alive with other new skinnies, alive with other Combiners speaking your language and offering compassion mingled with enthusiasm.

You've never looked or felt better; your hair gleams, your eyes glisten, your skin radiates. You wake up invigorated; you need less sleep; and best of all you feel great about yourself. You are all that you hoped you could be. You have grasped the core of the good life and all it has to offer.

While each week that passes reinforces skinny and undermines fat, never forget from whence you came. Fat and lethargy are as near as tomorrow; they will stop at nothing to reclaim you. Nothing. That is why the unconscious of the Beverly Hills Diet Lifetime Plan is so urgent. Now that you have embraced the good life, *hold on*. Don't give in and don't ever give up. Don't dwell on your fat consciousness; you did that long enough. Just know that it's there, poised to prey on your vulnerabilities. Revel in the Forever of skinny, hold on tight, and don't let go. Rejoice in it, appreciate it, and enjoy it. You've earned it.

You know, I need your success, too. You're my reason for doing all this. Your success is my success. You are the living, breathing proof that there is a cure for fat, that skinny isn't a transient phenomenon, that Conscious Combining means eternal slimhood. You've helped change the statistics.

Your victory is living testimony to the wonders of the Beverly Hills Diet Lifetime Plan. Your success shouts it out. Your glow breathes life into Conscious Combining, giving hope to millions of fatties who are waiting to see, waiting to hear, those who needed more proof, those less eager to be on the cutting edge than you.

We've no only discovered how we can be as thin as we'd like for the rest of our lives, we've done it. And if we can do it, so can others. Help us fix the numbers for all to see, take up the challenge, and join me in Pineappleland. Let's shout our victory to the world.

Let me welcome you into the world of Forever with our double golden pineapple pin, our symbol of Forever. You have become part of a very special network, a network of skinnies, and now that you are wearing the pin, we will be linked together always. You see, I don't really want to let you go. And believe me, I'm not going to.

Send me a copy of your records from your Workbook to Wonderland for your six months: the dates, your weights, the Food Formulas (yours and mine), your reaction to the exercises, and your comments, and I will send you your badge of success, the double golden pineapple pin. I will also respond with information about the Beverly Hills Diet Network, the plans in store and the ways to plug in.

And stay tuned, because I'm not through with you yet. As long as there's ink in this pen and a ribbon in my typewriter, I'm going to keep on writing. Next to come is The Beverly Hills Diet International.

So, now you're on your own. I'm not worried, though; I know you can do it. But if you ever need me, I'm here; I'll always be here for you. I'll never let you down, I'll never let you get fat again. Just uphold the badge of the golden pineapple and be true to yourself. Covet your pot of gold, because you've earned it and you deserve it! And now you have it all, hamburgers and hipbones, cheesecake and cheekbones. You are indeed a Beverly Hills Lifetime Plan maintainer of the first order.

CONGRATULATIONS, SKINNY, YOU'VE DONE IT! AND I'M REAL PROUD OF YOU.

Call or write: Judy Mazel
                 The Beverly Hills Diet
                 270 North Canon Drive
                 Beverly Hills, California 90210
                 (213) 858–7292

Glossary

THE TONGUE OF THE
GOLDEN PINEAPPLE

Those of you who read the first book, *The Beverly Hills Diet* (and if you haven't, I'm assuming you will now) have assimilated a new language, the tongue of the golden pineapple.

We no longer eat food. We *do* it. Or we go *on* it. We talk about Mono Meals, miscombining, and fruit days. We're on Food Formulas and doing an Open Carb. We resort to antidotes and precidotes.

The rest of the world is dying to know what a watermelon day actually *is*. "I'm on strawberries," you may murmur to a friend, "because I want to stay enzymatically open. Tomorrow I'm scheduled for an OD, so I'll be sure to follow it with an Open Protein. What are you on today?" The world is fascinated. "What are you talking about?" everyone wants to know.

But our language isn't so secret anymore. The golden pineapple is catching on and going public. Now when I walk into The Polo Lounge in The Beverly Hills Hotel, the maître d' gently inquires, "Are you on a protein day or a carb day, Miss Mazel?" It wasn't long ago they openly scoffed when I ordered two veal chops alone unto themselves ("No salt and clean off the grate before you cook them, please"). I sit in Ma Maison devouring bread, and Patrick or Fernand appears, smiling. "You must be on carbs today." And at the Bistro Garden they don't even flinch when I order a triple raspberries. They know I'll be back for their duck salad or chocolate soufflé another time. It's actually getting easy to communicate in the tongue of Conscious Combining.

In this advanced primer to the good life, we've embellished our basic vocabulary. But the Beverly Hills Diet Lifetime Plan speaks for itself with new words, new terms, and it shouts to be heard. Are you listening?

AMINO ACIDS   Building blocks derived from protein sources

ANIMAL PROTEIN   Protein derived from animal sources

ANTIDOTE   A follow-up food to enzymatically correct any negative side effects

BAIN-MARIE   A method of cooking in which two pots are used, as with a double boiler. The bottom one holds hot water, the top the ingredients to be cooked or warmed

BAKED BLIND   Refers to a tart or pie shell which is baked without a filling. The shell is held down with buttered aluminum foil and beans

BALANCED DIET   A regimen in which you are getting the proper balance of nutrients to promote and maintain health and slimness

BEVERLY HILLS DIET PROCESS, THE   Includes burn, feed, and wash
- *Burning* is the process in which enzymes are used to burn up and digest fat and extra protein.
- *Feeding* is the process in which minerals are being supplied to your body in highly concentrated doses to offset a mineral imbalance and to reestablish the harmony of the cells.
- *Washing* is the process in which fruit is used to eliminate extra fluid, chemicals, burned-up fat, and protein from your body.

BHL   Beverly Hills Lifestyle. The lifestyle that encompasses the good life Beyond The Golden Pineapple. The lifestyle that insures eternal slimhood by having as its eating foundation the Beverly Hills Diet Lifetime Plan and the technique of Conscious Combining.

BEYOND THE GOLDEN PINEAPPLE   The land of Forever. The state wherein you have internalized and synthesized the BHDL, where Conscious

Combining has become unconscious, as easy and natural as buttoning your shirt or driving your car. The land where the Beverly Hills Diet Lifetime Plan and Slimhood reign supreme.

BLOATER   One who is particularly susceptible to salt, one whose body ballons in response to it.

BLOWING IT   Miscombining either with or without permission

BRAN   Flakes derived from wheat or rice. The outer fibrous hull is used by the body as an elimination aid.

BROMALINE   The active enzyme in pineapple and strawberries, which interacts with and stimulates the hydrochloric acid in the stomach to digest fat

CARBOHYDRATES   Carbohydrates break down into glucose, which provides our body with energy. They are our fuel, the gasoline on which we run.

CLEANSING   Detoxifying. The process whereby toxins are eliminated by our bodies. It's accomplished on the Beverly Hills Diet through the burn, feed, and wash process.

COLD-PRESSED OIL   Sometimes called expellor pressed. Processed oil extracted from its source by a pressing method rather than a heating method.

CONSCIOUS COMBINER   Person who combines food to achieve the ultimate nutritional value afforded by those foods. A person who knows what digests well together and what doesn't and who chooses to eat accordingly.

CORRECTIVE COUNTERPARTS   Digestive foods that interact and offset hard-to-digest foods

DAIRY PROTEINS   Proteins derived from dairy sources, such as milk, cheese, eggs, and yogurt

DFC—DEBILITATING FAT CONSCIOUSNESS   That state of mental being that keeps you fat in a variety of different ways, that perpetuates fat thoughts and thus fat itself; examples, using a vacation as an excuse for blowing it, repeating to yourself, "I know I'll get fat again!"

DIGESTIVE PROCESS   The process whereby your body uses and processes food to maintain life and to provide it with energy.
  • *Digestion.* Step one in the digestive process. The stage at which food is turned into nutrients.
  • *Absorption.* Step two in the digestive process. The stage at which all nutrients are absorbed into the blood and sent to the cells.

- *Metabolism*. Step three in the digestive process. The stage at which all our cells are nourished and our body burns up energy.
- *Elimination*. Step four in the digestive process. The stage at which the unused waste products are eliminated. The main vehicles of elimination are urination, bowel movements, perspiration, and breathing.

DISTILLED SPIRITS   Includes all grain alcohols—vodka, tequila, bourbon, Scotch, rye, sake, and beer

EATER   A person who loves to eat and lives to eat

EATING EXPERIENCE   The Conscious Combiner's meal not defined in terms of breakfast, lunch, and dinner but rather separated by two or three hour increments

EMOTIONAL QUOTIENT   The tally of specified foods required to feed your heart and soul. When you attain your EQ, you will have banished your DFC.

ENZYMATICALLY OPEN   A condition in which you have not limited yourself to having to eat a specific food

ENZYMES   Little chemical reactors that speed up chemical reactions in our bodies. They either appear in the food we eat or are promoted in our bodies by the food we eat. Enzymes take human food and turn it into body food.

FAT   When you have five pounds or fifty pounds to lose. Fat is whenever you can't get on the scale and say "I'm perfect."

FAT CONSCIOUSNESS   That self-perpetuating way of thinking that makes us and keeps us fat

FAT QUOTIENT   The amount of food you can eat and still maintain your weight

FATS   Fats ultimately break down into lipids, the carriers of vitamins A, D, E, and K. They provide our body with stored energy.

FATTENING   Foods that are hard to digest or indigestible

FOOD FORMULA   A weekly compilation of perfectly ordered food combinations to ensure eternal slimhood. Geared to comply with your fat, nutritional, and emotional quotients.

FRUIT FLING   A three-day fruit escape to cleanse, stabilize, comfort, or moderate

GAINER   A food that will inevitably cause you to gain weight.

GETTING SALTED When salt is added to your food, without your knowledge, after you have requested "No salt, please."

GLUCOSE The energy form derived from carbohydrates

GOOD LIFE That state of perfection in which you are blessed and protected by the golden pineapple, the state of eternal slimhood, where you are no longer consumed by fat and the DFC

HERB A plant valued for its flavor and scent; used for seasoning or medicinal properties. Examples: basil, oregano, rosemary, and thyme.

INDIGESTIBLE Those foods that are impossible for our body to break down into nutrients because of the combination in which they are ingested or because of their intrinsic molecular makeup. These foods ultimately become clogged in our bodies and cause our fat.

JULIENNE The cutting of food into fine strips approximately 3 inches in length

LAST SUPPER Eating as if it's the last meal of your life

LECITHIN An essential fatty acid, a natural substance that always appears in conjunction with cholesterol. It's not only found in food but is present in every cell in your body, particularly in your nervous system. Its action is that of an emulsifier. It is the essential part of fat that allows it to be digested.

LEGUMES A food category made up of foods that are half protein and half carbohydrate. They are highly indigestible because of their innate miscombination.

LIAISON Used to bind or thicken sauces or soups by addition of a thickening ingredient. Most frequently, the liaison is egg yolk whisked into heavy cream.

LIPIDS Stored energy derived from fat sources

MAINTENANCE Maintenance means forever. It is the establishment of a firm weight from which you do not vary on a weekly basis by more than three pounds.

MALTOSE A sugar formed by the first stage of carbohydrate digestion

MARTYR A person who sits at the table and just drinks coffee or tea while watching everyone else eat and saying he isn't hungry when he is

MAXI CARBS Molecularly speaking, the most complex category of carbs. Also known as the starches because of their complexity and because they can be converted into flour. They take the longest of all the carbs to digest.

MENSCH   A human being

MIDI CARBS   Carbs with a molecular structure more complex than that of the simpler mini carbs but not as complex as the maxi carbs

MIND/BODY SPLIT   When the mind and the body are disconnected; a condition in which you don't feel your body or experience it as it really is

MINERALS   Inorganic compounds necessary for life

MINI CARBS   The most easily digested of all the carbohydrates

MISCOMBINATION   Foods that according to the principles of Conscious Combining do not digest well together. For example, combining proteins and carbohydrates

MISHIMISHIMA   A total miscombination—sugar, salt, chemicals, grease, the works. Its literal translation: a strange death.

MONO MEAL   A meal consisting of a single food

NONPHYSICAL EXERCISE   A mental exercise that is an integral part of the Beverly Hills Diet and the Beverly Hills Diet Lifetime Plan that is designed to propel the individual to confront, acknowledge and let go of the fat person while simultaneously instilling the pride and self-confidence of the skinny person

NUT PROTEIN   Protein derived from nuts and seeds, including avocados

NUTRIENT   A substance needed by a living thing to maintain life, health, and reproduction

NUTRITION   The science or study of the nourishment of humans

NUTRITIONAL QUOTIENT   Based on government standards, the balance of foods required to energize a healthy human. The tally of proper foods so you can feed your body along with your heart and soul.

NUTRITIONAL YEAST   An inactive yeast specifically designed as a food supplement to provide the body with B vitamins, amino acids, and minerals

OPEN   Choice of any three (except relating to Open Human)

OPEN CARB   A combination of three carbs, not more than two of which are maxi carbs

OPEN DESSERT   Dessert instead of a meal. If it is in lieu of a midday meal, two human portions of any dessert you choose. If it is in lieu of an evening meal, three human portions of any dessert.

OPEN FRUIT Fruit combined with wine, champagne, or brandy. One fruit only. Fruits do not combine with one another.

OPEN HUMAN Eating like a mensch (see "MENSCH") with one hand and one bite at a time while watching a skinny person and imitating him or her bite for bite

OPEN MEAL Meals not restricted to a single food

OPEN MISCOMBINATION There are two types:

1. One protein and one carb. Follow the rule of eating the protein last. Eat the carb first, and once you've taken your first bite of protein, don't go back to the carb.

2. Those foods—entities unto themselves—that contain both a protein and a carb and thus exist only as a miscombination. (see MISCOMBINATION)

OPEN PROTEIN The combination of any three proteins from any category, excluding nuts. Nut proteins combine with nothing.

ORGANIC Natural, without chemicals or preservatives

OUTSIDER A naturally thin person, a non-eater, a person whose soul is as removed from food as ours is attached. An Outsider eats little, skips meals *without realizing it*. A person who is worthy of pity because he is missing one of life's great pleasures.

PAPAIN The active enzyme in papaya, mango, kiwi, and persimmon. It interacts with and promotes the secretion of pepsin in our stomach to digest protein.

POSITIVE TALKBACK A Nonphysical Exercise that teaches a person a positive response dialogue for answering typical negative comments regarding their weight loss and their diet

PRECIDOTE Opposite of an antidote; it precedes or comes before a meal and enzymatically prepares you for it

PROTEIN Proteins break down into amino acids, the building blocks from which our flesh, blood, and muscles are made.

PROUD SHEET, THE A Nonphysical exercise in which one reinforces and instills pride and self-worth by keeping track of one's achievement

PTYALIN The enzyme secreted in the saliva and promoted by chewing that is essential for the digestion of carbohydrates

RAW BUTTER Butter made from unpasteurized milk

RESNICK OPEN Drinking instead of eating

ROUX   A mixture of flour and butter, usually of equal proportion, which is cooked to a specified degree, either white, golden, or brown

SECURITY   Being perfect and knowing you have the rules and tools to stay that way forever

SEEING YOURSELF AS OTHERS SEE YOU   A Nonphysical exercise in which the mirror is used to effect a realistic self-visualization by looking at yourself for extended time periods and using mental imagery

SESAME SEEDS   A high-protein, high-calcium, high-fiber food which is an important part of the Beverly Hills Diet

SHARON ASSIGNMENT, THE   A Nonphysical exercise which forces the person to confront, acknowledge, and let go of that fat person by revealing their negative feeling about being fat to strangers

SKINNY   Perfect. Whatever weight is perfect for you and no one else. Skinny means being able to get on your scale and say, "I don't have to lose one more pound." Skinny is a Forever state.

SKINNY VOICE   When your head says no and your heart says go, it's the voice that stops you

SLIMHOOD, ETERNAL AND OTHERWISE   Attaining the State of Skinny

STRAIGHT   Not miscombining

SUBSTITUTE   A food one eats in place of a recommended food *only* in a dire emergency

SUCROSE   The sugar obtained from sugarcane or sugar beets

SWEETENERS   All sugars, syrups, and honey

THREE QUESTIONS, THE   A Nonphysical exercise which enables a person to accept positive reinforcement by asking three people what they like best about him or her

TOXINS   Poisons, the residue of which is trapped in our bodies because of uneliminated waste products and chemicals

"TRADITIONAL" BALANCED DIET   Breakfast, lunch, and dinner or eating proteins, carbs, and fats at the same meal

UNCONSCIOUS COMBINING   When conscious becomes unconscious and combining is internalized

VICTIM   One who unnecessarily places himself in a potentially fattening position

VITAMINS   Some of the compounds necessary for the maintenance of life

WHOLE GRAINS   Unrefined grains from which the germ and the bran have not been removed

WIDE OPEN Also known as Pig-Out, in sharp contrast to an Open Human. Rather than eating like a mensch, with one hand, one bite at a time, a Wide Open is splurging with wild abandon, with permission, added pounds, and a commitment that you will do whatever you have to do tomorrow to lose it. An almost-never in the world beyond the golden pineapple.

WIDE OPEN CARB A combination of as many carbs as you want, with no limits on even the number of maxi carbs included. Not recommended for carefree maintenance.

WIDE OPEN PROTEIN Eating as many proteins as you want at a given meal from any protein category. Not recommended for carefree maintenance.

Index

Mental Rules, 51–56
menu planning, 66
    favorite foods in, 58–59, 123
    weekly, 92–93
    see also "Doing Your Own Thing"
        week
midi carbs, 82
mineral supplements, 75–76
mini carbs, 82, 96
Minnelli, Liza, 8, 15
miscombinations, 8, 117, 128, 133,
        188
    condiments in, 86, 87
    counteraction of, 28
    defined, 26
    desserts as, 109, 110
    fat caused by, 26, 28
    legumes as, 83
    see also Open Miscombinations
Mitchum, Robert and Dorothy, 15
Mobley, Mary Ann, 4, 25
Mono Carbs (MC), 87, 99, 102, 116,
        129, 147
Mono Fruits (F), 87, 129
Mono Meals (MM), 87, 116, 128, 147
    psychological benefits of, 160–61
Mono Proteins (MP), 87, 101, 105,
        116, 124, 131–35, 147
Morgan, Jaye P., 15
Morris, Phyllis, 112

nectarines, 65
Neufeld, Mace, 133–34
Nonphysical Exercises, 6, 33–35, 78,
        148–49, 150, 155, 160–62,
        167, 172–73, 178–79
    goal of, 33, 148–49
nut proteins, 66, 81
nutrition, 310
    "balanced" meals, days, and weeks
        in, 91
    BHDLP weekly intake and, 92–97,
        131, 309
    individual needs and, 125
    Senate Committee
        recommendations for, 91–92
nuts, 66, 69, 88, 94, 108, 316
    in desserts, 110
    Nonphysical Exercise for, 178–79
    portion control for, 108
    when to eat, 108

oil, 59–60, 66, 94, 307
    in cooking, 59, 94
    seasoning of, 60
Open Breakfasts, 94
Open Carb (OC), 87, 96, 100, 103–
        5, 106, 109, 116, 124, 131–33,
        147
Open Desserts (OD), 47, 89, 108–
        10, 116, 309–10
    portion control for, 109
    protein eaten after, 109–10
Open Fruit (OF), 87
Open Human (OH), 47, 70, 90, 94,
        116, 118, 124, 125, 133, 195–
        96
    Nonphysical Exercise for, 167
    preparation for, 66–67
Open Meals, 32, 47, 65, 116, 127,
        128, 133, 146, 147
    same food family in, 67
Open Miscombination (OM), 66, 70,
        88–89, 94, 116, 124, 131–33
    two types of, 88–89
Open Protein (OP), 64, 88, 101–2,
        105–6, 107, 109, 116, 124,
        131–33, 147

Palmer, Bill, 15
papayas, 69, 84, 95, 112, 117, 120
pasta, as served in restaurants, 172–
        73
peaches, 65
pears, 65
pepsin, 48, 49
phosphorus, 86
photographs, before and after, 142–
        43, 144
physical exercise, 73–74
pickled foods, 86
pineapple, 64, 69, 84, 95, 112, 117,
        118, 120
plateaus, 31, 35–36
P.M. Swing, 112
portion size, 23, 99, 108, 109, 128,
        186
potassium, 86, 124
precidotes, 28, 32, 47, 58, 65, 66,
        79, 84, 118, 124, 131
pregnancy, 308
preservatives, 65, 68